THE REPAIR
OF THE WORLD

THE REPAIR
OF THE WORLD

The Novels of Marge Piercy

Kerstin W. Shands

Contributions in Women's Studies, *Number 145*

GREENWOOD PRESS
Westport, Connecticut • London

Library of Congress Cataloging-in-Publication Data

Shands, Kerstin W.
     The repair of the world : the novels of Marge Piercy / Kerstin
W. Shands.
          p.   cm.—(Contributions in women's studies, ISSN 0147–104X   ;
no. 145)
     Includes bibliographical references and index.
     ISBN 0–313–29257–4 (alk. paper)
     1. Piercy, Marge—Criticism and interpretation.   2. Women and
literature—United States—History—20th century.   I. Title.
II. Series.
PS3566.I4Z94   1994
813'.54—dc20   94–5149

British Library Cataloguing in Publication Data is available.

Library of Congress Catalog Card Number: 94–5149
ISBN: 0–313–29257–4
ISSN: 0147–104X

First published in 1994

Greenwood Press, 88 Post Road West, Westport, CT 06881
An imprint of Greenwood Publishing Group, Inc.

Printed in the United States of America

The paper used in this book complies with the
Permanent Paper Standard issued by the National
Information Standards Organization (Z39.48–1984).

10 9 8 7 6 5 4 3 2 1

To Fredrik,
Molly,
and Hanna

Child, where are you heading with arms spread wide
as a shore, have I been there, have I seen that land shining
like sun spangles on clean water rippling?
I do not know your dances, I cannot translate your tongue
to words I use, your pleasures are strange to me
as the rites of bees: yet you are the yellow flower
of a melon vine growing out of my belly
though it climbs up where I cannot see in the strong light.

Marge Piercy, "The sun," *To Be Of Use*

Contents

Acknowledgments

I began my research on Marge Piercy's work in the mid-1980s. Since then, parts of this book have been written in New York, in Lawrence, Kansas, and in Uppsala, Sweden. During 1993, I had the rare good fortune of being an American Council of Learned Societies Fellow at the University of Kansas, where I was immersed in a highly stimulating and supportive environment. I am deeply appreciative both of the funding from the American Council of Learned Societies and of the inspiring milieu the University of Kansas provided, as well as of its outstanding libraries, all of which was of immense benefit to my research. Several people have had an input on this book:

First and foremost, I thank Marge Piercy, whose work has opened doors to new worlds to me for a decade, for her generous assistance and helpful commentary on my manuscript. Marge Piercy's cooperation also helped make my bibliography as complete as possible.

I give heartfelt thanks to Pia Thielmann, a Piercy scholar at the American Studies Program at the University of Kansas, for her challenging, expert scrutiny of my text in different versions and for her innumerable perceptive comments. Professor Elizabeth Schultz at the Department of English, the University of Kansas, read my chapter on *Woman on the Edge of Time* and welcomed me to join her seminar on Marge Piercy. Professor Sue Walker at the Department of English, the University of South Alabama, read parts of my manuscript. I was also able to discuss my work with Sylvia D. Stone, Women's Studies Program, the University of Kansas, and valued her comments. Lisbeth S. Saab, doctoral candidate at Uppsala University, read the introduction with refreshing enthusiasm and candor, and I am grateful for her detailed and insightful comments.

I also wish to thank Peter Coveney, senior editor at Greenwood Press, for his helpful advice during the completion of this manuscript, and my copyeditor, Wanda Giles, for her vigorous scrutiny of both language and ideas in the final manuscript.

I thank my husband, Frederick D. Shands, for perceptively and patiently critiquing more than one draft of my manuscript. I also wish to express my appreciation to Åsa Gezelius, Chicago, for strong friendship and for her staunch and spirited support of my research.

I give special thanks to Lynn Porter, keyboard operator, Pam LeRow, office specialist, and Paula Malone, director, at the University of Kansas Word Processing Center. Their help through innumerable drafts was invaluable, as was their invariably friendly and patient instruction while I was learning to master a different computer program. I am particularly grateful to Lynn Porter for her professional assistance with the final formatting of this book.

I owe my biggest debt of gratitude to the director of the Women's Studies Program at the University of Kansas, Professor Sandra L. Albrecht, whose support has been crucial. Apart from her always stimulating and encouraging professional discussions and her introducing me to the extraordinarily inspiring network that is the Women's Studies Program at the University of Kansas, she and her daughter, Molly, made the year we spent in Lawrence altogether memorable for me and my family.

In "What Rides the Wind," Marge Piercy has written about the need to "see and feel the connections," "that sense of being part of a web—a social network of labor and society, a total community of rock and lizard and bird and coyote and person, a maze of past from which we issue and the future which issues from us" (62). Writing this book, I have indeed felt part of a "network of labor and society," and I have been thinking about that "maze of past from which we issue." My dedication, however, is to "the future which issues from us": to my darling, six-year-old Fredrik, and to my precious goddaughters, Molly, three, and baby Hanna.

Abbreviations

Introduction

Send me your worn hacks of tired themes,
your dying horses of liberation,
your poor bony mules of freedom now.
I am the woman sitting by the river.
I mend old rebellions and patch them new.
                    Marge Piercy, "Let Us Gather at the River," *Stone, Paper, Knife*

Remarkably prolific, Marge Piercy is becoming an increasingly distinguished writer in the United States, even though her name may still not be "a household word like Drano or Kleenex," as she once put it with her wonted pragmatic bluntness (PCBQ 219). Among those who have read her work, opinions of it have been divided. Her detractors have scorned her aims to reach out to a wide group of women readers and her explicit political stance. But for countless readers, her novels have been part of a *rite de passage* toward increased awareness of the asymmetric encoding of power in both private relations and in a largely male-defined societal and cultural context. Piercy's aim is succinctly summed up in her epigraph to one of her collections of poetry, *To Be Of Use*:

For the give and take
for the feedback between us
for all the times I have tried in saying these poems
to give back some of the energy we create together
from all the women who could never make themselves heard
the women no one would listen to
to all the women who are unlearning to not speak
and growing through listening to each other.

Inscribing the issues and dilemmas of contemporary feminism, Piercy's oeuvre comprises novels, poetry, essays, pamphlets, and reviews (she has written about, for example, Alice Walker, Margaret Laurence, and Margaret Atwood). Her way of placing 'invisible' conflictual ideological constructs in relief and of thus rendering visible the sites of alterity within a dominant discourse, together with her varied and often subtly delineated gallery of characters, emblazons neofeminist questions discussed during the most recent decades. Of her poetry, Margaret Atwood has written: "Piercy is committed to the search for honesty, however painful; to action, however futile; to getting it said and getting it done, however awkward the result may be" (277). A comment by Thomas Pynchon, writing on *Dance the Eagle to Sleep*, is in the same vein: "Here is somebody with the guts to go into the deepest core of herself, her time, her history, and risk more than anybody else has so far, just out of a love for the truth and a need to tell it" (as quoted in *The Earth Shines Secretly* n.p.). According to Atwood, Piercy "is a serious writer who deserves the sort of considered attention which, too often, she does not get" (272), and Rachel Blau du Plessis categorizes Piercy as a "shrewd, articulate, and serious [woman novelist]," "who could . . . become the Brecht of the women's movement" (1979 1, 4). Valerie Miner wonders "why Piercy's work is so often relegated to the shelf of 'ideological fiction,' whereas the parochial fatalism of such writers as Ann Beattie is found under 'literary fiction'" (B3). Miner sees Piercy as "a raw, tough, willful, magnificent novelist and poet" whose "original vitality" unfortunately is not appreciated by dull WASP critics more interested in "personal pedigree" and "the correct education," and concludes that "if in fact marinated cynicism is the climax of post-modern literature, themes of hopeful engagement will be easily dismissed." Piercy has been overlooked by the literary establishment and has not been included in the traditional canon, even though she is sometimes included in the reading lists for women's literature courses.

Piercy's fiction—"a tough and dreamy tendentious literature," as Thomas Moylan has put it (1981 136)—is well worth exploring both for its challenging political perspectives and, to an increasing degree as one goes through her fiction chronologically, for its formal and structural aspects as well. The body of criticism on Piercy's work is growing, and I will refer to it throughout this study. In terms of separate articles, Piercy's fourth novel, *Woman on the Edge of Time*, has elicited the incomparably largest corpus of criticism. Among the most important book-length studies of Piercy's fiction are Pia Thielmann's 1985 master's thesis, published in Germany in 1986 as *Marge Piercy's Women: Visions Captured and Subdued*; it discusses the images of women characters in Piercy's fiction up to her 1984 novel, *Fly Away Home*; and Patricia Marks's 1990 dissertation, "Re-Writing the Romance Narrative: Gender and Class in the Novels of Marge Piercy," which analyzes four of

Piercy's novels—those which, in Marks's opinion, are feminist narratives transgressing the traditional romance narrative. To my knowledge, however, a comprehensive mapping of Piercy's prose into the 1990s has not yet been produced. This book aims to be an inclusive, readerly exploration of Piercy's fiction and its most urgent themes. In constructing this study, which will be both an elucidation and an evaluation, my considerations will be primarily cultural-ideological but also literary and aesthetic. I believe that by tracing Piercy's central thematics through all of her novels to date, in particular her depiction of power patterns and of a battle between what I see as a fundamental principle of connection, creation, healing, or what Piercy calls the "repair of the world," versus a principle of separation and destruction, our understanding of Piercy's writing, as well as her place in literary history, may be increased. I hope this book will offer new insights into Marge Piercy's writings and their place in American neofeminist thought. To stay within its scope, I will have to leave many stones unturned. It is my hope, however, to inspire readers to pursue new paths of research into Piercy's rich and extensive work.

Before turning to in-depth discussions of Piercy's novels, I would like to begin with a presentation of Marge Piercy and her place within American literature. I will trace her roots primarily to Walt Whitman, whom I see as a spiritual forefather of Piercy.   Then, I will point to some important characteristics of her writing, both formal elements and political credos. In order to elucidate Piercy's place within a female and/or feminist cultural community, and her predominantly realist fiction, I will, moreover, bring in a discussion based on Rita Felski's *Beyond Feminist Aesthetics: Feminist Literature and Social Change* (1989). Felski analyzes two different positions in American feminist literary criticism and attempts to construct a third, the trope of a feminist public space encompassing literature by women and feminist politics, dialectically, although not unproblematically, intertwined. This discussion will also clarify the theoretical assumptions of the present study.

Marge Piercy, born on March 31, 1936 in Detroit, Michigan, is white, of a working-class background, Jewish on her mother's side and Welsh-English on her father's, though he professed no religion. She was "A Depression baby [who] was often hungry during the first few years of her life" (Gould 298-99). Piercy's autobiographical essay in *Contemporary Authors* 1984 (267-81), and Sue Walker's "An Overview (31 March 1936-)" also provide biographical information.   She was always closer to her mother, and the physical resemblance between Piercy and her mother is striking. Prolonged illness in her childhood changed her from a streetwise tomboy into an avid reader. A highly gifted girl who participated in various committees to improve matters at school, she won a scholarship to the University of Michigan, which, however, she had to supplement by working at various jobs during her college years. She developed a pioneering interest in mother goddess religions (something that was considered "mad" at the time). She was "totally uninterested in sororities" (personal letter from Marge Piercy, April 26, 1993). This is how Jean Gould describes her: "She was considered one of the brilliant, gifted but dangerous radicals on campus. She was very persuasive: a dynamic brunette, with a great shock of dark hair, flashing dark eyes, and a generous mouth from which bursts a robust laugh; she was—and is—a forceful personality" (300).

Piercy's own self portrait has a more pungent flavor: "I was a garlic among the Anglican-convert lilies. I felt the wrong shape, size, sex, volume level, class, and emotional coloration" (PCBQ 117). In "Fame, Fortune, and Other Tawdry Illusions" she writes, "Joanna Russ says it's my body type and my style that gets me in trouble. Nobody tries to make her play mommy. . . . She's tall as the Empire State Building, lean and elegant, and dresses tailored. I am five feet four (almost), *zoftig* [*sic*], and dress more or less peasanty" (PCBQ 221).

Just as in high school, her extracurricular agenda at Michigan was impressive. In 1957, she graduated with an A.B., then got an M.A. from Northwestern University in 1958. She did not complete her Ph.D. In "Through the Cracks: Growing Up in the Fifties," Piercy has denounced the conformity of the 1950s, the lack of support for "alternative" lifestyles, and the absence, particularly glaring for women, of a subculture. In the same essay, she expresses her dismay at the class-ridden college life, as she experienced it: "a never-ending education in the finer distinctions of class insult and bias" (PCBQ 115). In many respects, Piercy, as a college student, was ahead of her times, and it was not always a cheering prospect, since "there was nobody to write for, nobody to communicate with about matters of being female, alive, thinking, trying to make sense of one's life and times" (118-19). She married Michel Schiff, a graduate student in physics and later a particle physicist, but at the age of twenty-two "broke out of the box of [her] marriage" (PCBQ 119). She married again in 1962, this time a computer scientist named Robert Shapiro, and lived an unconventional, open relationship in Greece, San Francisco, Boston, Brooklyn, New York's Upper West Side, and finally, Cape Cod, where the marriage ended.

Having come to writing early in life—she began writing seriously at the age of fifteen—she tried to eke out an existence as a free-lance writer, living on Wilson Avenue in Chicago, not an easy life. During her marriage to Michel Schiff she went with him to Paris, and lived in the 10th arrondissement for a few months. Her next domiciles were in Boston and San Francisco, then in New York, before she settled on Cape Cod in 1971 because of bad health. In Wellfleet, she lives "like a peasant . . . on a couple of acres where we grow all our own vegetables and some fruit, and freeze, dry, pickle, can, rootcellar the surplus for the whole year" (PCBQ 21). This move has had beneficial effects on her writing: "Living in Wellfleet, I have learned a whole new language of the natural world that I am part of, and that has changed and enriched my work" (21-22). Her writing has been influenced and supported by people around her, most notably by her third husband, Ira Wood, a writer, with whom she has collaborated on a play, *The Last White Class* (1980).

If we are to place Piercy in American literary history and trace her roots, it is Walt Whitman, rather than Ralph Waldo Emerson, who is Piercy's most important literary and spiritual forefather. Piercy herself has written: "Everything that moved me at first contact (Whitman, Dickinson) turned out to be déclassé or irrelevant to the mainstream, the tradition" (PCBQ 114). Comparing Emerson and Whitman, Camille Paglia has written that Emerson's "doctrine of self-reliance, by which America declared independence of European culture, is also a rejection of a female past" (1991 601). Walt Whitman, on the other hand, "revives the cosmology of the ancient mother cults," and by him, "American poetry's opening towards woman was achieved" (602). Paglia writes that Whitman "wants to assimilate all beings into the self, imagined as a capacious sac"; "His technique is identification, the Dionysian empathic," obvious indeed in the first stanza of "Song of Myself" ("For every atom belonging to me as good belongs to you.") I see Piercy's poem "They inhabit me" (from *My Mother's Body*) as particularly influenced by "Song of Myself," both in its affirmation of the Dionysian, of nature, of Apollonian refuse, and in its searching identification with a variety of living creatures. In stanza eleven, the voice becomes that of a racoon:

> I am racoon. I thrive in woods,
> I thrive in the alleys of your cities.
> With my little hands I open
> whatever you shut away from me.
> On your garbage I grow glossy.

The "promiscuous all-inclusiveness" Paglia sees in *Leaves of Grass*, and the manner in which "Democratic Dionysus broadens significance to refuse, chips and scraps," the way in which "Dionysus' polymorphous perversity breaks down Apollonian categorization and hierarchy" (1991 603) could be seen as operative qualities also in Piercy's novels. The same could be said for Whitman's vision of the poet as prophet or liberator, his protest against the bourgeois and against Puritanism. Paglia writes of Whitman that "his weaknesses also come from his Dionysianism, which offends Apollonian form and decorum. At his best, he has the sublimity of Pindar; at his worst, he is screechy and cornball, like a carnival barker." The reference to Pindar aside, the assessment is valid also for Piercy. Piercy's description of her discovery of Whitman, moreover, is actually quite Dionysian: reading his poetry, she "experienced inebriation and an intense loosening, a revelation of light and heat and identity" ("How I Came to Walt Whitman and Found Myself" 98).

After reading this introduction, Marge Piercy has emphasized that Emily Dickinson is as important to her as Walt Whitman (personal letter from Marge Piercy, April 26, 1993). Other primary literary influences on her art, according to Piercy's own statements, are the Romantics (Lord Byron, Percy Shelley, John Keats), William Blake, William Butler Yeats, James Joyce, Muriel Rukeyser, William Carlos Williams, Pablo Neruda, Edith Sitwell and Edward Arlington Robinson. Somewhat surprisingly, she adds Alexander Pope to her list—although she does have in common with Pope a passion for occasional poetry and "a strong regard for the technical elements of poetry" (personal letter from Marge Piercy, April 26, 1993). Simone de Beauvoir was an early and "tremendously important model" (*Contemporary Authors* 272), especially as a role model for Piercy among those who wrote political fiction (*Daughters of de Beauvoir* 114). Allen Ginzburg, furthermore, "liberated [her] imagination at a critical time, 1959," and in the 1960s, her "reading style was heavily influenced by Black poets" (PCBQ 305). An important friend is Joanna Russ, whose work Piercy admires (see, e.g., Piercy's foreword to Russ's *The Zanzibar Cat*).

Piercy's fiction is a departure from the classic American literature which, in the words of Camille Paglia, "suffers from a sex problem" that "began with the banishment of the maternal principle from Protestant cosmogony." Paglia adds that "the absence of the mother from pioneer American values imaginatively limited a people living intimately with nature" (1991 572). In Piercy's work a maternal principle is indeed celebrated and a Puritan ethic challenged. Her philosophy reaches out to the spirituality and ecology of Native Americans, such as the Plains Indians' culture in which visions are an integral part, as opposed to American society in which visions are punished (PCBQ 16). Some of Piercy's novels actually stem from visions, *Dance the Eagle to Sleep*, for example, from a vision she captured in the poem "Curse of the earth magician on a metal land," and *Woman on the Edge of Time* from a vision rendered in a sequence of eleven poems in *Circles on the Water*, "Laying down the tower." Piercy says, "I am not embarrassed by the sense I have at times of being a conduit through which a poem forces itself." The Tarot has also been an important source of inspiration, in which she sees "an incredibly rich treasure of images that have been in Western cultures and particularly heretical Western culture for a long time" (PCBQ 314). Diane Freedman's dissertation, "An Alchemy of Genres" (147-59) and Eleanor Bendix (101-10) elucidate the Tarot influence on "Laying down the tower." Furthermore, Piercy sees her own poetry as part of an oral tradition (PCBQ

134), upon which she touches in "Thinking of Homer at twilight," in *Mars and Her Children*):

> Homer worked in an oral tradition,
> as did my story-telling grandmother whose eyes
> were white as boiled egg with cataracts,
> but I write. Conventionalized dense squiggles
> are how I translate the world, how I
> transform energy into matter into energy.

As one might deduce from her latest novels and her articles in Jewish journals such as *Shmate*, Piercy's Jewish heritage has become increasingly important to her. In *Summer People, Gone to Soldiers*, and *He, She and It* in particular, Jewish ritual is vitally important. *Gone to Soldiers* made Piercy feel more actively engaged in Judaism. She feels strong links to her orthodox grandmother, but unlike her grandmother, and her mother, who "seemed to have a highly personal relationship with G-d," Piercy "cannot imagine a world that contains both the Holocaust and a personal omnipotent G-d" ("The Dark Thread of the Weave" 189). Earlier in her writing career, her Jewish identity was more submerged, even suppressed. In this respect, Lisa Albrecht has grouped Piercy with another writer, Ruth Geller, and on the basis of interviews with the two, writes that "both spoke of the denial of this part of themselves because of anti-semitism and cultural stereotypes. As Jews, who are often characterized as loud, pushy and opinionated, these women had a difficult time being both strong women and Jews simultaneously. Thus, they opted to be invisible as Jews" (1984 166). The great-granddaughter of a rabbi, Piercy was raised a Jew both by her grandmother and her mother. "One of the only two Jews in the school," she writes, "I was beaten up with monotonous regularity" (*Contemporary Authors* 269). She has only married Jewish men, stating that "a mixed marriage was more than [she] personally could handle" (272). In a review essay entitled "The Repair of the World" (1984), Piercy protests the view that Judaism is for women a particularly oppressive and staunchly patriarchal religion, a view she finds reiterated by the noninitiated: "A great deal of nonsense is talked and written about Judaism by those who are not Jews, and it becomes at times extremely tedious. The general consensus among many Christians and among many feminists seems to be that Judaism is a quaint relic or else the apotheosis of patriarchy, and that the attachment of Jews to our identity is a form of masochism or a sign of unheightened consciousness" (5).

In her discussion of *On Being a Jewish Feminist: A Reader* (1983), Piercy relates how Jewish feminists are changing the received traditions (*halakah*), one example being the custom that only a son says Kaddish for his dead parents, something many women would like to do. After the death of her mother, Piercy herself sought out a woman rabbi in order to learn how to say Kaddish for her mother. Piercy also mentions how the story of Lilith, Adam's first wife—Gershom Scholem claims she "irritated the Lord of Creation by demanding equal rights" (1965 163)—is becoming more important for Jewish feminists, both as heroine and as demon, as are the goddess religions of the Middle East, important in the early Jewish communities before monotheistic Judaism. New rituals or observances are being incorporated into the old, such as Rosh Hodesh, a women's half holiday when there is a new moon, a theme treated in "At the new moon: Rosh Hodesh" (*Mars and Her Children*), which begins:

> Once a two day holiday, the most sacred stretches
> in the slow swing of the epicycling year;
> then a remnant, a half holiday for women,
> a little something to keep us less unsatisfied;
> then abandoned at enlightenment along with herbals
> and amulets, bobbe-mysehs, grandmothers' stories.
>
> Now we fetch it up from the bottom of the harbor,
> a bone on which the water has etched itself,
> and from this bone we fashion a bird, extinct
> and never yet born, evolving feathers
> from our hair, blood from our salt, strength
> from our backs, vision from our brains.

In her autobiographical essay, Piercy has stated that she is "passionately interested in the female lunar side of Judaism" ("The Repair of the World" 268). What I see as central themes in Piercy's work, for example, the affirmation of a maternal, healing, and nurturing principle, could be linked to Jewish thought, to what Piercy refers to as "the repair (tikkun) of our whole way of being in the world" (6). At the end of this introduction and before we turn to an analysis of the novels, I will return to and attempt to highlight the most fundamental themes in Piercy's fiction.

But let us leave the thematics in Piercy's oeuvre briefly for a glance at ideas of form as related to a feminist discussion. Within contemporary feminist literary criticism a fear of closure, of any kind of "straitjacket," has been central, as have discussions related to concepts of women's language as fluid and nonlinear as opposed to the rational, linear, 'male' sentence. Drawing parallels between writing and sexuality, exemplified in Monique Wittig's *Les Guérillères*, Rachel Blau du Plessis has written about "that multifocal female body and its orgasmic capacity, where orgasms vary startlingly and are multiple" ("For the Etruscans" 278)—a vision of female sexuality that is affirmed in the third stanza of Piercy's "You ask why sometimes I say stop" (from *Circles on the Water*):

You come in a torrent and ease
into limpness. Pleasure takes me
farther and farther from shore
in a series of breakers, each
towering higher before it
crashes and spills flat.

"Multiclimactic, multiple centers of attention" are valorized by du Plessis, since "the 'female aesthetic' will produce artworks that incorporate contradiction and nonlinear movement into the text" ("For the Etruscans" 279, 278). Wittig's text is exemplary in "her lists, her unstressed series, no punctuation even, no pauses, no setting apart, and so everything joined with no subordination, no ranking. It is radical parataxis" (278). Classical notions of plot, furthermore, have been questioned by feminists. Josephine Donovan discusses feminists' ideas "that the Aristotelian notion of plot as progressive movement from beginning to middle to end is at odds with the traditional woman's fundamentally repetitive and cyclic existence" (101). Donovan suggests that the plotlessness of Sarah Orne Jewett's *Country of the Pointed Firs* (1896) "is an essentially feminine literary mode that expresses an inductive, contextual sensitivity . . . Jewett's greatest works concern an escape from the androcentric time of history into transcending gynocentric space." Tania Modleski has likened the form of soap opera, with its fragmentation, interruptibility and open-endedness, to women's lives (1982 98-99), linking it to "Luce Irigaray's description of woman's 'rediscovering' herself in 'a sort of universe in expansion for which no limits could be fixed and which, for all that, would not be incoherence'" (ibid. 105, quoting Irigaray's *Ce sexe qui n'est pas un*). In their decentering format, soap operas resemble women's lives, work, and pleasure, which is "already decentered—'off center,'" and could be seen as "not altogether at odds with an already developing, though still embryonic, feminist aesthetics." Modleski's thought is in line with Maria Kinder's suggestion "that the 'open-ended, slow paced, multi-climaxed' structure of soap opera is 'in tune with patterns of female sexuality'" (98; see Maria Kinder 1974-75).

In some respects, Marge Piercy's writings could be related to the above discussion of a female or feminist aesthetics, in others not. *Small Changes*, especially Miriam's narrative, has been compared to soap opera: both are open-ended and depict small worlds (see Elaine Tuttle Hansen 1985). Reviewing *Summer People* in the *New York Times Book Review*, Stephen Schiff, derogatorily, places that novel in the category of soaps (26). Like soap opera, Piercy's prose is slow-paced and woven from multiple threads. It is bulky, opaque, too-much, Dionysian rather than Apollonian. One critic has placed Piercy's wordy style on the opposite side of the spectrum from the crystalline clarity and precision of Virginia Woolf (Wallin 34). According to this critic,

Piercy is an altogether "contemporary" writer, who incorporates and scrutinizes all the messy and chaotic aspects of contemporary life, just as the voice of "The homely war" (in *Circles on the Water*) advocates:

> Better, I thought, for me in my rough being
> to force makeshift connections,
> patches, encounters, rows,
> better to swim in trouble like a muddy river rising
> than to become at last all thesis
> correct, consistent but hollow
> the finished ghost
> of my own struggle.

But Piercy's novels, although sometimes of a decentering format, are not plotless, and, although not transparent or unambiguous, compared to Wittig's texts, Piercy's prose is straightforward and more easily accessible. Most of Piercy's prose seems to fall into the category of social realism. Yet, as critics have observed, she occasionally subverts her own realist narrative by a counterpositing of utopian, self-reflexive, or kaleidoscopically fragmented writing. As Anne Cranny-Francis writes about *Woman on the Edge of Time*: "three intersecting narratives—realist, utopian, dystopian—construct a complex text in which Piercy deconstructs dominant ideological discourses, examines the interpellation of the individual in ideology and one of the principal means by which ideology is naturalized into the lives of individuals, the realist narrative" (137). Cranny-Francis also comments on the self-reflexivity of this novel: "The intersecting narratives of *Woman on the Edge of Time* produce a text which constantly reflects on the mechanism of the realist narrative, which is one of its own mechanisms" (139).

The claim sometimes made that Piercy's novelistic art falls wholesale into the category of transparent social realism is thus far from correct. I would agree with the assessment of Patricia Marks, who discusses the romance narrative as a connecting structural link between four novels by Piercy:

> The complexity of Piercy's construction of the muted discourse has been overlooked not only by literary critics in general, but also by feminist critics who argue that her writing is not sufficiently experimental or avant-garde. However, Piercy's double-voiced narratives reflect a highly innovative use of different historically defined narrative forms to create new narrative structures that push the boundaries of the realistic novel beyond its limits of so-called transparency. (iv)

Marks argues persuasively that, in the four novels she discusses (*Small Changes, Woman on the Edge of Time, Braided Lives* and *Fly Away Home*) Piercy is re-writing the traditional romance script in a way that revitalizes realism through hybrid combinations of narrative forms and through a destabilization of conceptions of Woman as Other.

Challenging both the ideas of what constitutes postmodern fiction and the exclusion of feminist historical fiction from the postmodern canon, Marleen Barr places Piercy among feminist postmodernist writers (71). "Much postmodern fiction written by men has," contends Barr, "a bleak, trivializing perspective on human life. In contrast, feminist fabulators insist that individual women's lives are important; they optimistically portray female protagonists who successfully revise their lives to conform to specifically female narratives—and their optimism in regard to women deserves, as much as male authors' bleak commentary upon humanity, to be called canonical postmodern fiction" (186). In Barr's analysis (which touches upon *Small Changes* and *Gone to Soldiers*), Piercy's fiction exposes rather than conceals the boundaries between 'reality' and 'fiction,' a claim with which I would agree and which I find even more pertinent to an analysis of *He, She and It*. In *Gone to Soldiers*, Barr perceives an exposition of patriarchal 'fictions' about women's wartime achievements contrasted against a rendering of women's real, but unfamiliar exploits.

While many neofeminists during the 1970s held up the authority of experience as a cornerstone in realist writings by women, during the 1980s, in particular, the anteriority of experience was increasingly questioned. As multiculturalism and plurality became *paroles d'honneur* and as the self became visualized as ultimately ungraspable, forever flexibly in process—and certainly not in process towards the mature, hard-core, clearly delineated adult identity envisaged by earlier developmental psychologists—the concept of 'womanhood' became increasingly problematized. Many theorists now preferred to call their field "gender studies" rather than "women's studies." To bring men into the feminist project seemed both laudable and necessary at this point, although not unproblematic, as evidenced in the dialogical anthology *Men in Feminism*. No longer was it, moreover, entirely "politically correct" to speak about feminism, since there were so many and varied *feminisms*. In this debate, among all the fluid and intersecting modalities theorists now had to consider, where was 'woman' or 'women'? A quotation from Judith Butler seems representative of the predominating fear of essentialism: "If one 'is' a woman, that is surely not all one is; the term fails to be exhaustive, not because a pregendered 'person' transcends the specific paraphernalia of its gender, but because gender is not always constituted coherently or consistently in different historical contexts, and because gender intersects with racial, class, ethnic, sexual, and regional modalities of discursively constituted identities" (as quoted in Modleski 1991 18). While Elaine Showalter had introduced the concept of "gynocriticism" in the 1970s, in the 1990s, Tania Modleski perceived also a "gynocidal" feminism. Half tongue-in-cheek and half seriously, she has entitled one of her books *Feminism Without Women*: "'Feminism Without Women' can mean the triumph either of a male feminist perspective that excludes women or of a feminist anti-essentialism so radical that every use of the term 'woman,' however 'provisionally' it is adopted, is disallowed" (14-15). But, as Modleski observes, there must be "a way to hold onto the category of woman while recognizing ourselves to be in the *process* (an unending one) of *defining and constructing the category* (which, as noted earlier, includes very disparate types of people)" (20).

However tormented or tortuous, I believe that there is a crucial link between experience and writing. As Lisa Albrecht found of the women writers she interviewed, they "said again and again that they write to locate self-identities and understand the multiplicity of these identities. They write to make valid and real the lives they have been historically denied" (179). Piercy's fiction does not belong to a confessional or autobiographic genre. In her own words: "my major impulse to autobiography has played itself out in poems rather than novels," but she adds, "I have never considered myself a confessional poet" (PCBQ 18). She says, "I rarely use a protagonist to speak my mind or my politics. I feel that the book as a whole is making a statement," adding that "to me the truth of the novel isn't in what any character says, but rather in the whole of the fiction. As a known feminist I find critics often naively imagine I am putting my politics directly into the mouth of my protagonist. That I could not possibly be amused, ironic, interested in the consonances and dissonances" (PCBQ 148). Even though aspects of her life do surface in her texts, her most autobiographical novel being *Braided Lives*, they are easily submerged in her wide gallery of characters and actions. Among Piercy's characters are people from all walks of life, such as convincingly realized real estate developers, computer specialists, housewives, revolutionaries, and 1960s or 1970s counterculture youths. Some of her novels could be classified as novels of development, an important genre in feminist literature. In Piercy's case, Judith K. Gardiner's hypotheses concerning the relationship between reader and text as well as of how a woman writer works seem applicable, that is, "[a] female author is engaged in a process of testing and defining various aspects of identity chosen from many imaginative possibilities. That is, the woman writer uses her text, particularly one centering on a female hero, as part of a continuing process involving her own self-definition and her empathetic identification with her character" (187). Issues of ethnicity, gender, and class are predominant in Piercy's oeuvre. Her protagonists are often people on society's margins; they may be homosexual or lesbian or bisexual; they may be oppressed, poor, persecuted, of ethnic minorities. Implicitly stating her own perspective, Piercy writes in a review of Gail Godwin's *A Mother and Two Daughters* that "the world of the affluent is presented as if it were all women's situation, instead of a small minority's" ("Godwin Details Strains" 3). Never neutral, Piercy's narrative agonistically sides with the disadvantaged, oppressed, or exploited. Her prose belongs to the didactic insofar as it wishes to engage and to exhort to action. Marge Piercy wears political bias as a badge of honor. It is perhaps this explicit, emphatic political stance that most significantly separates her work from that of many other women writers of this period.

In the 1980s and the early 1990s, when women's social and political gains seemed uncertain, such a stance retained its urgency. On the one hand, the position of American women was seen as practically equal to men's, feminist struggles thus appearing less necessary. Some observers even felt that feminist movements were not only unnecessary but even detrimental to women's well-being. Reactionary forces analyzed by Susan Faludi in *Backlash: The Undeclared War Against American Women* (1991) claimed that women who had followed feminist ideas and struggled to have careers as well as families had made a terrible mistake. These women, ominous voices asserted, suffered from burnout after having believed that they, like men, could have both—incited to such beliefs by feminism. Moreover, backlash voices implied, career women would not just suffer from burnout, but would end up both infertile and husbandless—ideas uncannily echoing warnings issued by nineteenth-century ideologues promoting the idea of separate spheres. What Faludi shows in her book is that such "facts" were based on faulty, incomplete, or nonexistent research, willingly enlarged by the media, such as the mythical dearth of eligible men available to highly educated women and the myth of an epidemic of infertility. In *Summer People*, a character observes that "The women's magazines were full of stories of women who waited too long and proved infertile" (142). When the "facts" were proven wrong, the correct results of the finished research were given short shrift in the media, the faulty myths thus being allowed to live on. American media and movies were full of negative depictions of single women or career women as well as of the feminist movement, and feminism seemed to be taking a step backward in terms of political influence. After the election of Bill Clinton as president in 1992, Barbara Ehrenreich provocatively asked, "What Do Women Have to Celebrate?" (*Time* Nov. 16, 1992, 55). She pointed out that in 1992, only "3% of the Senate and 6% of the House of Representatives is female, proportions that lag embarrassingly behind most European nations," and commented: "Women's issues, such as domestic violence, never came up in the presidential campaign, and when abortion did intrude into the vice-presidential debates, Admiral Stockdale undercut his own pro-choice statement with a grumpy plea to 'get on past this and talk about something substantive'" (55-56). In 1993, Ehrenrich's title could be applied to the latest research on gender, which suggested that girls were shortchanged in American education and that this led to a loss of self-confidence: "Girls participate in class discussions at only an eighth the rate that boys do, and researchers find links between this silence and the depression and suicidal feelings that strike girls three or four times more often than boys" (Schrof 43).

Turning to Piercy's place within a female and/or feminist cultural community and to her political agenda, I will now bring in a discussion of the idea of a feminist public space as theorized by Rita Felski in her *Beyond Feminist Aesthetics: Feminist Literature and Social Change* (1989). At least during the 1980s, there seems to have been within feminist literary theory two sides or positions, that is, one Anglo-American and the other French-influenced. This polarization in many ways resembles the debates between realist and modernist positions in the 1930s, with socialist realism on one side and avant-garde or experimental art forms on the other. This debate is continued today, in Felski's view possibly recharged by Roland Barthes's notions of "readerly" and "writerly" texts, which makes for a dichotomy between 'passive' readers of easy, transparent, illusion-creating realism and 'active' readers of difficult experimental writing (156). "The critique of realist narrative as a form which conceals its own ideological status by presenting itself as a mirror of reality has gained wide-spread support. . . . Consequently a 'conservative' realism is counterposed against a 'radical' modernist or avant-garde art, which is perceived to challenge rather than affirm dominant modes of representation" (156-57). Realism is thus seen as a "closed form," a view Felski protests by pointing to the ongoing interpretation of nineteenth-century literature, which is so little unambiguous and transparent as to lead to a host of different and contradictory readings. Moreover, one may ask whether there *is* an avant-garde today. Perhaps avant-garde forms have been digested by and incorporated into contemporary cultural institutions: the avant-garde's continual celebration of the new "can be seen in this context merely to echo the fetishization of novelty and fashion which is the hallmark of a capitalist consumer culture built upon constant innovation and instant obsolescence" (160).

Within American feminist literary criticism there is, or has been, an "instrumental theory" that is reflectionist and looks for "pragmatic political use-value" in a text (3). Being reductionist, this "first position" cannot create a satisfying literary theory, although it has brought attention to the ideological content of texts in a useful way which opposes formalism. This kind of literary criticism may work best with 'straightforward' realistic texts and with thematic investigations of, say, images of women in literature. The feminist content of nonrepresentational art forms is less easily appreciated. The "second position" of French-influenced feminism looks to form itself as a subversive agent and promotes experimental form as a means to undermining dominant discourses. Such readings "foreground notions of desire and *jouissance* rather than cognition" (4), *l'écriture féminine* being an example, and Julia Kristeva's theory of the semiotic another. However, as Felski argues, in my view correctly, there is no obvious link between experimental form and "anything inherently feminine or feminist": if one looks at *l'écriture féminine*, "the only gender-specific elements exist on the level of content, as in metaphors of the female body"—thus the two cannot just be equated as "marginalized dissidence vis-à-vis a monolithic and vaguely defined 'patriarchal bourgeois humanism' which is said to permeate the structures of symbolic discourse" (5).

The theme of self-discovery, individual and collective, within American women's literature has been unduly disparaged by the second position: "a literature which articulates female experience is a legitimate cultural need of an oppositional movement," writes Felski; here is "a medium which can profoundly influence individual and cultural self-understanding in the sphere of everyday life, charting the changing preoccupations of social groups through symbolic fictions by means of which they make sense of experience. . . . Its significance is obscured by the assertion that experimental writing constitutes the only truly 'subversive' or 'feminine' textual practice, and that more conventional forms such as realism are complicit with patriarchal systems of representation" (7).

A major problem with the second position is that it perpetuates the old dichotomy between realism and modernism, it "[draws] upon static oppositions" (161). But whether texts are 'radical' or not does not reside merely in their formal qualities, but also has to do with how they are received by different audiences, what their *effects* are. Felski wants instead to shift the attention to the frameworks of reception (161), which would be a third alternative to the two positions outlined above. Perhaps Felski herself reproduces an unnecessary dichotomy between these two positions. But I do think that Felski rightly assesses the second position as "[relying] upon a vague homology between literary structures and social and political structures such as realism and patriarchy" (8), and her attempt to construct a third 'space' seems to me a worthwhile pursuit. Advocating a dialogue between feminism and women's literature, Felski looks to "the historical emergence of a feminist counter-public sphere" (154). It is Felski's contention, with which I would agree, that feminism as a social movement must be an important factor in the analysis of feminist literature, without resorting to simplistic reflectionism.

Felski builds her concept of a feminist public sphere upon Jürgen Habermas's ideas of a bourgeois public sphere. This sphere was, as Felski elaborates, a progressive force in its claim that rationality, rather than birth, should determine one's possibilities of participation in state affairs, a group or "discursive community bound by shared assumptions" (164), something that smoothed over actual differences in terms of social status and, of course, the fact that this "discursive community" was male. Habermas wrote about this subject in 1962; since then other theorists have studied more recent examples of discursive communities with the conclusion that they no longer boast universal claims but focus on specificity: there is thus a "plurality of public spheres" (166). A feminist public sphere is one of these, and it shares some traits with the bourgeois public sphere outlined by Habermas. It, too, assumes a shared identity: gender-based oppression is its focal point despite other vast differences of ethnicity, class, nationality, or sexual preference. It is able to accommodate these differences since there is no core theory to which all must subscribe, and it is precisely this shared, "general sense of commonality" (167) that explains the importance of a feminist literature in which that identity, or the quest for it, is explored.

As Donna Haraway has observed, in recent U.S. feminism there has been "a growing recognition of another response through coalition—affinity, not identity" (155). Other critics have also emphasized that the relationship between feminism and feminist criticism has to be a dialectical one, a "double, doubling commitment," as Catherine Stimpson puts it in "Feminism and Feminist Criticism" (116). The first phase of feminist criticism has been "deconstructive" while the second phase has been "reconstructive": "Feminist critics have knitted up a woman's tradition" (117). Looking back over the female tradition, Stimpson hears "intervocalities" and sees "intertextualities"—*within* the bounds of a female literary tradition, permeable boundaries thus extend backward, and Stimpson suggests that "the knitting up of a female heterodoxy [is] at once independent and interdependent" (119).

The above discussion of a feminist public space has relevance for a comprehension of Marge Piercy's perspective, as expressed both in her fiction and in her essays. As Joyce R. Ladenson has observed, "Piercy's interest in radical politics, especially feminism, is also significant from a comparative perspective because it places her already prodigious canon together with women novelists who share similar concerns—namely such writers as Agnes Smedley, Tillie Olsen, Zora Neal [*sic*] Hurston, Harriet [*sic*] Arnow, Meridel Le Seur [*sic*], Grace Paley, and Alice Walker, among others" (1991 112). The dialectics of political struggle and the creation and reading of literature are foremost concerns for Piercy. "The women's movement," she writes, "has encouraged cultural work and also provided a home for thinking and working on the relationship between form and content, between tradition and oppression, between invention and communication" (PCBQ 173). Piercy, whose novels are sold in supermarkets and drugstores, wants to reach out explicitly to women readers. About the response she gets to her writing from a large group of people, Piercy has written: "Publishing books, especially about women, brings letters that can break your heart: women losing custody of their children, women shut up in mental institutions because they rebelled against being an unpaid domestic or took a female lover, women in all shapes and colors of trouble" (PCBQ 219). She says: "I want to reach people who don't go into bookstores. So that means mass paperback is very important to me" (PCBQ 25), something that has led to criticism by some smaller presses: "At every college where I go a feminist will demand to know how I dare publish with New York houses rather than the local Three Queer Sisters press—as if the point of feminism isn't to try to reach women who don't agree already, rather than cozily assuming we are a 'community' of pure souls and need only address each other" (PCBQ 227). Piercy, in fact, warns against ghettoizations of literature (PCBQ 250).

As an *engagée* writer, Piercy inevitably has received various labels. Several critics (such as Martha Masinton and Charles G Masinton, 311) see her as "a radical feminist." Considering her celebration of a feminine, or maternal, principle, that assessment appears to be correct, but radical feminism can also imply secession from men, and in that respect the label is faulty in Piercy's case. According to Piercy's own pronouncements, she sees herself as a committed radical artist, and says: "I want to argue in defense equally of women who want to work to create a female culture and of those who want to contribute to what has been a male culture and change it to a broader, less oppressive culture" (PCBQ 3).

There may reside a contradiction in being a writer, which is a solitary profession, and a political activist, which means public involvement. For Piercy, this is not the case, although her strong involvement in political movements initially took too much out of her and even left her ill. In the 1960s, she was engaged in the leftist movement, but like many other women, she ended up disenchanted with the sexism within it. This dissatisfaction made her leave the movement and turn, instead, to feminism. Time and again, in essays and interviews, she has emphasized the strong links between her involvement in the women's movement and her literary creativity, both in the sense that her political engagement has empowered her as a writer and that it has influenced the form and the content of her writing. To place the label "leftist" on her writings is to do them a disservice, however. The fundamental conflict in Piercy's work is not between "left" and "right," however one defines those positions, but between an openness to change on the one hand and a resistance to it on the other, and between a detached and an engaged stance. Marge Piercy's work is both spirited and vitally alive, sometimes chaotically so, along Dionysian rather than Apollonian lines, and also in the sense of it being uncongealed, in process, as well as being a literature "living" for people: its "*use*" for living, for encouraging self-discovery and political awareness, is a primary concern for Piercy. Of her poetry she has stated: "I make poems for people as people bake bread for people and people grow corn for people and people make furniture for people" (as quoted in Hicks 1973

543-44); "I write poems for specific occasions, viewing myself as a useful artisan. I have written poems for antiwar rallies, for women's day rallies, for rallies centering on the rights and abuses of mental institution inmates" (PBCQ 16). In "Circles On The Water" Piercy writes: "I imagine that I speak for a constituency, living and dead, and that I give utterance to energy, experience, insight, words flowing from many lives. I have always desired that my poems work for others. 'To be of use' is the title of one of my favorite poems and one of my best-known books" (PCBQ 18-19).

Rather than a liability, Piercy's political engagement should be seen as a central aspect in her fiction. Sometimes compared to the work of Doris Lessing, Piercy's work falls within the category of political literature, a *littérature engagée*, or, more particularly, within the category of feminist literature. The marriage between literature and politics has rarely been an easy one. Not unlike the Puritans in the seventeenth century, twentieth century politicos have harbored suspicions against fiction, and the literary establishment, striving for the lofty and universal, has turned up its nose at writings that smack of partisan politics. Mordantly, Piercy herself questions notions of what *are* political novels, observing that because of a reviewer's bias the implicit politics of a novel may pass unnoticed:

> People tend to define "political" or "polemical" in terms of what is not congruent with their ideas. In other words, your typical white affluent male reviewer does not review a novel by Norman Mailer as if it were political the same way he would review a novel by Kate Millett. Yet, both are equally political. The defense of the status quo is as political as an attack on it. A novel which makes assumptions about men and women is just as political if they're patriarchal assumptions as if they're feminist assumptions. (PCBQ 34)

Susan Kress has commented on the tensions and dangers facing the politically engaged writer who cares about her books both from an aesthetic point of view *and* wishes to communicate an urgent message: "How does such a writer achieve distance from her own (acknowledged) strong emotions? Conversely, how does such a writer ensure that rage is controlled but not eradicated?" (109). As concerns the novels of Marge Piercy, Kress's answer is that "each work represents a different solution to the committed novelist's search for appropriate form."

Marge Piercy has indeed been seen as an "artful polemicist" (West 10). At the same time, the political slant of her art must not be overemphasized at the cost of the formal qualities. As she has stated, "Art works on many different levels. The political is one of its dimensions. Art is not a totally rational thing. A work of art whether it is a piece of music, a painting or poetry speaks to you on many pre-rational and irrational levels. It speaks to you on all levels of your knowing and being. Some of those are rational and political and some are not" (PCBQ 206). Piercy's poem "Athena in the front lines" (*Circles on the Water*) is a comment on the creation of art:

> Wring the stones of the hillside
> for the lost plays of Sophocles they heard.
> Art is nonaccident. Like love, it is
> a willed tension up through the mind
> balancing thrust and inertia, energy
> stored in a bulb. Then the golden
> trumpet of the narcissus pokes up
> willfully into the sun, focusing the world.

Piercy's massy, miasmic style should be savored in chunks rather than morsels. Not seldom tomes, the novels surveyed in this book, altogether comprising approximately 6,000 pages, indeed span a broad spectrum. Reviewing *Summer People*, Patricia Craig makes the comment that "while the vogue in England is for brevity and irony, Americans are drawn towards narrative amplitude" (997). Often, a great deal of research goes into Piercy's novels. For *Woman on the Edge of Time* "an enormous amount of research" was necessary (*Contemporary Authors* 277); for *Vida*, both library research and interviews were required "as well as studying files of defunct underground papers" (280), and for *Fly Away Home*, there was "a great deal of time spent exploring Boston neighborhoods and watching the impact of particular landlords, and hours and hours down at the Registry of Deeds."

Piercy's first novel, *Going Down Fast* (1969), takes place in Chicago in the 1960s and depicts the problems of racism, sexism, and urban renewal schemes. *Dance the Eagle to Sleep* (1970) examines the dangers inherent in the credos of extremist leftist "revolutionary" groups, a depiction departing from the real-life struggles of Students for a Democratic Society, more commonly called the SDS. *Small Changes* (1973) focuses more clearly on women's dilemmas, with the characters placed in a social and economic context. In *Woman on the Edge of Time* (1976), Piercy develops a triple exposure of American society, one picture being of the present, another of a utopian place, and a third of a disturbing dystopia. In *The High Cost of Living* (1978), Piercy has created a heroine who, aware of the difficulties for a woman to succeed in a male-dominated field, chooses a 'male' road toward achievement, at the same time as she is critical of the power struggles inherent in contemporary male-female relationships and drawn to women's values and a budding women's culture. *Vida* (1979) describes a pursued and persecuted woman revolutionary's life. *Braided Lives* (1982) is a glance backward by a forty-year-old woman scrutinizing her life, and especially her years at college. It is a *Bildungsroman* which reflects upon what it was like to grow up in America during the 1950s. *Fly Away Home* (1984) contrasts a principle of connection and (re)creation against a principle of separation and destruction just as it contrasts power and powerlessness through the protagonist's sense of loss, confusion, and crisis and her development toward a feeling of rebirth. The masterpiece among Piercy's novels is *Gone to Soldiers* (1987), in length comparable to George Eliot's *Middlemarch*. A comprehensive and gripping account of World War II based on extensive research, it is told from the points of view of ten different characters, moving between, for example, the Jewish *Résistance* in France, the race riots in Detroit, and the horrors of combat and concentration camps. *Summer People* (1989) presents an unusual and intense triangle drama taking place on Cape Cod. In this novel, Piercy depicts problems which have been discussed more recently by feminists: the shadow side of the ideas of solidarity and empathy among women, ideas of sisterhood above all: the hidden envy and hostility, the competition and jealousy that may lurk in the most inspired sisterhood. In *He, She and It*, Piercy weaves together two tales, a historical one set in Prague in 1600 and the other a science fiction adventure set in America in 2059. At the same time as this novel is an engrossing adventure story, it celebrates and affirms Piercy's most fundamental themes. In her most recent novel, *The Longings of Women* (1994), three women characters' ways of responding to patriarchy's marginalization of and violence against women are explored. Two central themes are enmeshed: women's literal or metaphorical homelessness and struggle to build spaces of their own and female violence against men, grenades thrown from the edgy margins of placelessness toward a self-defined center.

Marge Piercy is, unlike many other contemporary women writers, an explicitly political writer. In "The Dark Thread of the Weave," she writes: "I think the Holocaust made me feel that being political is a necessity and that only fools and the very naive permit themselves the luxury of remaining aloof from the political process" (182). As I stated above, however, the battles fought in her fiction cannot be boxed into traditional, leftist versus rightist, positions, but rather have to do with an openness versus a resistance to change.

Throughout Piercy's work, there is an ongoing battle or dynamics between two different forces or principles, a battle that takes different shapes and has different outcomes from novel to novel. I thus do not see a progression from defeat to triumph, just different ways of elaborating or working out the dynamics illustrated. Since Piercy is a feminist writer, one might see the dynamics she is illustrating as a male-female battle. That is sometimes a motif, but on a fundamental level it is only part of the dynamics. While the dynamics involve an opposition between characteristics or values such as caring, compassion, nurturing, empathy, and healing on the one hand, versus force, lack of empathy, division, isolation, and destruction on the other, it is hazardous and untenable to label such characteristics 'male' or 'female' since that may carry essentialist implications. To use labels such as 'feminine' and 'masculine' can be equally misleading for the same reason: 'feminine,' moreover, may associate to characteristics such as passivity, weakness, frivolity, and so on, which, rightly or wrongly, are associated with our cultural constructions of femininity. A term such as 'maternal' or, the kind of "transformed maternal thinking" Sara Ruddick believes "could make a distinctive contribution to peace politics" (137), comes closer to what I want to capture, and I do use this term to convey connotations of caring and compassion. Running like a scarlet thread through Piercy's oeuvre, positive change is associated with a maternal, healing, and nurturing principle, while patriarchal values are depicted as oppressive, destructive, and at times even associated with death. The question of whether feminine or maternal characteristics and values are biologically or genetically determined has not yet been satisfactorily or definitively answered and will perhaps never be. It is, on the other hand, irrefutable that certain values or characteristics have been culturally assigned to women, that is, the connotative rather than denotative aspects of motherhood: empathy, caring, compassion, motherliness, nurturing. "At least women have been conditioned to be tender," Piercy writes, also stating that "tenderness, compassion, and altruism are valued by men and women, but men almost exclusively benefit from women having these traits" ("Asking for Help Is Apt to Kill You" 26). 'Maternal' and 'paternal' are not really opposites, 'maternal,' however, is insufficient as a term indicating a pole on Piercy's spectrum, even in the larger context in which I use it, that is, not limited to biological motherhood or even to women. Terms such as 'Alpha' and 'Beta,' indicating relational dynamics, also seem too limited for an overall, organizing scheme, as is also the case with ideas of 'muted' versus 'dominant' worlds, concepts that I do, however, find useful in my analysis of, for example, *Summer People*. Principles of 'creation' versus 'destruction,' which I also use, are problematic, since destruction can be necessary and not necessarily negative. As Donna Haraway has put it: "Consciousness of exclusion through naming is acute" (155). Should we even use the terms 'masculine' and 'feminine' at all? Do they imply that we accept certain attitudes and limitations that lead us to overgeneralize and oversynthesize? What terms *are* workable? A masculine dominant does not consistently apply to the male or to masculinity or even to any existing group, but is necessarily fictional. Purposely, in this study, I will not employ a single set of terms but will use most of the terms above (with the exception of Alpha and Beta), also since what I want to indicate are *currents*, not fixed features, in Piercy's fiction. What becomes increasingly clear and convincing in Piercy's novels and often expressed through spatial metaphors and water imagery as well as birth metaphors, however, is the movement toward and commitment to the repair of the world, underlying which is a principle of connection as opposed to a principle of division, distancing, and isolation.

In Piercy's work, sexual difference is not obliterated but respected, even relished. But an artificial division into male and female worlds or into muted and dominant groups is exposed as oppressive and linked to a principle of separation as is the ideology of androcentric essentialism that is the rationale for patriarchy. Gender roles are a very important facet of Piercy's dynamic scheme of principles and will be a salient part of virtually every novel discussed. Part and parcel of the repair of the world is the repair of women's domains and the healing of the false dichotomies between 'good' and 'bad' constructs of Woman. Some passages in Piercy's novels could be seen as extolling ancient matriarchal principles including mother goddess worship, a celebration of ancient female wisdom—as in the portrait of Dinah in *Summer People*, as in the mother stone encountered by Abra in *Gone to Soldiers*, or the birthing stone Chava, the midwife, offers women in labor in *He, She and It*—but the fundamental qualities are not inherently or essentially female but human qualities, qualities that are integral to Piercy's larger scheme of an impulse toward connection and continuity.

In the following chapters, I will demonstrate that these are qualities that are celebrated as life-enhancing and life-saving in all of Piercy's fiction. "Most of my novels," writes Piercy, "are not centered upon one particular individual. The center is thematic" (personal letter from Marge Piercy, April 26, 1993). Through a presentation of Piercy's characters as well as of imagery, plot, and structure, I will now turn to an elucidation of Piercy's visions and a distillation of her most urgent theme: the repair of the world.

Chapter 1

Going Down Fast

The man said, We must make a new world, and the woman said, Honey, you
so right, why don't you start with me?

Going Down Fast 274

Set in Chicago in the early 1960s, *Going Down Fast* depicts the effects of
racism and sexism in a patriarchal, capitalist society and the problems that
arise from what is called urban renewal. The characters are part of a 1960s
counterculture generation, concerned with fighting the system, finding their
identities despite parental interference, siding with a black or a working-class
culture and making underground movies. As in Piercy's 1984 novel, *Fly Away
Home*, the focus is on the ethical problems connected with urban renewal
schemes.   In *Going Down Fast*, it is the University of Chicago that is
aggressively trying to expand its territory, thereby threatening a struggling
black neighborhood—recalling Piercy's poem, "Half past home" (in *Hard
Loving):*

> Among the houses of the poor and black nearby
> a crane nods waist-high among broken bedrooms.
> Already the university digs foundations
> to be hallowed with the names of old trustees.

Going Down Fast, a "savage novel" in John Leonard's view (1969 45), is
Piercy's first published novel: before this she had written six rejected novels.
Of this novel she has written:

> That had the least women's consciousness of any of my novels, but then it
> was written from 1965 to 1967 when I had the least of any time in my
> life. . . . *Going Down Fast* marked the first time I had written with a male

protagonist, in part, other than in short fiction. The novel is told from two major viewpoints and a number of minor ones, and is a fairly classy example of what you can do with multiple viewpoints in showing political process and the exercise of power and powerlessness. (PCBQ 213-14)

Far from being uninteresting—in Jack Hicks's view it is "a very solid first work" (1981 143)—*Going Down Fast* is an auspicious literary debut, although perhaps less engaging than other novels by Piercy in that character formation is here less convincingly realized. Piercy's formal devices of shifting viewpoints to examine the same incident are part of the message, as are the occasional experimental stretches, as when one character's part is broken up by computer-like captions which disrupt the narrative. These formal devices draw attention to the text's signifying practices, the form being inseparable from the content and indicative of the fragmentation of the lives described: the breakdown of a neighborhood and the crumbling of the sense of continuity and hope for the future. Ambiguous features are inherent in the formal qualities and in the presentation of the characters. Susan Kress writes that *Going Down Fast* "is a novel which, in reflecting the political and personal convulsions of the sixties, takes its shape from imagery of fragmentation and disintegration" (110), and finds that "the book offers numerous examples of those who are deliberately or accidentally broken by the system." As Kress continues: "no authoritative, omniscient narrator tells this story. Instead, a restricted narrator filters it through the consciousness of a number of characters, sometimes in sequential, sometimes in parallel time. The formal narrative strategy suggests that out of such times, out of such characters, come only partial visions, fragments and approximations" (111). Underlining the motif of disparity and fragmentation in *Going Down Fast* is a recurring imagery of jarring contrasts, such as cleanliness/washing/water and ash/dust/dirt. In one of Leon Lederman's movies, his Belle Dame Sans Merci is pictured "in what looked like a large ashtray, washing herself" (GDF 161). As Anna ventures out in Chicago one January day, "The streets were filled with a gray froth like dirty eggwhites" (GDF 281), and later, she notices that "an unclean gray rain had fallen" (GDF 310). This mix of light and shades of darkness, life and death, is linked to the lives and deaths of Black Jack, Rowley's hero, and of Vera Jameson, as well as to the problematic racial intermixing, a central concern in this novel along with issues of gender and class.

Pia Thielmann, a socialist-feminist critic, argues that "the female characters do not learn, change, or develop during the novel," and wonders "what is feminist about this book?" She thus finds little inspiration in this novel for women who seek spiritual guidance, unless one chooses to read it as a cautionary tale illustrating how destructively women can act toward each other (71). It is indeed questionable whether *Going Down Fast* should be classified as a feminist novel, yet here already can be detected seeds of an ideology that Piercy later develops more fully, an ideology suggesting that a maternal principle of connection and caring has been suppressed in capitalist patriarchy. *Going Down Fast* attempts to elucidate the negative effects of this suppression. Feminists could therefore applaud the principles underlying the work even though they might find individual characters disappointing.

The ambiguous title of this novel gives rise to multiple associations: does it refer to some kind of accelerated breakdown? To a sinking ship? To a collapse of structures, or perhaps to the creative destruction preceding rejuvenation—the first page of the novel, with its raw, physical descriptions of the cranes, the noise, the sledgehammer, the workmen in action recalls August Strindberg's poem "Esplanadsystemet." The title also invertedly alludes to the father of Rowley, one of the characters, dying from cancer and "going down slow" (GDF 109).

As I will highlight in the next few passages, *Going Down Fast* indeed presents a group of fragmented characters, whose lives are marked by breakups, divorces, unwanted separations, and worlds in collision. Colliding in this novel are male and female worlds, which might be visualized, with a term from Shirley Ardener, as "dominant" and "muted" worlds. While gender roles are not the main focus, a male-female dynamic that is sometimes a battle underlies the overall symbolism of the novel, informing its major themes. Not infrequently, sexuality is depicted as obsessive-compulsive and in opposition to what characters' conscious minds desire. Anna Levinowitz, one of the major characters, says: "When I'm interested in a man my brain shuts off" (GDF 40), perhaps a necessity in her relationship with Rowley, in which, tossed about on the waves of his decisions or infidelities, she is mostly able to react rather than act. Inherent in the title is undoubtedly an ambiguous sexual allusion, continued in the first page of the novel with its picture of a house and a humanoid crane: "The crane, taller by a couple of stories, was eating [the house]" (GDF 7), in the meaty smell from the stockyards. A Dionysian chaos is depicted here, a sparagmos, a tearing apart of old structures in "a murky late afternoon August green, moist as a swamp," and, in Leon Lederman's imagination, Anna's eyes are "melting" (GDF 8). Leon and Anna, who will later engage in a relationship with each other, are watching the house and crane. Anna is depicted thus: "Naked face watched the walls crumble. She held herself across her full breasts. Her mouth looked as if it might be slightly open. He imagined her eyes melting" (GDF 8). In the "Naked face . . . full breasts . . . mouth . . . slightly open . . . melting" one may see intimations of the "transcendent liquid ecstasy" enjoyed by Shira in *He, She and It* (HSI 118). Yet no transcendence is achieved here. Leon thinks that Anna would identify with "The walls, of course, or something behind them" (GDF 8), an ambiguous thought indeed, but one which becomes more clear as Anna's destiny unfolds. While she does experience a rejuvenating attraction for Rowley and humorously fantasizes about a sign to hang out, "a great neon phallus, here lives Rowley the Rod, Satisfaction Guaranteed" (GDF 11), and feels a "pleasurable terror" (GDF 44) in the first meeting with him, Rowley the Rod and other men are rod-like cranes in Anna's life, knocking down her walls. The shapeshifting ambiguity of the sexual metaphors in *Going Down Fast* illustrates, on one level, the push-and-pull dynamics of the male-female encounters depicted, both a "pleasurable terror" and a battle for versus a resentment of women's not yet fully articulated desire for equality, while, on another level, tying in with the ambiguities of the stage of transition described. Anna's sexualized image of skyscraper and horizon suggests a desire for balance and mutuality: "The skyscraper was invented here, a thrust skyward to counter the thrust of the horizon" (GDF 286). That "The day felt clean and generous" (GDF 286) further enhances the positiveness of her picture of the cityscape as man and woman in inverted missionary position, an image, furthermore, echoing the lines in Piercy's "The skyscrapers of the financial district dance with Gasman" (from *Breaking Camp*):

The skyscrapers are dancing by the river,
. . . .
Standard Oil and General Foods have amalgamated
and Dupont, Schenley and AT&T lie down together.

Anna, a poor but principled college teacher, is among those characters whose homes are threatened by demolition, and whose lives are frayed and fragmented. Cut adrift after a divorce from Asher, she is, at the outset as well as in the end, involved with a blues musician, Rowley. She soon breaks off with Rowley, after his having succumbed to the charms of Caroline Frayne, and slowly becomes involved with Leon Lederman, a divorced avant-garde filmmaker, and moves in with him. More marked by friendship than by passion, this relationship is not unproblematic, since Leon, too, is in love with Caroline and even pictures himself as her savior, the one who can make the fragments of Caroline coalesce and who can "keep her from coming apart into little plastic pieces" (GDF 227).

The son of an abusive, unsympathetic father, the ne'er-do-well Leon is in the end "caged," committed to an asylum, because of what his father sees as mental instability, but which may only be the instability of straddling muted and dominant worlds. Leon may be sideswept into a muted world by a society that lacks comprehension for his avant-garde art, but as a husband, he inhabits a dominant world self-righteously bent on controlling the other half, even with violence, if necessary. Typical of avant-garde film of this time, Leon's movies are fragmentation and instability (perhaps) made art, a collage of "commercials and bodies, politicians and penises, the world with red paint running over" (GDF 160). But is he really mentally unstable? Or is it that the (dominant) world is not yet ready for Leon, for his "good human material and strength and caring and willingness" (GDF 219)? Manifestly, and through parables, Leon is made to mouth the implicit mottoes of *Going Down Fast*, the principles of caring and connection, interestingly rendered through spatial imagery as Leon tells Anna: "What matters is handling others not like things but setting up a connection. A live circuit. You have to keep trying to get through. When you give up, you're dead: walled in" (GDF 48).

Anna returns to Rowley, or he to her, something that Thielmann's analysis deplores, since it happens before Anna has had a chance to restructure her life on her own: What remains negative, in the view of Thielmann (65), is Anna's being a male-oriented woman. While Anna is not entirely lacking in woman-identification, that identification is highly ambivalent, as indicated in her selection of and view of a goddess image: "a photograph of the Cretan great goddess, in shape like a chesspiece: not the well-known barebreasted figure from the empire but a later back-country goddess of a defeated power with stoic face and pillar body, arms stiffly raised past the head in blessing or surrender" (GDF 24).

Rowley's relationships, too, are marked by fragmentation and disruption. Apart from his relationship with Anna he is for a time involved with Caroline Frayne, who gets pregnant by him and whom he then abandons. Caroline turns back to her fiancé, Bruce, who beats up Rowley for his undesired contribution. Rowley also has a brief affair with Vera Jameson, a fiercely independent black woman, before returning to Anna. An important part of Rowley's rite of passage is his search for continuity and connection in his looking for a musician, Black Jack, for Rowley a hero who has given inspiration and direction to his life. At the end, his vision is "of darkness, pain and despair" (Kress 111). Through his choice of music Rowley aligns himself with the marginal, the downtrodden and exploited—but he does not belong with them. Even though he lives in the "Cracks, crevices," the "interstices of a rich society," that society "paid him to entertain it and to preserve pieces of its urban folklore for future entertainment" (GDF 214).

Caroline Frayne, the focus of desire of Rowley and other male characters in *Going Down Fast*, is playing the role of the 'dumb blonde,' whose pliable behavior and "innocent slutty look" (GDF 51), calculated to please men, does not, however, bring the rewards it is supposed to; neither does it lead to any sense of female solidarity. Vera Jameson is, in several respects, Caroline's opposite. Inscrutable and appearing as if carved out of one piece, Vera herself resembles the masks she creates. Disguising and revealing, the masks, mostly "constructed of household trivia," mimic and wryly comment on society: "Wall of faces. Wall of judgments. Society which must jar and rub on her, cuff and molest her, insult her daily in banal and trumpeting ways, she looked back at through its blind faces" (GDF 84). Rowley, from whose perspective we view the masks, puts down the abstract level of "society" as cause for Vera's discontent and tensed withdrawal. While fancying himself as an embattled rebel against society, however, he is part of that troubled society which makes Vera wish she could wear an Arab veil so that male animals on the street cannot wipe their eyes on her, as she puts it. In Anna's view, too, Rowley is indeed part of a society that divides women into "good girls and fallen women" (GDF 156). Revealingly, when Vera makes a mask of Rowley, "The mask was all leer and droop, part hound, part lecher and smug with satisfaction" (GDF 85). Vera's masks can be seen as the protective shields held up by the muted world of America's "marginal" people: women and minorities, the powerless, against the ruthless manifestations of power of the dominant groups or its guards. In a scene in which issues of race and gender intersect, Rowley and Vera are stopped by police when walking in a cemetery. The police are "staring at Vera. How she must feel it, the simple threat of rape" (GDF 174). Rowley fails to see that the nature of power is neither pure nor simple, and that from certain "other" perspectives he could be seen as implicated in the same power dynamics as the two policemen, which elicits in Vera a spatially rendered attitude described as a "childish mask of no-one-home" (GDF 197). Vera reaches a horrible end as she dies in a fire. In Thielmann's view, this is because she represents a threat to patriarchal society (69). Granted, Vera is an uncompromisingly autonomous character, almost a witch figure high up in her apartment house and surrounded by her strange masks, but as a grade school teacher she is also a nurturer. The school building could be seen as a hierarchical structure that makes its teachers paint the schoolchildren institution gray and which extinguishes the life-saving maternal principle of connection society actually desperately needs. As a parallel, Anna's building is torn down at the end of the novel.

More peripheral characters are Asher and Sheldon, both of whom represent a principle of separation and hierarchy. Asher is Anna's ex-husband, a man fearful of commitments and a representative of rationality who will lecture Anna on her irrationality (GDF 43). Hierarchically, Asher has "ideas of wifehood" (GDF 44) and of what constitutes female beauty (GDF 43) that Anna, while married to him, attempts to live up to in order to gain his approbation. Anna's marriage to Asher, and traditional marriage in itself, is likened to a cage in Leon's story: "A man got himself a pretty bright-colored bird because he liked the way it sang. He took it home and put it in a cage, but it wouldn't eat or drink, and finally it got so small it flew out like a mosquito through the wire mesh. That goes to show you, the man said, I should've invested in a better cage" (GDF 48-49). While Asher is part of a dominant group, Anna belongs to a muted world, whose reaction to Asher's chilly dominance is "*squashed* fury" (GDF 44, my emphasis). Sheldon represents white male capitalist patriarchy. Rowley and his visions are cut off from and contrasted against that of Sheldon, who lacks compassion both in his personal life—he is Leon's unsympathetic father—and in his exploitative attitude toward society. In his dreams for a "new City," for example, he seems to have abjured all sympathy for the people who will be evicted (GDF 244-68). In his son's view, "Sheldon sounds like a vulture, he acts like a vulture, he thinks like a vulture. He even smells like one" (GDF 45). What Sheldon dreams of is "Light, cleanliness, order, totality" (GDF 244), which will triumph over the Dionysian "vulgarity and chaos" (GDF 248)—as in Piercy's poem "The track of the master builder" (*Hard Loving*):

> Fortresses, dungeons, keeps,
> moats and bulwarks. Palaces with mirrored halls;
> rooms whose views unfold into each other
> like formal gardens, offer vistas and symmetry.
> Skyscrapers where nobody lives filled with paper.

Sheldon envisions a city recreated with the needs of corporate men in mind: "Beyond, the garden cities, and beyond that ring, the industrial and research belt, then fancier wooded suburbs for semi-country living" (GDF 248).

Throughout the novel, spatial metaphors of houses or images of construction/demolition illustrate the relations between the muted and dominant worlds of class, race, and gender. Anna's street, for example, is "like a bright grimy fringe on the green carpet of middle-class housing" (GDF 27), while, on the lake, there is a "largely vertical" area of "new glass walled skyscrapers. Cliffs of money on the lake" (GDF 42)—lines associating to Piercy's poem "Gasman invites the skyscrapers to dance" (in *Breaking Camp*):

> Lonely skyscrapers, deserted tombs of business risen
> and gone home to the suburbs for the night,
> your elevators are forlorn as empty cereal boxes,
> your marble paved vestibules and corridors
> might as well be solid rock.
> Beautiful lean shafts, nobody loves you except pigeons,
> nobody is cooking cabbage or instant coffee in your high rooms,
> nobody draws moustaches, nobody pisses on your walls.
> Even your toilet stalls have nothing to report about the flesh.
> You could be inhabited by blind white cavefish.
> Only the paper lives in its metal drawers humming like bees.

In her essay "Masculine and Feminine Cities: Marge Piercy's *Going Down Fast* and *Fly Away Home*," Christine W. Sizemore argues that in these two "urban novels," "Marge Piercy addresses the question whether women can create feminine spaces, places for themselves within the city" (Sizemore 90). In American literature, writes Sizemore, women have either been excluded from the city or have been its victims. While men have planned and built the cities, women have suffered from the violence generated within the social and urban schemes. Sizemore sees this as a particularly American condition and points out that women novelists in other countries do not always portray the city as negative: portraits of London, for example, are often vastly more positive.

In *Going Down Fast*, Sizemore sees a picture of "the negative tradition of women's lack of place in the city" (91). Relying upon Jessica Benjamin's concept of intersubjective space, Sizemore contrasts the spaces of masculinity, the individual, phallic towers celebrated by Asher and Ledermann, with the relational, other-directed or other-involved spaces of femininity.   Male individuality denies connection more than it affirms it: "The male characters in *Going Down Fast* who are involved in urban renewal all fit Benjamin's description of the male personality as emphasizing separation, autonomy, and rationality" (93). Asher and Lederman are equally fascinated with skyscrapers, Asher being "the primary example of the dominating, separatist male personality" who "behind his façade of rationality . . . is afraid of difference and connection with other people" (94). Sizemore links the visions of these two characters with the modernist architecture created by exemplars such as Patrick Byrne and Richard Keeley, an architecture that is "authoritative, rational, and elitist" (95). Along the lines of the architectural critic Jane Jacobs, Marge Piercy is, instead, focused on neighborhoods and on people.

The fate of Anna and that of her building may be interpreted in different ways. She can be viewed as defeated in the end, a victim of patriarchy whose building falls because of capitalist greed. Or her demolished home could symbolize a necessary tearing down of negative, obsolete structures and thus signal new beginnings. In Kress's view, "Piercy does propose a modest personal, if not political, affirmation at the end of the book" (Kress 111), in that Anna and Rowley are together again in February, with the first thaw of the Chicago winter (112). As far as Leon is concerned, "What came off him more and more strongly as [Anna] knew him was a sense of waste, of good human material and strength and caring and willingness, wasting" (GDF 219). Throughout the novel, the battle of principles of separation and hierarchy versus connectedness and empathy rages, but remains unresolved. However, with *Going Down Fast*, Piercy has set the stage for a battle that will continue in her novels to come.

Chapter 2

Dance the Eagle to Sleep

> Words, words! You just mix them around and make boxes with them to hold
> your head in. I ask something real, and you give me back an abstraction.
> Plastic Man!
>
> *Dance the Eagle to Sleep* 143

In a recent book entitled *The Dream and the Nightmare: The Sixties' Legacy to the Underclass*, Myron Magnet has depicted the 1960s counterculture as responsible for the most appalling problems in America, such as the escalation of drug abuse and crime, poverty and homelessness. The legacy of the counterculture, in Magnet's analysis, included a set of values devastating to blacks and the lower class. Hard work, responsibility and discipline, marriage and family, all of this was scorned by the counterculture, which celebrated free love and drugs. Magnet argues that whereas young people from the middle class were able to enjoy their temporary dwelling on the margins of structurelessness, young people from the lower class were not, instead remaining permanently mired in a morass of drug abuse and joblessness. This leads Magnet to conclude that it is the fault of the liberal counterculture of the 1960s that the lower classes are stuck in the quagmire in the 1990s. The generation of the 1960s, as Camille Paglia has commented, "heroically broke through Fifties conformism but . . . failed in many ways to harness or sustain its own energies" (1992 vii).

While I would question Magnet's wholesale assault on the 1960s counterculture, it did have some aspects which, if magnified, could cause considerable damage. Some of those aspects are historicized in Marge Piercy's second novel, *Dance the Eagle to Sleep*. Set sometime in the future, *Dance the Eagle to Sleep* documents the rise and fall of an ill-fated group of young revolutionaries, the Indians, who secede from society to form farms and paramilitary warrior groups with the aim of overthrowing oppressive American society—the Eagle. In part, *Dance the Eagle to Sleep* is an acerbic post-mortem on the struggles of Students for a Democratic Society, more usually called the SDS, an organization to which Piercy herself belonged but the abstract rhetoric of which she grew increasingly disenchanted with (See "Active in Time and History" and "The Grand Coolie Dam"). Piercy's poem "In the men's room(s)," is a rendering of how a youthful self tries to squeeze itself into a left-wing intellectual world, a self-absorbed male arena, where, "To be certified worthy of high masculine discourse/ like a potato on a grater I would rub on contempt," and where the men "were talking of integrity and existential ennui/ while the women ran out for six-packs and had abortions/ in the kitchen and fed the children and were auctioned off" (*Circles on the Water*).

Comparing *Dance the Eagle to Sleep* to *Going Down Fast*, Susan Kress writes: "*Dance the Eagle to Sleep* offers the next stage in revolution, and proposes a very different kind of artistic form. If the characters in *Going Down Fast* have gone down to the bottom, have stripped themselves of illusion, and have analyzed their situation, then those in *Dance the Eagle to Sleep* suggest some ways of acting on that analysis, some ways of rebuilding" (112). *Dance the Eagle to Sleep* has been seen as a dystopia (Sargent 23) and as "a science fiction extrapolation" (Moylan 1982 136). Evoking the period parlance of the 1960s youth culture and its idealistic but limited perspectives, it paints a disturbing and depressing scenario. John Updike has suggested that "Piercy's tale is less persuasive than it might have been and therefore politically inefficient" (according to Hicks 1981 149); in Updike's words, Piercy "resorts to a hurried sociological tone, makes people talk like press handouts, and declines to linger upon sensual details" (147; also quoted in Hicks 1981 149). But despite such flaws as what Hicks has seen as "a wide streak of rhetorical preaching and posing," there are interesting aspects: one might agree with Hicks that "the fiction's weaknesses, perhaps even more than its virtues, are instructive and exemplary" (144). Despite its flaws, it was "Praised by left liberal critics in *Nation, Commonweal*, and *New Republic*" and is, according to Hicks, "politically informed and convincing. The force and detail of Marge Piercy's analyses are valuable" (149). John Leonard in the *New York Times*, who finds that Piercy's "prose crackles, depolarizes, sends shivers leaping across the synaptic cleft," sees it as a "frightening, marvelous book!" (1970 39).

Perhaps more pointedly than any other of Piercy's novels, *Dance the Eagle to Sleep* discusses questions of the difficult and debated relationship between art and politics, "the question of how," in Hicks's words, "art may most effectively move people to share or act upon a political belief. More exactly, how can fiction best convey a political vision? How can political concepts, values, and judgments be submerged in fictional forms, be translated into compelling patterns of character in action with which people can identify?" (Hicks 1981 149).

Through an analysis of characterization, imagery and plot in *Dance the Eagle to Sleep*, I will show how Piercy creates an ideological panorama rife with tension. *Dance the Eagle to Sleep* is the story of the Indians, the group of teenagers who wish to avoid the Nineteenth Year of Servitude, a year of service to the state obligatory for nineteen-year-olds not pursuing scientific studies, a part of The Plan, a "task force on youth problems":

> Most guys still ended up in the Army, and a great many went into the street patrols and the city militia. But a number were channeled into overseas aid and pacification corps, the rebuilding programs in the bombed-out ghettoes, and the pollution clean-up corps. Girls who weren't pushed into the nursing corps worked in the preschool socialization programs in the ghettoes or as teachers' aides or low-level programmers for the array of teaching machines. Of course, students in medicine, engineering and the sciences just kept trotting through school. (DES 10-11)

The novel is told from a variety of perspectives: that of Corey, the half-Indian leader of the movement; Billy, a high school whiz kid and later leader of a group of warriors; Sean/Shawn, a young rock musician; Jill/Joanna, a runaway teenager; Marcus, leader of a black gang that has fled society altogether and lives in a state park. In Piercy's own words, "the emphasis is on significant episodes of a collective action. There are five major characters, four of them viewpoint characters and one seen only from the other's eyes" (as quoted in Hicks 1973 543-44). Hicks finds that while the "central characters share a marionettelike quality early in the novel, they become less wooden and more convincing in action" (1981 147). In the view of Susan Kress, in *Dance the Eagle to Sleep*, "Piercy seems to have come to the conclusion that if she wants to express a coherent alternative to a capitalist system, she will need to locate the energy for that vision in a different group of characters, and channel that energy through a different formal structure" (112).

Originating in the powerful summons of Corey's nightmare vision of being attacked by an eagle, this revolutionary movement deteriorates into a more oppressive force than the society it set out to destroy. As seen in the characters' uncertainty and ambivalence, it is a time of transition during which it is crucial not to be pushed onto the wrong path. *Dance the Eagle to Sleep* demonstrates what happens if extremist doctrines prevail. The portraits of the Indians are of young people in transition, with a great deal of confusion and ambivalence. Some dialogues among the women characters show an incipient questioning of the roles men expect them to play. When the confusions are not dispelled, conflict arises out of the double standard, as when Joanna deems it necessary to sleep with Shawn in a distorted affirmation of her fledgling independence, something that leads to a crisis of trust with her lover, Corey, even though Corey himself routinely sleeps with other women.

As pointed out by Hicks, "Joanna is the major female character. Like the other four, she is virtually a sociological type . . . the most static of the cast, revealed to us in skeletal form; indeed, her 'brainwashed' character remains unconvincing throughout the novel. She too serves as the handiest mouthpiece for the preachiest of political lectures" (1981 146). In Thielmann's view, Joanna actually develops backwards (74). Initially, Joanna is shown to spurn women's traditional roles:

> It depressed her that she could only define herself in negatives. She was not like her mother. She was not like her father. The conventional masculine and the conventional feminine were for shit. The primary business of those base ladies was to talk about each other. What her mother knew could be contained in a greeting card and consisted of You're Supposed To's and Don't You Dare's. It could be summed up as "Don't sit with your knees apart, Jill [Joanna's real name], you're a big girl now."
>
> She did not want to be somebody else's wife or somebody else's mother. Or somebody else's servant or somebody else's secretary. Or somebody else's sex kitten or somebody else's keeper. She saw no women around who seemed to be anybody in themselves. They all wore some man's uniform. She wanted to be free, and free meant not confined, not forced to lie, not forced to pretend, not warped, not punished, not tortured. (DES 54)

To find a way out of the enclosure, however, is not easy. Joanna wonders, "how could you know what you wanted if you never had seen it?" (DES 56). "What pulled her was getting out of the hate machine and getting to a place where people were gentle to each other, didn't bug each other, shared what they had, shared their food and their bodies and their music and their space and their kicks. She would not grab at anybody or let anybody fix hooks into her. Women mostly wanted to take some man, turn him into a house and go sit in it." Lacking role models, and not having been brought up to be independent, Joanna does not fare too well in her journey toward freedom. Her environment, whether at home or when she has run away, is somehow too overwhelming, and her struggles to find her own road and to find out what her true needs are, are in the end thwarted. Joanna is in reality no more 'free' than her mother. Her feelings of powerlessness render her unable to refuse a sexual encounter she does not desire as sordid payment for staying overnight—"Old creep. She hadn't been using anything of his, sleeping on his kitchen floor. Hadn't even been eating there. The body tax. To be obliged to have sex with someone was about the only thing that could kill it" (DES 58)—or makes her embarrassed if she does desire a man enough to take the initiative: "She had never been aggressive before. She had always asked the man if he wanted to, if he hadn't asked her first, and then let him" (DES 68). "She felt enormously embarrassed. She had seduced him, raped him almost" (DES 69). When she becomes "Corey's girl," she lets her identity become submerged under his, allowing Corey's needs to determine her role and behavior within the relationship and also within the group. In her relationship with Corey, Joanna is the provider of maternal sustenance and support, which he is all too willing to exploit. Thielmann argues that Piercy's portrait of Joanna as the Mother and the Whore enables a female reader to scrutinize those stereotypes and see where she stands herself (75).

Jill/Joanna remains a confused and ambivalent character of conflicting 'new' and 'old' ideas. In a dream, the black boys in the state park rape her, and "she became their queen and their slave" (DES 125), a vision that captures her real situation as a woman, a servant who is simultaneously put on a pedestal. Furthermore, her ideas on masculinity remain ambivalent. Apparently, she despises Corey for not being 'man' enough to execute Chuck. "[Corey] forgave himself for not shooting Chuck, but he saw that Joanna did not" (DES 120). It is after this episode that Joanna reveals to Corey that she had "made it with Shawn once." Caught in a raid in the end, Joanna is put through a manipulative sort of psychoanalysis, for which 'cure' her unformed identity and inner uncertainty and ambivalence make her a prime candidate. Co-opted into the society of the 'Eagle,' renouncing all struggle and regressing to being Jill again, Joanna expounds on the perils she has escaped:

> It was the whole matter of my penis envy. I had no good female models. I wanted to be a boy and I tried to turn myself into one. For instance, sleeping around and running away from home and trying to reject myself—pretending my name was Joanna, pretending I could become someone else. My name is Jill, and I wish you'd use it. Wanting to be a warrior—what was that but wanting to be what my father was? It was that whole fixation on the Army. But there was a positive side in me, even then. For instance, Dr. Hayes pointed out that I was captured because I was in Tunnel D with the babies. That was my effort in a crisis situation to act out my femininity. (DES 210-11)

Another ambivalent and complex character representing both positive and negative values is Corey, in high school a dealer who had learned that there were "only the powerful and the powerless" (DES 23). Of his girl-friend, Ginny, he thinks, "Publicly and privately, she was his property" (DES 25), and he dreams of Asian women, who will let him be the master and retain the initiative: "Tough and silent as a shadow, she would follow him" (DES 28), while at the same time despising his mother and sister "for their clinging weakness" (DES 29). Still, he realizes his own part as well as that of society in women's oppression, as evident in his diagnosis of Ginny's situation, thinking that "she was too conned by the system and by him to challenge anything." Even while his own discovery of an Indian heritage parallels women's search for a history and traditions of their own, his awareness never develops far enough to include women's situations. It is Corey's Indian heritage that makes him reject an ultra macho, paramilitary stance adopted by other members of this "tribe." As both the title of the novel and the association to Piercy's "Curse of the earth magician on a metal land" cited below (from *Hard Loving*) suggest, Corey's way is a more gentle one, aiming toward creation, not destruction.

> This is butterfly's war song about to darken into the fire.
> Put the eagle to sleep.
> I see from the afternoon papers
> that we have bought another country
> and are cutting the natives down to build jet airstrips.
> A common motif in monumental architecture in the United States
> is an eagle with wings spread, beak open
> and the globe grasped in his claws.
> Put the eagle to sleep.

In his relationship with Joanna Corey also reciprocates, he wants to be good to her, and at the zenith of their time together, "he would tell her that she was making him human. She would say that they were giving birth to each other" (DES 128). Claiming in the beginning that the tribe is just that—a "tribe"—he asserts that they are (or should be) "Past couples. Past the nuclear family that works so well as a hotbed for breeding neurosis" (DES 75), he nevertheless develops a possessiveness about Joanna. He says to Chuck, a more traditional member of the tribe who, despite the possibility of punishment by death sells the Indians' type of drugs at higher prices and keeps the difference himself, because he wants to buy a car so that he can impress girls, whom he calls chicks: "The man taught you to take women like tissues, and wipe yourself in them and throw them away" (DES 118). Yet this assessment does not lead him to scrutinize his own attitudes and behavior. Corey chooses male values in the end; his retreat to a mountaintop is a traditionally male choice of spiritual retirement. In an inversion of the story of the princess on the glass mountain and a merging of this story with Corey's eagle metaphor, Corey flees from his last encounter with brainwashed Joanna: "Claws in his chest. The air was glass. It was crushing him as he ran blindly, and a choked scream escaped him like an injured bird drag-flapping off, like a wounded crow" (DES 212). In climbing up the mountaintop, Corey is associated with a patriarchal principle, as is Avram in *He, She and It*. In Carol Ochs' words: "In patriarchal religions, God, if he is not in the highest heavens, is at least atop a mountain, such as Olympus or Sinai. In matriarchy, where God is identified with the earth, one descends to address the gods" (104). Choosing isolation rather than connection, Corey loses his last surviving friends. The Indian way of Dancing the Eagle to Sleep is lost, co-opted by the dominant discourse. Possibly, Corey's positive characteristics will live on in his and Ginny's child, born at the end of the novel.

A third major character is Billy Batson, with a first name associating to billyclubs and whose last name associates to hitting/batting and to bats, thus carrying connotations both of violence and lunacy, as well as to a shadow side of socialist ideas. "Named for the human weakling in which comic book superhero Captain Marvel hid" (Hicks 1981 146; see also DES 39), Billy is one of those students who are "tracked" for science in grade school, where the students are tracked for life. "Sometime in high school, already your fate was settled, your social class was established for the rest of your life . . . If you weren't in the academic track and the fast classes, nobody would try to teach you much, just keep you busy" (DES 48-49). It is in the depiction of Billy that Hicks finds "Piercy's rhetorical excesses" to be "especially blatant" (1981 146).

At the outset, Billy is not a negative character. Helping to teach Joe, "a certified slow learner" (DES 41), he discovers that Joe is not a slow learner at all, and that Joe, moreover, may have something to teach Billy, too. "He had seen himself as Joe's liberal teacher, but Joe was giving him more real and more useful instruction than he was giving Joe" (DES 41). Being a more isolated person, Billy envies Joe his net of connections, "his easy rapport with his family and his brothers and sisters," and begins to realize that "in a fancier way he was just as trapped and manipulated as Joe" (DES 42). Billy gets into the high school rebellion instigated by Corey. The courses they create echo the 1960s counterculture and women's consciousness-raising groups. "Corey said that people were finding out that what each of them had thought of as his personal problem that he must solve in his life, was not personal at all but a common problem" (DES 51). Billy, however, undergoes a negative development. Opting to join the warriors and to adopt male values, he chooses a road to destruction. He never takes seriously what he did learn from Joe or from Ginny. As Thielmann points out: "Billy, the scientist among the Indians, turns into a soldier and goes as far as to use the same expressions for his cause as used by the 'Hate Machine,' such as 'power,' 'battle discipline,' 'defense/offense,' 'general,' and 'army'" (115). John Seelye, who has compared *Dance the Eagle to Sleep* to *Lord of the Flies*, also sees in Billy an Ahab, "whose disillusionment with the System turns into maniac hatred" (25).

Shawn's attitudes and actions are not always commendable or even justifiable (as when he shoots Chuck), but he is a more flexible and open character from the start, and his choice of reaching out and embracing feminine or maternal values or a principle of connection allows him to survive.

More open to women's perspectives from the beginning, he listens to other boys in school talk about girls, "and the talk choked him. A girl will let you know, she knows what she wants, he would have said" (DES 9). As a rock musician he is immensely popular. "At age eighteen, Shawn was officially loved by sixty thousand four hundred and eleven girls registered in his fan clubs" (DES 7). What is important for him is his sense of connection to his audience. When he enters a relationship with Mrs. Kapp, an 'older' divorcée of twenty-six, it is not primarily for her physical appearance, but out of a genuine desire for communication, because "he had to stay human" (DES 12). A character full of contradictions, he ultimately sides with Ginny.

As mentioned above and as suggested in the titles of two chapters ("How Joanna Accepts a Chain" and "Corey Holds on to the Ball"), the women in this novel do not improve their lots by joining the Indians. The movement suppresses any feminine or maternal values and extols a macho stance of force and hierarchy. "They were always whipping each other into more-and-more-militant thrusts of rhetoric. Nobody dared seem less revolutionary than anybody else. Their language was all of armed struggle, while they had not one plane or tank or bomb" (DES 140). Like the boys, the girls are slotted into their roles, but they are treated with less concern: "The girls wanted to learn karate and self-defense too, but they complained that no one would teach them seriously. They said the boys did not care if they learned or not, yet they had much greater need" (DES 50). In the verbal battle, the women lose out. "In some tribes the women might as well have stayed out of council, for they were ignored and afraid to speak" (DES 140).

> Of course most of the girls were just names: "Nancy, Lena, Sue, Gloria, Hilary..." They got stuck with all the inglorious daily jobs that made the place run. Unless a girl thrust herself forward insistently or forced herself into the warriors, she could spend her tribal life washing dishes and peeling potatoes and changing babies. A few men like Shawn disliked the sexual roles and consciously crossed over to help care for the babies. But the girls who did not push hard, found themselves quietly pushed down. (DES 129)

This depiction echoes assessments Piercy has made of the New Left: "Most prestige in the movement rests not on having done anything in particular, but in having visibly dominated some gathering or in manipulating a certain set of rhetorical counters well in public, or in having played some theatrical role" ("The Grand Coolie Dam" 16). In the same article, Piercy also comments on the difficulties women had (or have) with using political jargon. One of the few who not only perceives this pattern but who actively challenges it, Ginny emerges as the one who really changes and who pushes others to change. Bitterly, she realizes that all her caring is insufficient to prevent Corey's death. For a while, because of the developments within the movement, she sees men as her enemy and wants to be left alone. "She told them they were in love with apocalypse, like all men, more in love with myths than with any woman" (DES 217). She argues that "Men are always floating castles on a cloud of hot air!" (DES 219) Male politics irritate her. She allies herself with nature—with a mythical natural world as it existed before the division into "strutting snarling males and their nurturing suffering females" (DES 222). Perhaps a new era—"try it again!" (DES 222)—will bring more balance and harmony. Taken quite literally, the ending certainly is overly optimistic, but if one chooses to read the story of the Indians as a metaphor (as does Thielmann), it has a symbolic value: "The baby lived and she lived and it was day for Marcus and for him, it was day for all of them" (DES 224). In Hicks's view, "The tale ends on the tiniest of glimmers" (1981 148), whereas Kress asserts that "the symbolism is heavy-handed; dogma weighs down the imaginative structure; and the book comes to a kind of visionary dead end" (114).

Why do the efforts to create a new society fail? Initially, "liberation" (DES 12), "rebellion, freedom, sex" were the guiding stars (DES 13), leading away from threats to women of "being raped or beaten or hit on the head or cut up with a knife" (DES 17), away from the lack of empathy of parents (DES 19), away from distorted teachings of history that suppress or rewrite the history of Native Americans. Corey's original vision is of a world reborn into harmony and cooperation, into a bodily wholeness and communion/connection between people and land. Corey visualizes a "mothering, fathering buffalo" that will inspire him and his tribe to conquer the eagle, the all-American emblem of strength and power. Billy sees America as the glass mountain he remembers from the fairy tale about the princess who lived at the top of the mountain and who sadistically solicited knights to ascend the slippery slope to woo her (DES 40). Already from the start Billy sneers at Corey's plans, visualized through a maternal metaphor, of building a nation "in the belly of this one," based on "community" and "cooperation" (DES 44) and with associations to boundaryless and life-giving water: "We're water. Only if they can scare us and freeze us can they break us up. We're water and we can flow together" (DES 52). Billy's response is "Rhetoric. Bullshit. You have no analysis and no strategy. You have no program" (DES 45). The idea of getting rid of the teacher's chair and assembling in a circle does not appeal to Billy, who remains an aloof outsider also at the nude ritualistic dancing. Billy's adherence to principles of separation and hierarchy, to the "male warrior style" (DES 89) that shuts out women's voices is disastrous, as is the demagoguery and dictatorship that develops. As Norm Fruchter writes in *The Village Voice*, "the tribes have developed only opposition identities which can verify revolutionary credentials only by the willingness to fight and die. . . . and therefore the self-necessity to define themselves as revolutionaries can only be achieved by the escalations of militancy, a self-destruct spiral" (36). A myopic faction of warriors is formed, Fire People against the Water People. Seelye's comparison of this novel to *Lord of the Flies* is indeed apt: if anything, the Indians are suffering less from a lack of program or strategy than from a lack of connection to all the real people, the unemployed, "fucked over," "robbed" (DES 138), who are not prepared to become Indians or to take comfort in quotes from Lenin or Mao. Their jargon effectively separates and alienates them from ordinary people, and in a new little hierarchy of zealotry, the Indians deem themselves to be superior to the very people they wish to save from the claws of the Eagle.

A turning point in the plot and a move away from the original credos of cooperation and community toward a divisive principle allows Billy to view Chuck and his actions as entirely cut off from and inimical to those of the tribe. The idea that Chuck could be reeducated or simply kept on the farm or that they may all be sharing in the responsibility for Chuck's actions—that "no one had noticed and no one had cared" that Chuck took the wrong road, are not considered (DES 112). The others are not willing to trust Chuck, and the council turns into a wrestling for power, control, and prestige with "a dangerous feel to the room. It was necessary to do something to heal the collective" (DES 113). But even Corey is drawn into the struggle for power, and "bleakly" admits that "power corrupts" (DES 114). While Joanna chooses to cling to the illusion that Corey lacks interest in power and only cares altruistically for the group, Ginny is the only one to question Billy's development toward military discipline and violent measures, the madness that gradually takes over, and the offensiveness replacing their initial defensiveness. Ginny comes up with alternative solutions everyone can benefit from: instead of killing Chuck so that he cannot sell the tribe's recipe for drugs, she suggests that they simply give the recipe away. Bureaucracy, however, stands in the way: they cannot go against the decision of a council, and Billy and the warriors, moreover, use the income from drugs for buying weapons, in a not so ironic replication of the culture they claim to repudiate.

Through these characters' lives and fates Piercy illustrates the value of adopting 'male' or 'female' methods or characteristics in a battle for a better world, with a possible triumph for the latter. Whether or not one chooses to interpret the ending—Ginny's giving birth to Corey's child, assisted by Marcus and Shawn—as indicating hope for the world, a return to humane values and to respect for nature, *Dance the Eagle to Sleep* does suggest that certain characteristics, praised or denounced as 'male,' and what I have called a principle of separation and hierarchy, must be renounced if the world is to survive. An awareness of and reassessment of gender, as well as a conscious personal choice as to value systems, in reality neither 'male' nor inherently 'female,' must be made. Moreover, no matter how detested a political system may be, to imitate its methods in striking back is no solution. Violence only breeds more violence. Fancying themselves a vanguard, these warriors in their actions and attitudes reflect only the shadow side of the society they wish to overturn. In terms of awareness of gender roles, furthermore, these "revolutionaries" are not so revolutionary after all: women's roles have been left unexamined, and women are no less exploited or despised than in the society they have left behind, in which "the sexes were segregated and sharply delineated in function" (DES 11). The options available to women are seen by Joanna as two: the mommy/madonna or the whore, who "would lie on a pink cushion with her bush carefully airbrushed out and millions of sad men would jerk off all over the page in preference to having anything to do with real hairy women" (DES 55)—both images, however, of the mommy/madonna and the whore, being in reality equally airbrushed and unreal. The men's attitudes sometimes approach Nazi positions in their contempt for weakness and in their wish to relegate women to *Küche* and *Kinder*, if not *Kirche*. The women "belong" to their men, and the men retain leadership and initiative, despising methods that are not "masculine," paramilitary, violent, aggressive—methods that lead to death and destruction in the end. As if commenting on *Dance the Eagle to Sleep*, in 1972 Piercy wrote: "The counter-culture has a long way to go before it's a real counter-culture for women. . . . Dropping out, digging the primitive and the tribal too often goes along with women as beasts of burden and a whole ragbag of patriarchal myth and heaviness, the creation of a hierarchy outside the mainstream that is even a bit cruder and meaner and more ruthless" ("Tom Eliot meets the Hulk at Little Big Horn" 66).

But as in other novels by Piercy, in *Dance the Eagle to Sleep* there is choice. Women who become warriors can adopt male values; men can (at least partially) reject destructive values, as do Corey, Shawn, and in the end, Marcus, who, unlike his comrades, survives because he chooses to trust and follow a woman (Ginny). The closing scene shows how Shawn and Marcus have cast off their "shells" of cultural conditioning; aiding in Ginny's giving birth, they are adopting values that they have hitherto considered primarily womanly. In John Leonard's words: "Miss Piercy can come up with no better ending to their experiment than John Steinbeck settled for in 'The Grapes of Wrath'—the birth of a new child, the image of motherhood and renewal, the precious increment of unsullied consciousness. It is not enough, but it is all there is" (1970 39). After all the preceding internecion, there is thus a somewhat hopeful note—a vision of connection, empathy and cooperation replacing earlier distrust and discord, a vision echoed in the last stanza of "The spring offensive of the snail" (*Circles on the Water*):

Yes, for some time we might contemplate
not the tiger, not the eagle or grizzly
but the snail who always remembers
that wherever you find yourself eating
is home, the center
where you must make your love,
and wherever you wake up
is here, the right place to be
where we start again.

Chapter 3

Small Changes

> Then Miriam, the prophetess, the sister of Aaron, took a timbrel in her hand; and all the women went out after her with timbrels and dancing.
>
> Exodus 15:20

Along with *Braided Lives*, *Small Changes*, more clearly than other novels by Piercy, describes and analyzes gender roles and relations, vividly reflecting women's, and in some cases, men's increased awareness and change, the slow pace of which is alluded to in the title of the novel—the slow exodus out of patriarchy.

Critics have praised *Small Changes* for its exploration of several different lifestyles tried out by women during this time (see, e.g., Schulder). In *Feminist Fabulation: Postmodern Fiction*, Marleen Barr places Piercy among "feminist fabulators," who "create protagonists who socially reposition themselves after rewriting patriarchal discourses (i.e., fables) about women. By doing so, the authors simultaneously critique the process of excluding women from postmodern discourse and reposition themselves as postmodernists according to their own terms, not according to the terms of stellar male theorists" (1992 185).

It was a difficult novel to write, according to Piercy herself; she says "all through 1970, I was trying to start it . . . trying to find, somehow a vocabulary of actions that would define what I wanted to say about women . . . and somehow to figure out how to deal dramatically with all those small ways that women were oppressed" (as quoted in Albrecht 91). In *Parti-Colored Blocks for a Quilt*, she describes her project thus:

> *Small Changes* was an attempt to produce in fiction the equivalent of a full experience in a consciousness-raising group for many women who would

never go through that experience. It was conceived from the beginning as a
very full novel that would be long, almost Victorian in its scope and detail.
I wanted, I needed that level of detail in the lives of my two protagonists.
The novel is as much about who is doing the housework at any given point
as it is about who is sleeping with whom. (214-15)

In Piercy's short story "Do You Love Me?" the 'safety' of marriage is
connected with thoughts of death in the female protagonist's mind. Within the
androcentric culture depicted in *Small Changes*, too, marriage becomes a
suffocating institution for women, who are shown to slowly drown in an ever-
engulfing sea of demands, arising not out of an original loving bond but from
the culturally imposed roles that usurp the initial, real emotional connection.

The way in which the female characters are taught to focus on marriage
frames the novel structurally, reinforcing the image of marriage as entrapment:
in chapter 1, ironically entitled "The Happiest Day of a Woman's Life," a
lamb (Beth) walks into the lion's den (marriage with Jim); in the last chapter,
an unmarried woman sets her desperate hopes on somebody else's husband—to
ensnare the coveted prize, a Man, and to survive within 'the Man,' that is, the
system, this exploited and pathetic paramour-to-be, isolated, and of an unraised
consciousness, must leap into the extramarital fray and wreck a marriage.
Within these structural brackets, Piercy elaborates on relations to men and to
'the Man' from a female and feminist perspective. Women are just beginning
to become more visible—at least to themselves, even though the traditional
gender roles are barely beginning to be transformed. The sexual revolution has
brought no real change, however, but is seen by female protagonists as more
to men's advantage than to theirs; "It was only a revolution for men," as
Dorine says (SC 421). Spatially rendered, the struggle sometimes seems
overwhelming: "The whole commerce between men and women was too
complicated and exhausting, composed of boxes and blind alleys and dead
ends," as Beth expresses it to herself (SC 455). In this chapter, I will
approach Piercy's ideological tenets through a close reading of, primarily, how
her principal characters are depicted, but with a look also at some minor
characters of importance. As Piercy has stated: "One of the tasks of minor
characters in novels, of course, is to present the development of the
themes—or the counterpart to themes—played out by the major characters"
("Active in Time and History" 100-01).

I will begin with Miriam's perspective. Piercy's sense of a "demand that
[she] speak for those largely unspoken for" (PCBQ 168), seems to me
epitomized in the portrait of Miriam Berg, a portrait echoing that of her
namesake in the Bible, where Miriam is the sister of Moses and Aaron, a
woman prophet, who wonders why God will speak to Moses, but not to her.
This displeases God, who punishes her by giving her leprosy. As told in the

Bible, Miriam's story suggests that it is presumptuous for a woman to want to enter into a colloquy with God (see Eklundh 19).

Anita Goldman's study of "Our Biblical Mothers" relates the following (76-87): Miriam is the first woman in the Bible who, rather than being fettered by husband and children, moves in the public sphere, participating in the creation of history, not passively but actively, and she is also the first woman in the Bible of deep and fervent faith. Already as a young girl she shows presence of mind and initiative, guarding her brother, Moses, by the river. Goldman also links Miriam to two strong midwives, who spited Pharaoh by not killing newborn boys. After the drowning of Pharaoh's army in the Red Sea, Miriam leads the women on, singing to them. Originally, singing and dancing were connected with rites offered to the Great Goddess. There is also a "midrashic theme that the well which provided water for the Children of Israel in the desert was by virtue of the merit of Miriam," a well that was "artesian, overflowing of its own, not needing to be primed or pumped" (Polen 7).

The portrait of Miriam has been cut down in the Bible: only fragments remain, which have to be filled in from sources outside the Bible. According to Anita Goldman, the suppression of Miriam's story must be seen as a strategy of the priests to eradicate mother goddess cults. It is also Goldman's thesis that the Bible was written as a part of a patriarchal, anti-woman battle against an older, woman-dominated mythology (18). Miriam's singing is silenced. Her name (Hebrew *mar*) is usually interpreted as *bitterness*. From what does her bitterness stem? Goldman suggests that it has to do with her relationship to God: Why does God only speak to Moses and not to Miriam and Aaron? In demanding that God speak to her also, Miriam is demanding equality. Yet while both she and Aaron are objecting to Moses' authority, only Miriam is punished. Miriam might have additional reasons to be bitter: Mosaic law, created through Moses, involves countless instances of discrimination against women, beginning in childhood and continuing in marriage and divorce. The priesthood, with its special relation to God, is reserved for men. However, Goldman underlines Miriam's special position within Jewish oral tradition as the only woman placed practically on par with the most prominent patriarchs in the Bible.

In *Small Changes*, the story of Miriam resonates with biblical undertones. Intertextually, one might see Miriam (together with Beth) as the first of Piercy's heroines who are heralding women's difficult exodus out of patriarchy. As someone who wants to have people tangled up with each other, sharing things, and with her wonderful, nourishing bread, Miriam is embracing a principle of caring and connection. With her grandmother's patchwork quilt, she also represents generational continuity. Miriam's journey to womanhood is delineated against the background of her early socialization with its sine qua non imprinting of sex stereotyping, "Mark had a future before him; Allegra and she had only prospects, which meant husbands" (SC 94), a stereotyping reinforced by her reading matter: "Most plots consisted of a hero going through adventures.   Once in a while there was a heroine instead, but her adventures then were men she met and got involved with" (SC 97).   Her brother has been raised to expect his sisters to iron his shirts (SC 126).   This conditioning goes a long way toward explaining why such a feisty and independent woman as Miriam in the end turns into a submissive housewife, initially the last thing she would want.

Miriam's journey is affected by relationships with three male characters, all of whom are well drawn.   In Alix Kates Shulman's novels, to take another feminist writer as an example, men hold themselves superior but are in fact limited and ludicrous.   In Piercy's work this is rarely the case.   As Anne Michelsen puts it, "Men in Marge Piercy's *Small Changes* play a far more important role than is usually found in the works of women writers. Portrayed frequently as types in the Dickensian sense, they do not, however, fall into the category of eccentrics as Dickens's men (and women) sometimes do. Piercy's male characters have a vitality of their own imparted to them by the writer—but a vitality which, when directed towards women, is shown to be destructive" (178). Even for Marie Lucille Fucci, who takes exception to what she regards as "a novel that is social propaganda," "simplistic solutions to complex problems" and the ignoring of "even rudimentary psychology," the male characters in *Small Changes* are acceptable, "admirably drawn, without any attempt to fit them into categories" (36). Male characters in *Small Changes* are vitally alive, and they are essential to the story. All male portraits in *Small Changes* are nuanced, vividly drawn and convincing—even the 'villains' are definitively human and understandable.

The most positive male portrait is that of Phil Boyle. Described as the brother many women wish to have, a growing human being, ultimately he comes to embrace a principle of connection and cooperation: "Only Phil ever really talks with Miriam, but then Phil is an unusual man, the exception that proves the rule. A hustler with words—as are women (SC 521)—Phil is beaten down by the establishment, undergoes a conversion, and in the end recants his old phallogocentrism . . . He chooses to withdraw from the dominant discourse and becomes a carpenter" (Hansen 213).

Among all the men, significantly, Phil alone enters into the narrative with his own point of view within the otherwise all-female perspectives. Initially, Phil appears to be an irrepressibly irresponsible character, forever experimenting (in drugs, women, work), an occasionally self-destructive character. However, he becomes a man who is linked with development and progress rather than stasis, with openness to change rather than rigidity. For Miriam, he is an initiator and an enabler.   As her first sensual and knowledgeable lover, Phil comes to play a key role both in Miriam's development as a woman and as a student. She loves the person she is with Phil (SC 110), because she feels that person is her true self. Phil aides in her quest for selfhood, whereas the man she later marries, Neil, comes to hinder it. Using a maternal metaphor, in a letter to Phil, she calls him her "good fairy godmother" (SC 112), whose magic properties shine all the more against the dull experiences she endures with other men while at college, such as the Four-Stroke Man or the Renaissance Man (SC 113-14). As opposed to these men, who fail to see Miriam as a whole human being rather than a sex object, Phil embraces her in a more complete way. "Only with him could she loosen her emotions, separate the strands of her desperation. She carried herself like a knot to him, her hand clasped sweating on the book she was toting with her to his apartment, to the hospital, back and forth: what she was supposed to be studying that summer for her fall course, the Theory of Complex Variables" (SC 133).

True, Phil is not free from chauvinistic strutting, as in the braggadocio he displays before Jackson after having seduced Miriam (SC 100-3). On one occasion, he hits Miriam and another time, when she is half asleep, he rapes her. But as Phil develops, he begins to reevaluate his life and his past. Having been raised by his mother and having witnessed his father's violence against her, he has perhaps come to identify more with women than the other men in the novel. Growing up in a harsh, lower-class environment, he is expected to prove his manhood by exercising brutality against women. In a passage occurring after he has been fired from his job, a memory comes back from an episode in which he was to participate in a gangrape. He watched the other men take their turns but was then unable to rape the woman himself (SC 285-89), a humiliating experience which leaves a mental scar causing occasional erectile dysfunction. "Part of him mocked the idea of manhood that consisted of torturing a girl in an alley and part of him judged with his peers that he was less a man for not being able to get it up when they could. Part of him still thought he had failed" (SC 289). "Piercy's representation of this rape scene is," as Marks observes, "representation of how our culture equates violence with power, and power with sexual domination" (73). In the view of Nancy Topping Bazin, "His inability to decide whether he feels more guilt because he intended to participate or because he suddenly became impotent and could not is symptomatic of the moral confusion of the American male. Other rapes are mentioned in the novel: Jim rapes Beth, Tom Ryan rapes Miriam, Jackson rapes Sissy, and Miriam's psychoanalyst, in a sense, rapes her mind. These incidents establish rape as the image that best represents the sexual politics displayed in the novel" (Bazin 36). After Miriam's marriage, Phil comes back into her life and they set up an enterprise baking and selling bread together. When the bread burns—as does Miriam's house—the dead end nature of her marriage is made clear, as well as the end of her relationship with Phil.

Miriam's second relationship is with Douglas Jackson, who is absent in the beginning of the novel, off on 'inner' journeys in Mexico. "Just as Piercy posits Beth and Miriam as halves of the mythical female self," writes Kathleen Halischak, "she offers Miriam's two lovers, Phil and Jackson, as halves of the male self" (64), an image that associates, I think, to the symbol of the snake with two heads occurring elsewhere in Piercy's fiction, an image that reinforces Piercy's central themes of dual impulses. Introduced as an unusual man, Jackson is dedicated to following his own conscience and exploring nonconventional lifestyles, stripping his life bare of all unnecessary trappings and pursuing his own truth, wherever that might take him. "Acerbic, often cruel, Jackson is," in Halischak's view, "as reticent and unyielding as Phil is gregarious and giving" (66). According to Michelsen, Jackson is a thoroughly negative character: "There is an unrelieving no-goodness about men like Jackson . . . . Jackson has few or no twinges of social conscience, and is consistent in his aim to achieve economic and sexual superiority" (178); he is "constantly squeezing himself into the conventional male stance—authoritative man, formulator of rules," and he has one principle, "unless you control women, they will control you . . . Dour, bitter Jackson is a Dickensian character who remains the same in every respect. As with Dickens' characters, defined by their obsessions and passions, Jackson's constrictive bitterness dominates him more or less to the end" (180). But Jackson (he prefers to use his last name) is an intriguing, complex man, likened both to Christ and to Abraham Lincoln. He can be both an uncompromising judge and a father figure. A rugged, stubborn and proud man, he is sensual, yet ascetic and devoid of vanity. Less handsome than Phil, he is shown to be magnetically attractive to women, a primordial male exuding sexuality. In Beth's perception, he has a "strong homely face. Lines etched the mouth and eyes, making a texture that drew her fingers to want to touch lightly, like carved wood" (SC 72).

Miriam's passionate, tempestuous love affair with Jackson is convincingly real in all its stages of obsession. Touching the very core of her being, he makes her lose control. Her whole life changes; her love for him becomes "an abdication" (SC 188); "She felt like a battlefield. She felt as if an enormous force had picked her up and turned her around, moving the masses of her along new fault lines, fracturing her being" (SC 189). Through water and space metaphors, the alluring, swirling instability of their relationship is conveyed: "Falling into a river where the currents took her and spun her around and dashed her onward, a river where she rose and fell under an alien power, where she might drown . . . She fell into it, she leaped into it. Something in her came to and snapped, saying, He is The Man. He is it. This is more real than anything gone before" (SC 190). With the rationalization that his desire is the strongest, Jackson 'takes' her from Phil. In his opinion, "It's a plain thing, a man and a woman. People invent fancy things when they're bored with each other . . . [Phil's] relationship to you is no different in kind than his relationship to me. That's not what you need as a woman. That's not what I want about you" (SC 191-92). "There was a terrible simplicity indeed about [Jackson]" (SC 192). Despite all this apparent simplicity, however, Jackson is unequivocally leading their dance: "When he withdrew, she was learning to step back too" (SC 233). Miriam learns to avoid thinking about such issues as 'equality'; "He had too much heavy will for controlling her" (SC 196). One example is matters of contraception: because of Jackson's preferences, Miriam must take the pill, despite unpleasant side effects about which Jackson scornfully tells her to be silent. His own convenience is uppermost.

When this relationship sours, the traditional gender roles of dominance and submission are partly the cause. Frequently unable to brook criticism, Jackson refuses to investigate his own role within the relationship with Miriam or in his previous, disastrous marriage, projecting all responsibility on to the women: "They're all so easy to get on with in the beginning. Women are always agreeable. For a while, for a while, for a while" (SC 172). Miriam's experiences or demands he trivializes in mock-chivalrous, mock-obsequious duets with the less-than-saintly Phil as a sparring partner (SC 254-56): "What's all this emoting about? O Philip, what new sin have you committed against womankind?" (SC 297). Their dialogue is amusing, but there may be more to it than mere jesting, since laughter can be "a strategy many men use to avoid considering viewpoints that are inimical to their interpretation of reality," according to Cheris Kramarae, who continues: "Analysis at the intergroup level suggests that laughter and ridicule can also be a defensive response through which a dominant group seeks to protect its threatened social identity" (64). The muted world of women's perspective is invisible to Jackson, whose uncompromisingly individualist stance and fear of being hurt precipitate a perhaps unnecessary breakup of his relationship with Miriam. Suffering from commitment phobia—"I do not feel married. If I did, I'd jump out the window. Any window, any fire escape, any loophole, any drain" (SC 274), he is nevertheless almost perversely committed to himself. Yet, in the end, it is this sense of unflawed integrity that makes Jackson an engaging and even hopeful character. What is questioned in this novel are the concepts of manhood he subscribes to (SC 464). Jackson is no total villain, something that is underlined above all in the scene of rapprochement between him and Beth, a character who comes to represent a female avant-garde committed to change. Much to Beth's surprise, Jackson desires her to stay in his house. By then, his house has changed, a result of improved finances but also suggestive of psychological changes. Jackson's introduction of some measure of beauty and comfort into his earlier forbiddingly austere bachelor's pad can perhaps be seen as an intimation of a budding openness to a female side within himself. While he understands that he has been trapped in his earlier marriage, he does not understand why or how to deal with it, only how to hurt his wife in turn—and escape. His refusal to look at his own part in relationships is problematic for the women involved with him; yet there is also something healthy in Jackson's refusal to repeat a mistake.

Initially the most gentle and congenial man in this novel, Neil (appropriately surnamed Stone), develops into the most oppressive husband. Rather than adopting any despicably macho stance or displaying overt verbal or physical aggressions toward his wife, this highly intelligent and educated career man nevertheless slowly comes to suppress his wife's growth through subtle manipulation. Neil, at the outset the most agreeable, and Miriam, initially the strongest, most flamboyant, and talented woman, choose to adhere to traditional gender roles of dominance and subordination and are thus led into a dead end marriage. As long as their relationship is based on equality, it flourishes. Working for the same computer company, they are both seen as highly competent and talented. Delighting in this sweet and gentle man after the tempestuous ménage-à-trois with Jackson and Phil (SC 275), Miriam decides that she wants it all (in a phrase that echoes the journal of Sylvia Plath at the beginning of her married life): "I want to be a good technical person and creative in my field, I want to be happily married, I want to be a good cook, I want to be a good mother and have lots and lots of babies—I want everything!" (SC 384). With marriage and parenthood, however, the positions begin to shift from horizontality to verticality. Quitting her job, Miriam becomes a full-time homemaker. Neil never questions the precepts of marriage he has inherited from his parents. Instead he gradually adopts them. Devoting more time to his career, while simultaneously increasing his domestic demands on Miriam, he embarks on a climb upward. The power balance shifting, the respect he formerly felt for her is converted into condescension. After all, he is the breadwinner, and what does she do all day?

Martha Masinton and Charles G. Masinton, who see *Small Changes* as "indeed doctrinaire and occasionally polemical," find that "Piercy's formulation of the feminist problem acquires validity through her recognition of the need for revolutionary change in society at large and through her careful attention to the details of the intricate relationship between sexuality and cultural role playing" (311). Marge Piercy herself has stated, as quoted above, that "The novel is as much about who is doing the housework at any given point as it is about who is sleeping with whom" (PCBQ 214-15). Careerless, the formerly eminently capable and work-involved Miriam becomes a housewife and accomplished hostess entertaining Neil's business associates. Economically dependent on her husband, she forfeits an important part of her own life and identity and starts feeling obliged to conform to Neil's wishes. "Why must she always be 'understanding' him? He didn't spend that effort studying her, he didn't need to. He knew what he expected of her and only grew worried when she failed to provide it" (SC 468). At the cost of her own personal growth she must please Neil or at least avoid displeasing him at all times. Meanwhile, Neil—whom Phil calls "the Man" (SC 464)—meta-morphoses, and the distance between the spouses increases both personally and ideologically, as the following quotation shows:

> Miriam dreamed and dreamed of something real and external to do. She could not go back to work. Every time that subject came up she had to agree with Neil that Ariane could not be turned over like a puppy dog to some hired person to sit with. She did help Neil with his papers more, but he had regular assistants for the classes and on his project. They regarded her as an intruder. Moreover, Neil wasn't writing papers about the kind of research she wanted to get into. It was all the big machine stuff she had washed her hands of. (SC 467)

In her portrait of this marriage, Piercy thus underlines the difficulties inherent in what is here called the 'system.' Some critics have deplored the depiction of Miriam's development into a dependent housewife as implausible, since she is so efflorescent at the outset. Sara Blackburn, for example, does not quite believe in the change, since it "takes place off-stage" (2). Neither does Blackburn see psychotherapy as a deciding factor in this development: "The author would have us believe that it was Miriam's psychotherapy that programmed her for this disastrous future—for Piercy, all modes of psychiatry are down-the-line death trips for women." In my view, Piercy chooses to place the redoubtable Miriam, the strongest of the female characters, in a traditional, submissive role as a housewife, something that almost crushes her seemingly indomitable, effervescent spirit, in order to emphasize how debilitating Miriam's *situation* is. This situation also means choosing between a career and a family, since American society does not accommodate parents of small children in providing parental leaves or child care, a situation essentially unchanged in the early 1990s, despite some improvements. According to a 1991 survey of working mothers done by the Families and Work Institute, "Only 16 percent said their supervisor was supportive when they needed to take care of family matters, and only 7 percent said their coworkers were supportive. More than half felt they had to choose between advancing their careers and devoting attention to their families" (Marill 84). According to experts quoted in this 1993 article, "Firings of new mothers are still as much of a problem as ever . . . the new laws have simply forced companies to cover their tracks better." In the work market, children are seen as potential disturbances disrupting the conveyor-belt pace. In her poem "The Disturbance" (*Stone, Paper, Knife*), Piercy addresses this issue:

> How seldom babies cry
> in the university. Where
> are they? Why don't fathers
> bring them to work in baskets?
> Have you ever studied while nursing?
> Have you written a speech while cajoling
> a baby raging with colic?
>
> A visitor from Alpha Centauri
> assumed humans are born full sized
> after examining our public places.
>
> Should we really just cram mother
> back into the broom closet with baby
> and go on with our business, grateful
> for all the mothers crouching in closets
> with babies chewing and weeping
> talking to walls quietly
> and disturbing no one else?

It is Miriam's 'impossible' role that distorts her relationship and stunts her growth. Neil's development from being a tolerant young man into a family tyrant and philandering husband is also delineated against Piercy's depiction of a cultural context; it is his choice of adopting the traditional values of his background rather than trying to transcend them that allows this benignly monstrous oppressor to emerge. "The key phrase she weaves about Neil is wreathed in the illusion which the author feels women so often delude themselves with: 'I know him.' . . . Unlike Jackson, who wants no commitment, Neil insists on a permanent relationship—marriage. As it turns out, Miriam and Neil are strangers who agree on nothing: politics, friends, role of wife, role of husband, the rearing of children, the handling of finances, etc." (Michelsen 189).

That Miriam 'knows' Neil indeed turns out to be an illusion. Perhaps she has, like Beth with Jackson, "made him up in part, while believing she was shrewd in perceiving him" (SC 505). "[Miriam] remembered believing when she had been getting to know Neil that his unwillingness to shed blood, his contempt for hunting and fishing and fighting, were a refusal to play traditional male roles. She did not think that any more. He disliked violence in words or action; he preferred a quiet tone of authority" (SC 470). Miriam may be less to blame for their dissolving union, since Neil holds the trump cards, but she is shown to be co-responsible. Miriam, who early in the novel contests her sister Allegra's notions on marriage, saying "I don't want to marry anybody! I don't want any marriage I've ever seen!" (SC 131), ends up precisely in the spot chosen from the start by Allegra: that of having to manipulate her husband rather than openly communicating her needs. Relying upon an essay by Karen Kollias that perceives three layers within the American working class, Patricia Marks sees in the different class backgrounds of Beth and Miriam a clue to why Miriam remains mired in a suffocating marriage while Beth does not (Marks 56). Miriam's marriage is a relinquishing of growth, although there are hints that wifehood will not eclipse development in other areas forever: for a while, she finds an outlet for her energy and creativity in setting up a home bakery with Phil (this enterprise is, however, crushed by Neil, who also forces her to give up her friendship with Phil), and in the end, Miriam aids in Wanda's and Beth's escape—a surreptitious declaration of independence on the part of Miriam.

Miriam's counterpart is Beth Phail, whose story is told in the biblical-sounding "Book of Beth." These two characters connect through the symbol of a fig, exchanged at their first meeting, a symbol associating to the fig tree of female possibilities in Sylvia Plath's *The Bell Jar*. Like most American women of her generation, Beth has been raised to look to marriage as the main avenue to fulfilled womanhood and to harbor romantic illusions of marriage as the beginning of 'real' life. The road toward women's selfhood, love and marriage, seems to exclude higher education, and Beth wrestles with women's classic quandary of choosing between achievement and affiliation. Incredibly, her marriage ceremony costs as much as two years of college—for which Beth has been told there was no money. In both Miriam's and Beth's stories, there are numerous clues to the novel's vision of marriage as entrapment visualized in negative spatial metaphors. "In Beth's case," writes Kathleen Halischak, "the cramped, unattractive apartment that never seems to be in order typifies the suffocating effect of her marriage to Jim, just as Miriam's large, unfilled, unfinished Victorian house engulfs and threatens to drown her in its over-burdening domesticity" (51).

As a contrast stands the positive image of the cave of mirrors Beth construes out of her mother's winged vanity when she is a girl, a protective cave into which only a shaft of light enters. Since spatial metaphors are important in Piercy's novels, as well as in fiction by other women writers both of the nineteenth and the twentieth centuries, I will make a brief digression aimed to provide a background. Many feminists have linked women's social and psychological conditions of limited space to their literary expressions. "As Mary Wollstonecraft complained in her gothic novel, *Maria, or the Wrongs of Woman*, young girls' lives were all too often cramped and confined," writes Tania Modleski (1982 62). Susan Brownmiller asserts that "the feminine environment has been a world of closed interiors, imposed limitations and cramped space. It would be strange if some instances if [*sic*] claustrophobia,

desperation and self-consciousness did not seep onto the printed page" (125).
The sense of enclosure experienced by George Eliot's heroines is continued in
subsequent writings by women. In literature surveyed by Annis Pratt, "Young
women heroes . . . [were] looking *into* a trap *from* a space of doomed
authenticity" (37). Pratt sees "the golden circle of marriage" as "a tarnished
enclosure" (45). In this literature by women she perceives "wifehood as a
cause or condition of madness," with "extended metaphors linking normal
households and insane asylums" (51). She also detects a frequent female
complicity, as with Joyce Carol Oates's women who "imprison [themselves]
within escape-proof enclosures" (49). Female protagonists, finds Pratt, react
by turning to a "spaceless world appropriate to rebellion against placelessness
in the patriarchy" (169). In this literature, Pratt perceives a "synthesis, or new
space" that "describes a world so alien to patriarchy as to be invisible, or in
Mary Daly's description, unhearable" (177).

In twentieth century literature by women, endings in flight from marriage
and from the traditional family are legion. Instead of trapping men to keep
them company in their enclosures, women characters wish to get away from
male-controlled spaces altogether. When Alix Kates Shulman's *Burning
Questions* features an androgynous fantasy it is, not surprisingly, called New
Space. Countless examples of spatial imagery in contemporary fiction by
women writers could be discussed. One writer, Diane Johnson, believes that
women actually write about "different subjects," and that they "set their novels
in houses, center them in families, things that correspond to the facts of female
life" (131).

In Marge Piercy's novels, spatial metaphors are highly significant. In fact,
not only *space*, but also a sense of *place* is vitally important in Piercy's work
(See Robert Bender 120-30). In *Woman on the Edge of Time*, one character
ends up in the wrong future and is isolated in a nightmare version of a
megacity, claustrophobic space dwindled into the infinitesimal and enveloped
by suffocating, hugely expanding, male-controlled outer space. In *Fly Away
Home*, to take another example, a house is a central symbol and an image of
rebirth and regeneration. And for Beth in *Small Changes*, the first priority
after leaving her husband is to find a room of her own, her own space. Beth's
cave of mirrors, remembered in the first lines of the novel, is an interesting
symbol of enclosure and openness, darkness and light, a double-edged
metaphor of female beauty, sexuality, and reproduction and of women's
journey towards the "light" of awareness, as well as, since it is her mother's
vanity, an evocation of a sense of continuity and connection. That this vanity
has "wings," moreover, associates to women's flight toward freedom, to a
transcendent immanence. In its womb-like enclosed open space, Beth's cave
of mirrors resembles the matrilinear courtyard house in *He, She and It*. The
similarities between Piercy's spatial metaphor of the cave of mirrors and the

cave metaphor analyzed by Sandra Gilbert and Susan Gubar in *The Madwoman in the Attic* and Mary Shelley's parable of the cave of the Sibyl, which, according to the authors, reconciles the negative association of the cave with a positive remythologization bear examination. The disintegration that women artists have experienced which has undermined their creativity is here healed into the life-giving symbol of the Cumean cave. Gilbert and Gubar see this cave as a feminist symbol of biological, spiritual, and literary creativity, protectively enclosed yet open to the sky—a sort of transcendence in immanence.

Beth's cave of mirrors is such a space of transcendence in immanence: it is a womb-like hidden place, yet slightly open to the sky, just like Mary Shelley's cave. But it carries yet another layer of associations: recalling an important spatial image in Virginia Woolf's *A Room of One's Own*, Beth's cave of mirrors carries allusions both to women's writing and a tradition of women writers, foremothers of women writing today, at the same time as it foreshadows Beth's development toward an exploration of love between women. Describing how her imagined author would write about an intimate relationship between two women, Virginia Woolf evokes its character of hidden substory, metaphorically expressed as unexplored, underground space: "For if Chloe likes Olivia and Mary Carmichael knows how to express it she will light a torch in that vast chamber where nobody has yet been. It is all half-lights and profound shadows like those serpentine caves where one goes with a candle peering up and down" (80). The *tripartite* vanity, furthermore, an image echoing the tripartite structure of the novel (divided into "The Book of Beth," "The Book of Miriam," and "Both in Turn") and the mirroring of women's lives into each other, evokes a sense of matrilinear continuity and fertility mythos in its association to the Persephone and Demeter myth, since Persephone, too, entered a "cave," the underworld, where she lived for a third of the year, spending the other two-thirds with her mother, Demeter. Since Piercy's linking Beth to the tripartite vanity and her surrounding Beth with female relatives emphasizes transgenerational female socialization, and since, as Madonne Miner has argued, "The first sentence [of the novel] metaphorically says that Beth sees herself mirroring her mother's pride: Beth *is* the mirror of her mother's pride" (16), I must disagree with Patricia Marks's vision of Beth as lacking a historical past (64).

In the mirror, Beth inspects herself in her wedding dress. As Kathleen Halischak has observed, "the dress functions as icon for the marriage: she is made to conform to its dimensions. Here, as throughout the novel, dress serves as an important emblem, manifesting the psychic reality of the characters" (55). Another significant symbol is the wedding cake, an image of enforced cultural codes: while both Beth and Jim want a chocolate cake, they are forced to have the usual "store-bought sawdust white cake" (SC 22), as unappealing as the dusty, standardized and tasteless roles they are urged to engorge. The obligatory wedding waltz is another, equally unappealing convention that does not suit this couple (SC 23). A culmination of their courtship, the wedding night, becomes an anticlimax for Beth, as well as a foreshadowing of her disillusion to come. "She was lying there with a new hole torn in her" (SC 26). Visualizing herself as a wedding cake, Beth feels that "they would come and slice her and take her home in white boxes" (SC 12)—a sinister, funereal image of female mutilation—and feels suffocated by the makeup session before the ceremony, symbolizing the denaturizing forces that suppress and distort her sense of her self.

In an interview, Marge Piercy has emphasized that "The men in *Small Changes* are always, except for Phil, seen from a woman's point of view. And they are seen, in a sense as men write about women, only insofar as they impinge upon women. That was very intentional. You don't, except for Phil, see them from their point of view" (PCBQ 135). Perhaps the most villainous of the men in the novel, Jim Walker insists on having a traditional marriage with a wife who waits on his every wish, despite her being in the work force, too: he insults her cooking, he is an inept lover, he makes no efforts to understand her attempts at change and real communication. For Jim, a wife is a possession (a conception dating back to English common law). The real Beth remains as invisible to him as the underlying patterns that rule their marriage. At times, he appears almost criminally insensitive and brutal, as in the rape scene. However, Jim is not actually breaking the law; raping Beth is merely an exercise of his legal rights as a husband, as the condescending (male) lawyer explains to Beth. Rape within marriage was not punishable by law in most states at that time, and it is still legal in thirty states (Faludi xiv). In consenting to marry Jim, Beth thus unwittingly subordinates her will and her sexuality to him. The saying "Marriage Is a Matter of Give and Take"—the title of chapter 2—for Beth turns out to mean that Men Take and Women Give. "She was studying him, learning him, trying to please him. . . . Yet Jim seemed to please her the same ways as before, or less: he aimed to please her with ritual gestures addressed to Any Girl" (SC 30). The wisdom she learns from the women in her family is to learn to tolerate a husband. "They complained about their husbands. They assumed a common level of grievance. That was being married. They saw a certain level of war as normal: women had to get things indirectly, wives had to plot and manage and evade" (SC 31). Very soon it becomes obvious that Jim's needs are to dominate the marriage (SC 33) and to thus take out the humiliations suffered at work on his wife. If Beth attempts to stand up for herself, Jim threatens economic repercussions. Her anger recoils into itself and she contracts, taking up even less space. As in the case of Miriam, Beth does not really know her husband: the spouses are disconnected, alienated from each other. However, the individuals are less at fault than the "whole mythology of love and marriage" (SC 37) with its infantilizing effect on women.

Resilient, but resolved to move beyond the rigid matrimonial corral and to construct her own boundaries, Beth fixes upon a turtle as a suitable symbol for her stubborn quest for a self as well as a metaphor for women's alignment with peace and veneration for life and nature, and for the slow and unglamorous struggle forward in the women's movement. This private symbol predates Beth's involvement in the women's movement, however; at this point, she believes herself isolated in her rebellion. In the selection of the turtle as a symbol, there may also be a reference to an African cosmology story in which, in the words of Carol Ochs, "God asks the stone if it chooses to have children. The stone chooses immortality. God next asks the turtle, who chooses to have children. Man, shamed by the turtle's selfless choice, chooses also to have children, and that is why he is not immortal" (20). In this story, it is not only mortality and immortality that are contrasted, but an image of connection—choosing to have children—and an image of separateness and of clearly delineated, hard boundaries represented by the stone. In "A shadow play for guilt" (from *Circles on the Water*) the image of the turtle is directly linked to the body: "But the body is simple as a turtle/ and straight as a dog:/ the body cannot lie." The turtle is thus a highly significant symbol that is integral to Piercy's most central themes.

Propelled by her humiliating marital experience, Beth escapes and begins a journey to a very different world in Boston, toward dignity and selfhood, and to increased awareness of social structures. Neither Jim's use of physical violence nor his legal measures—through the use of lawyers unsympathetic to women's plight—can make her return. Jim himself remains trapped, mired in stagnation and stereotype, barred from the social mobility he seeks, failing to see an alternative way out of his situation. Brought up in the working class and lacking both inner impetus and external guidance, Jim cannot transcend the rigid frames that press upon him, while Beth, on the other hand, *is* socially mobile, although not in a conventional, status-seeking manner. Their last meeting is for all that not lacking in sympathy and tenderness. The marriage being dissolved, at some cost for Beth, they can both perceive the core of good residing in each of them and remember their original loving bond (SC 21). With such a reconciliation the author seems to point to the innate possibilities in each human being for individual growth and for mutually enhancing bonds, in this case made more difficult or thwarted by the social situation in all its complexity.

During her literal and metaphorical journey to a new world, Beth takes temporary solace in other men, such as Tom Ryan, a twenty-five-year-old man personifying male ambivalence toward women. While humorous and tender, and appreciative that Beth is a real woman and not "one of those overdelicate females who can't walk on their feet . . . One of those held together with little gold wires and hair lacquer" (SC 52), he is also condescending (for example, in his etiolation of Dorine into 'Clorine') and nastily dismissive when threatened by a woman's professional competence (as with Miriam), as well as deaf to women's choices—as to whether Beth desires him at all, and as when he rents an apartment where he, only half in jest, assumes that Beth will spend most of her time in the kitchen (SC 75). Not surprisingly, Tom and Beth never quite connect. However, Tom's function in the plot is to introduce Beth to a new group of characters, and Beth's relationship with him shows some "small" but consequential "changes" in her development towards a re-construction of her own boundaries.

Only when she enters a love relationship with a woman does Beth discover "the first consistently pleasurable sex she had ever known" (SC 321). What develops into a lesbian relationship between Beth and Wanda is the only truly fulfilling love relationship in the novel. It may not be so much the lesbian component that makes it so, but rather the particular insights and commitments brought to the relationship. Wanda as a character represents a feminine or maternal principle of connection and sharing as well as a need for finding a way back to a woman-oriented perspective. "She talked about the need for women's rituals, for making each other strong, for giving each other power, for feeling each one her own beauty with each other. They must make their own strong clean rituals of giving birth and puberty and fighting and growing and sharing and dying" (SC 418). Together they will create a "theater that speaks for women" (SC 419), which is built upon a sense of connection by women getting out of their solitary cells and creating a body larger than themselves during their exercises—re-connecting, thanks to Wand(a)'s magic, with African goddesses and with women's rituals harking back to Paleolithic times.

Just as they will create a "theater that speaks for women," Beth is, analogously, creating a language that speaks for herself. Nancy Walker observes that for Beth, words are weapons used in the "battle for selfhood" (38). As Alan Shima remarks in his "pursuit" of language in the works of Adrienne Rich, Susan Griffin, and Beverly Dahlen, "Part and parcel of our dominant language conventions is the fact that the language of women is generally stigmatized. It is frequently judged as incidental, superficial, charming but inconsequential in its ability to affect our social and political lives" (24). Shima underlines that "Feminism's attention to concerns other than those established in the vocabulary of male power and privilege attempts to redefine the terms which conceptually govern women's identities and relationships. It is for this reason that the critique of language remains essential to the feminist enterprise" (33). In *Small Changes*, Madonne Miner has detected a wealth of "interesting examples of language split into various discourses along class lines" (17). She notes how "men assume denominational perogatives [*sic*] in relation to women: Beth's father addresses his wife and female children collectively as 'The Girls'; Tom christens Dorine 'Clorine'; Phil, Miriam's first lover, writes about her as 'Venus Berg.' In addition to these individual instances of men naming/placing women, Piercy also highlights larger cultural manifestations of this process as fathers give their names to daughters and husbands give their names to wives" (21).

Language is power. Beth has been lying to herself in her diary, writing a surface story hiding the covert activities she engaged in as a teenager. Rereading it, she realizes that her memories do not tally with what is on the page. In her free space in Boston, by contrast, she defines her own walls also in the sense that she writes upon them: the writing ought to be on the wall. She is redefining concepts that she earlier has taken at face value, such as love. She is deciding to say yes to herself, to become audible. As for Miriam, she "initially employs words as weapons in the private sphere; soon, however, she carries her battle onto more public ground. . . . Demystifying computer jargon and disseminating computer codes, Miriam alters the power structure of this language" (Miner 23). Miriam's mother, on the other hand, is never listened to: no one takes her "kvetching" seriously until it turns out that she is dying (see Nunnally and Petersen).

Almost as an aside, Wanda's ex-husband is introduced. A parallel to Jim, Joe is a working-class man, and, at first glance, an out-and-out villain. A chauvinistic Puerto Rican leftist, Joe abandons his wife and small children to devote himself to political and extramarital passions. However, in his case, too, there are extenuating circumstances; to survive in his Puerto Rican environment, Joe must adopt a brutal, macho manner. Despite Wanda's suffering in their marriage, she recognizes this and praises Joe for at least having taken *one* step toward change. Respecting his political integrity and with grit and grace proving her own, Wanda prefers to go to jail rather than pass on the information about Joe requested by the police. The following passage sums up her attitude:

> he isn't my worst enemy. The corporations that poison the rivers and make war profitable and the state that makes war—those are my enemies. This society taught him to take women and use them and throw them away. It taught him you marry a woman and then she gives you children and everything your heart desires till you trade her in on a prettier, younger model. This society taught him what it means to be a man—the fist, the balls, competing, winning, putting everybody down. (SC 491)

Here, Piercy's manifesto appears at its most clear. To be sure, the individual man may be a victim, too—perhaps no single story illustrates this better than "Do You Love Me?," in which a man recollects his relationship to his father and the expectations under which he suffered.   It is rather the negative elements of a principle of hierarchy, separation, and destruction that are the real villain.   When certain characteristics traditionally associated with masculinity are reinforced and upheld as the law, this becomes destructive for society as a whole.   If men begin to be aware of society's ideological assumptions, this is laudable, but the hierarchical structure still leaves room for them to oppress in their turn.   As long as that is the case, the plausibility for true equality within marriage will remain slim.   The fact that men are a controlling group in society will affect power relations also within the home, it is suggested.   That may be why Beth is described as "losing control" when making love with Jackson (SC 507).   For her, an "interesting, intimate struggle" is no longer worth it.   She says, "I don't want to love a problem. I don't want that difficult, interesting relationship. I want to love somebody and face outward and struggle to change things that hurt me and hurt others. I don't want to be fighting the person I'm supposed to be with" (SC 507).   And Beth is, indeed, increasingly, facing outward toward, as Kathleen Halischak has put it, "an ever-widening circle of personal and social awareness" at the same time as Miriam's life "is marked by an opposite, the constricting and strangulating noose of marriage" (74).   The two forces I see as fundamental in Piercy's fiction are opposed here: an impulse toward connection and repair and an impulse toward separation.

Pia Thielmann (whose study focuses on the images of women in Piercy's novels) argues that, at one point, when Beth has left her marriage and gone to Boston, her development is too rapid (90).   I would like to suggest the opposite: that although any journey towards deeper insights may take a long time, it will not proceed one ratchet at a time; there may also be sudden surges forward, especially because of drastic changes of circumstances—as is the case with Beth, who is thrown into a very different world.   This 'gap' also marks Beth's transition from being male-oriented to a shift in perspective, via a phase of low or neuter sexuality—a process hinted at in the description of her affair with Tom, in which she is still neuter, unfeeling, still not positively identified with women.   Further, I think that this structure may not necessarily mean that Piercy is not meeting "her own requirement of writing a *detailed* novel."   The very structure carries a meaningful message: the gap is *silence, invisibility*; it is a symbol of both Beth's neuter phase and her individual invisibility, as of any woman's before she can claim recognition for who she is.

In her analysis of Beth's development, Marleen Barr relies upon Todorov's theory of the fantastic, especially of how 'uncanny' events produce a 'hesitation' in the reader.   In Barr's interpretation, Beth's and other characters' 'hesitation' before 'the patriarchal uncanny' makes for a pause in which to recreate or rewrite herself.   In what Barr sees as Piercy's feminist metafiction ("fictions about patriarchal fictions"), the "hesitation yields positive female textual spaces for women's stories. . . . Their transformed (or rewritten) lives—transformations available to real-world women—are female-centered narratives about women vacating muted social spaces" (Barr 204), the 'hesitation' thus being "an emancipatory strategy" (205). Barr argues that Beth subversively attempts to "introduce the wild, alien space of women's culture within the dominant, familiar space of patriarchal culture" and that she attempts "to transform the fixed spaces pictured on Ardener's chart [of dominant and muted groups] into postmodern heterotopian zones" (202). Beth Phail, in Barr's analysis, "is denied access to dominant American space when she assumes a new identity to live with her lover, Wanda" (203).

Loving a woman is part of the solution for Beth, but while her own decision stems in large part from disappointing contacts with men, she is not advocating that all women follow her example. Clearly, it is not a solution for every woman; for, as Luce Irigaray expresses it, "that would lead to a new cloister in which we would be enclosed, constructed by our own hands" (243). Some critics have found Beth's and Wanda's relationship unconvincing or dissatisfying: Martha Duffy writes that Piercy "has set some stick figures in motion to illustrate her conviction that women would be better off if they organized their lives without men" (82), and Sara Blackburn finds that Beth has developed into "a lifeless mouthpiece for the principles of radical feminism" (2). Others have praised her characters for their vitality; Kathryn Lee Seidel, for example, writes that "Her women are superb," adding that "few other contemporary novelists have presented the range of women Piercy has," an observation with which I would agree (1986 675).

Meanwhile, to envision a New Man is apparently not without its difficulties. Attempts at a recasting or redefining of manhood easily become programmatic, as in the following, edifying passage:

> Men who had been involved in such a struggle were different in obvious and in subtle ways. They had different manners and different anxieties. In gross ways the house was unlike other communes: the men cooked too and the women also chopped wood and the men took care of the children and the women climbed up on ladders and worked side by side repairing the roof. One of the men, Alan, did needlepoint for pleasure. He was also accurate with the rifle. (SC 483)

Piercy's musings upon how she and other women were conditioned to respond to men during the 1950s are interesting as exemplifying what the New Man should *not* be:

> What we were trained to respond to sexually in men can be roughly divided into two types. One was the Sensitive Hood, mean, destructive, self-destructive, sadistic but suffering. The other was Iceman . . . The essence of

each was the inability to love, to feel in a useful way, while retaining the
ability (usually) to act . . . One is the Sinful Son and the other the Terrible
Father, basically Puritan ghouls, competitive, alienated, death-dealing and
empty, empty in the soul, useless to the preservation of life. Egoistic in quite
different styles: insensitivity trained by the grueling rituals of American
manhood, or narcissism ogling itself in the shine of the switchblade (usually
imaginary). (PCBQ 124-25)

In *Small Changes*, women's views of men undergo profound changes as they
begin to locate their own perspectives and find their own voices, something
that is also indicated in the narrative technique itself of *Small Changes*. Elaine
Tuttle Hansen, who raises the question of whether the women characters can
"control or escape [the dominant] discourse to speak of and for themselves"
(209), finds that the narrative technique used by Piercy includes

the subversion of conventional narrative openings and closings; the
intentionally didactic, oversimplified, even allegorical nature of the work and
its characters; the use of what du Plessis has called 'multi-personed or cluster
protagonists' to affirm the 'feminine' values of 'collectivity' and
'interdependence'; the rich (even 'exhaustive' and 'obsessively
observed')—details, often associated with stereotypically female interests such
as the way space is arranged in various domiciles, or the way 'life support'
activities are managed. (214-15)

Piercy shows how the dominant discourse can be utilized subversively in the
story of Beth (by inverting "the classic male story of education and
adventure") or paralleled by what is often seen as a more conventional female
form of narrative, that is, soap opera. Primarily, it is Miriam's life that fits the
soap opera model, and the "soap opera heroine is caught in predetermined
circumstances, unable to choose or to act on her own. She is constrained by
the narrative structure, and hence by the reader's foreknowledge, as much as
by her own all too predictable desires" (217). The result is important for the
reader's sense of perspective: "The effect is that in general we *see with* Beth,
where we often merely *see* Miriam," and Hansen concludes: "The feminist
Bildungsroman, built on a culturally male model, facilitates the representation
of a certain kind of revolutionary change, of individual growth and
development in a woman's life; the soap opera more accurately presents and
records ordinary women's experience" (220). According to Nancy Walker, the
soap opera's repetition and lack of resolution is present in the final chapters
of this novel, with their lack of finality (94).

For women, *Small Changes* suggests, salvation lies not in finding the right
male, but in the affirmation of a maternal principle of healing over a
patriarchal one of hierarchy and division: in this novel, male-oriented women
shrink, become invisible. Their helpfulness becomes exploited: unappreciated,

badly paid labor in typing pools, taken-for-granted whipping up of gourmet meals for the representational purposes of career-minded husbands, unpaid domestic labor, sexual catering to married men. The 'system' is often male in Piercy's novels, as, for example "the Man" in *Dance the Eagle to Sleep*. In *Small Changes*, its main representative is Miriam's husband, Neil—whom Phil, significantly, calls 'The Man.' For Beth, the system is embodied in her father, who "used to whip her with a wooden yardstick that stood in the corner of the kitchen" (SC 306). Later, her husband Jim takes his place.

Reviewing *Small Changes* in *The New Republic*, Diane Schulder writes that "Piercy is the first contemporary white American novelist to do what Doris Lessing has done in Britain: that is in articulating the subtleties of women's thoughts, she obliterates the dichotomy between the 'political' and the 'personal'" (31). Replete with period detail, the immediacy and intimacy of the dialogue in *Small Changes* more clearly than in Piercy's previous two novels is an appraisal of women's dilemmas of the time, spelling out Piercy's proposals for change and making abundantly clear how an individual's actions are rooted in her past and in her family background, as well as in the social and economic context. In a review in *Time* entitled "Stiff Upper Lib," Martha Duffy finds that in this novel, "the musk of female superiority is heavy indeed" (81-82). But the male portraits in *Small Changes* are never venomous no matter how brutal or faithless some of the male characters might be, since the narrative suggests that they are so because of socialization and earlier experiences. Even so, there is no pessimistic message that these earlier experiences need stunt an individual's growth forever. To the contrary, *Small Changes* evinces a firm belief in human beings' capacity to act on insights, to survive psychic damage and to grow stronger. The author affords a choice to her characters—to either deal with life in a constructive way or to stagnate. That choice, in *Small Changes* and in Piercy's next novel, *Woman on the Edge of Time*, is between an oppressive patriarchal principle and a maternal principle of healing and repairing the world. Those characteristics which help an individual advance, if not always thrive, in a capitalist patriarchy, are competition and aggressiveness, whereas a maternal principle that stands for compassion, emotional and physical nurturing—Earth Mother attributes, will point the way to a better world in the long run. Piercy does not discuss whether women innately possess such characteristics or are socialized to cultivate them. These qualities have been termed female or maternal because during our known historical times women have made, or have had to make, these values theirs; in Piercy's world, however, they are not, neither should they be, the monopoly of women.

Chapter 4

Woman on the Edge of Time

Knowledge rests not upon truth only, but upon error also.

Carl G. Jung 163

"[Telling] a tale of two cities," as Ihab Hassan puts it (104), *Woman on the Edge of Time* has been analyzed as a dystopia, as speculative fiction, and as realist fiction with fantastic episodes. "By her vivid and coherent descriptions of new social institutions," writes Rachel Blau du Plessis, "Piercy has answered the famous Cold War dystopias like *1984* and *Brave New World* which lament that there is no possibility of imagining an anti-totalitarian society" (1979 4).

In Piercy's own view it is *not* a utopia—"because it's accessible. There's almost nothing there except the brooder not accessible now. So it's hardly a utopia; it is very intentionally not a utopia because it is not strikingly new. The ideas are the ideas basically of the women's movement" (PCBQ 100). Sheila Delaney concurs: "It is a compelling realistic novel with utopian interludes" or a "Utopia in transition" (173, 176), whereas Margaret Atwood opines that "none of the reviews of *Woman on the Edge of Time* . . . seems even to have acknowledged its genre" (272). In Atwood's interpretation, it *is* a utopia, "with all the virtues and shortcomings of the form" (273). In Celia Betsky's view, Piercy's "utopia is more believable and moving than many renderings of contemporary reality. Like a latter-day D. H. Lawrence, she sees the future as a revival of tradition, eternal values and human ritual, heir to the primitive qualities of Connie's rural Mexican past" (1976 39). David L. Foster believes that *Woman on the Edge of Time* "[offers] an insight into the body, or form, or structure of feminist science fiction," one device of which, he suggests, is to "estrange" or "defamiliarize" the reader in certain passages of the novel (48, 52), a convention also pointed out by Anne Cranny-Francis

(110-119). Patricia Marks finds five distinct narrative structures in this novel: aside from realism and utopian/dystopian writing, she finds a pornographic aspect in the dystopia and a "narrative of the holograph" in the utopian section (Marks 15; see also Karen C. Adams 39 and Sue Walker 138).

As of 1982, *Woman on the Edge of Time* was the author's favorite among her own novels (PCBQ 169). "It is primarily a novel about Connie," says Piercy. "There's a lot about social injustice in it, and about how a woman stops hating herself and becomes able to love herself enough to fight for her own survival" (PCBQ 100). American culture is here shown to be on the edge of time, as is the protagonist, in a particular way: she inhabits what Teresa de Lauretis has called "the space-off," the "spaces in the margins of hegemonic discourses" (25). Not only does Piercy place her protagonist in a muted zone, but she employs a genre which itself has been a muted zone within literary criticism (Annas 143). Despite its "doubly fictional" nature, according to Chris Ferns, utopian fiction has largely been "the antithesis of postmodernist experiment" in remaining "obstinately non-self-referential" (453-54).

Hospitalized for schizophrenia, Connie, or Consuelo Ramos, is able to get out of present, oppressive time and mind-travel into the future. A thirty-seven-year-old Latina, she is at the bottom of American society, representing a host of victims suffering under the yoke of capitalist patriarchy: women, ethnic minorities, the poor, the uneducated, the old. As Cranny-Francis puts it, "Piercy's utopian figure . . . deals not only with the status of women as a group, but with the differences between women which make women of particular races or classes susceptible to different pressures, different kinds and degrees of oppression" (135). Connie's story is the story of victimization. While as a young woman she had dreams, ideas, ambitions, at the age of thirty-seven, what she valued or loved most in life has been taken from her, killed, or stolen by society: the men she has loved, her daughter, her intellectual and creative potential.

Connie's vows as a teenager not to grow up like her mother—"To suffer and serve. Never to live my own life!" draw sharp rebuke from her mother, who advises her that she will "do what women do." That is, accept that as a woman she is less valued than men—her brothers are a priority in the family—that her main concern will be raising a family and that she must therefore forget about going to college. Small wonder that Connie rejects the accouterments of womanhood: "Nothing in life but having babies and cooking and keeping the house. Mamacita, believe me—oígame, Mamá—I love you! But I'm going to travel. I'm going to be someone!" "There's nothing for a woman to see but troubles," is her mother's disheartening reply (WET 46).

Unfortunately, her mother has assessed matters correctly. Unfortunately, too, the mother gives Consuelo less of a chance to prove her wrong. Being resigned to her plight, she has abdicated her maternal power and comes to collaborate both in her own and in her daughter's oppression.   Having internalized patriarchal evaluations of sons as more valuable, she is unable to love her daughter as she needs to be loved.   "[Connie] wanted her mother's comfort.   She had wanted Mariana to come with her in her pursuit of knowledge and some better way to live.   She had never been mothered enough and she had grown up with a hunger for mothering.   To be loved as Luis had been loved" (WET 47).   Taken from Connie, her own daughter, moreover, will not be mothered by *her* mother.   According to feminist psychotherapists, it is not unusual that women live with a sense of loss of maternal nurturing that is neither conscious nor culturally acknowledged.   In a review of Phyllis Chesler's *Women and Madness*, Piercy reflects that "in modern patriarchal culture, the mother-daughter bond is broken.   Mothers have no land or money to give daughters: not pride or dignity or sense of self.   Mary is easy to identify with—power through receptivity, compassion, and the suffering womb—but Mary has a son, not a daughter" ("Asking for Help Is Apt to Kill You" 26).

Predictably enough, Connie's attempts to exit her blighted circumstances and to fulfill her dreams of a more rewarding life are continually thwarted, and her life becomes a catalogue of defeat.   She manages to go to college for two years, but being too poor to afford a typewriter, she assents to type the term papers of a white male student, and when she gets pregnant by him, she has to leave the college.   Another man she loves, Martín, is killed, possibly by the police.   With a man named Eddie she has a daughter, Angelina, but Eddie leaves her.   To survive, she has to commute to her brother's (Luis/Lewis) nursery in New Jersey.   She meets Claud, a black saxophone player and pickpocket, but he dies after having consented to letting the prison where he is incarcerated use him in medical experiments.   After this blow, Consuelo is inconsolable, taking to the bottle, using drugs, and finally, in despair, hitting her own child.   The daughter unfortunately falls into a door and breaks her wrist, whereupon she has to be taken to the hospital, which must report the injury and thus leads to Connie's losing her to a foster home.   Early in the novel, Connie has also learned what it means to lose one's freedom: when her niece, Dolly Campos, has sought protection at her place, and Dolly's prize pimp, the sadistic *cabrón* Geraldo (bringing with him a thug and a doctor) breaks in and beats her in order to force her to have an abortion, Connie attacks him with a bottle.   In his resemblance to an eagle (albeit temporarily, WET 24), Geraldo recalls the "eagle" of Piercy's second novel, representing an oppressive patriarchal society, to which, despite his being a marginal person in other ways, Geraldo is linked.   He punishes Connie by having her committed to the state mental hospital.   "The pimp and the mad doctor," writes Judith Kegan Gardiner, "thus stand as the two exemplary villains of this society.   Both profit from turning the private realms of sexuality and of mental fantasy into institutions of exploitation" (75). The pimp and the doctor, moreover, recall the "emperor" in Piercy's poem "The Emperor" (from *Circles on the Water*):

> You exiled the Female into blacks and women and colonies.
> You became the armed brain and the barbed penis and the club.
> You invented agribusiness, leaching the soil to dust,
> and pissed mercury in the rivers and shat slag on the plains,
> withered your emotions to ulcers,
> strait-jacketed the mysteries and sent them to shock therapy.
> Your empress is a new-model car with breasts.

In her review of Chesler's treatise, Piercy concedes that it "passed instantly into [her] bloodstream and brain" ("Asking for Help" 25), and that it changed her way of seeing. In fact, *Woman on the Edge of Time* can be construed as a fictional account of the factual horror story that is *Women and Madness*. Resembling a prison, Piercy's hospital could be seen as a metaphor for women's condition. In Margaret Atwood's words: "Some reviewers treated this part of the book as a regrettable daydream or even a hallucination caused by Connie's madness. Such an interpretation undercuts the entire book" (273). In Phyllis Chesler's study, "Men dominate clinic work, while women are the majority of the clients" ("Asking for Help" 26). In the mercilessly oppressive "confined space" (WET 23) of Piercy's mental hospital, a rigid hierarchy reigns, where feminine or maternal characteristics such as empathy, caring, emotionality are denigrated, and masculine/patriarchal values such as rationality and impersonality are validated. The depiction of the hospital in *Woman on the Edge of Time* has been compared to that in Ken Kesey's *One Flew Over the Cuckoo's Nest* (1962). The mental hospitals portrayed are similarly oppressive, yet there are distinctive differences. As Frances Bartkowski writes, "Piercy's novel adds a feminist component missing from the earlier book. Where Kesey's text is blatantly sexist and misogynist, Piercy condemns the patriarchal nature of this institution and its exploitative treatment of women and men, Black and white. In Kesey's novel, the symbol of control is a grotesque character, Big Nurse, an incarnation of the terrible mother archetype" (1982 85-86).

Part of a muted world, Connie's virtues and talents are invisible to a dominant world devoid of empathy: nobody really listens to her or really sees her. She is insulted, infantilized, and incarcerated: in a passage recalling a ride in Sylvia Plath's *The Bell Jar*, which the heroine experiences as being enclosed in a prison van, Connie is transported to a mental hospital feeling as if she were "carried blind in the belly of the iron beast" (WET 31). The ultimate rape committed by society (after performing an unnecessary hysterectomy after Connie's being raped by Claud) is when she is chosen for experimental brain surgery, purportedly to control her 'violence.' This harrowing operation signals a final suppression not of her violence, but of a female principle: "Suddenly she thought that these men believed feeling itself a disease, something to be cut out like a rotten appendix. Cold, calculating, ambitious, believing themselves rational and superior, they chased the crouching female animal through the brain with a scalpel" (WET 282).

It is not only Connie's perspective—her observation of the three different societies outlined in *Woman on the Edge of Time*—that is significant. Equally notable is how these societies view *her*. On the 'present' time level, she is invisible: she is perceived as too insignificant to merit an effort to really see and hear her. Her particular knowledge is not seen as worthy of exploration. Society's blindness to Connie's virtues stands for an androcentric culture's incapacity to absorb, and its tendency to denigrate, a feminine principle—to make it invisible. Not even Connie's niece Dolly, a male-oriented person, is able to hear Connie even though she badly needs Connie's advice and help. Only when Connie, prompted to vengeful action, resorts to society's own deathly weapons and murders the coldly rational and inhuman doctors in self-defense, do her actions elicit a massive response.

Most of Connie's relations to men on the 'present' time level reduce her to being a service institution or a commodity to use or abuse. She tells Luciente, her guide to the alternative society:

> We have a religious idea of being good—a bit like what you call good, being gentle and caring about your neighbor. But to be a good man, for instance, a man is supposed to be...strong, hold his liquor, attractive to women, able to beat out other men, lucky, hard, tough, macho we call it, muy hombre...not to be a fool...not to get too involved...to look out for number one...to make good money. Well, to get ahead you step on people, like my brother Luis. You knuckle under to the big guys and you walk over the people underneath. (WET 120)

On the whole, Connie remains mistreated and misunderstood. From her powerless and forgotten corner of American society the oppressive nature of a patriarchal culture is revealed most clearly and suffered most acutely. Beleaguered by the misfortunes that befall her, Connie tells Luciente, "All my life I been pushed around by my father, by my brother Luis, by schools, by bosses, by cops, by doctors and lawyers and caseworkers and pimps and landlords. By everybody who could push" (WET 98-99). Connie "had noticed before that white men got off on descriptions of brown and black women being beaten. 'Hay que tratarlas mal,' Eddie would say" (WET 94). She is sexually exploited, seduced and abandoned, abused by cruel and indifferent doctors because men's desires and authority are prioritized before hers. Because a pimp's word weighs more heavily than hers, she is locked up in an asylum, and her noncompliance only gets her into more trouble. "She could have used some of her mother's resignation. When she fought her hard and sour destiny, she seemed only to end up worse beaten, worse humiliated, more quickly alone—after Eddie had walked out, alone with her daughter Angelina and no man, no job, no money, pregnant with the baby she must abort" (WET 44).

To be sure, men who do not conform to the masculine ideals of Connie's society also end up victims, as do the two men she has loved and lost, the portraits of whom have some feminized elements. Martín is described as follows: "He had been beautiful, his body like the molten sun, coppery and golden at once, his body in which strength and grace were balanced as in a great cat. His body had been almost girlish in its slenderness—although she would never have dared to say that in any way, for that very thought expressed would have lost him to her—and masculine in its swiftness, its muscular tight control" (WET 243). Claud, the black saxophone player and one of society's despised outcasts, encounters a senseless death in prison. From Connie's perspective, he has admirable and lovable qualities: "He was a fine saxophone player. He was a talented pickpocket and he brought home good things for her and her baby. He had been as good to Angie as if she had been his own baby daughter. He had been good to her, too, a loving man. The sweetest man she had ever had" (WET 26). Claud, too, is on a bottom level of the hierarchy, which is perhaps what makes for an equal relationship between Connie and Claud, a balance suggested by their virtually equal-length first names of identical initials, names associating, moreover, to another pair of outcasts in society: Bonnie Parker and Clyde Barrow.

Having chosen the way of the white 'Anglo' male, Connie's brother, Luis, by contrast, has been amply rewarded in terms of material success. "The army had changed Luis. When he had come back, he had contempt for the rest of them. His anger and unruly pride had been channeled into a desire to get ahead, to grab money, to succeed like an Anglo" (WET 363). Luis has "hardened" (WET 364), betrayed her and his own origins (switching his name to Lewis), renounced qualities like empathy, and adopted the perspective of the predominant culture; these changes mean that he cannot really see his sister or sympathize with her problems. He has alienated himself and absorbed all the attributes that have assured his ascendancy in mainstream America, but he has thereby lost Connie's affectionate admiration and has even become a stranger to her: "this middle-aged overweight businessman in the dark gray suit and the wide tie with its narrow dim stripe, the round moon face bulging into jowls, the forehead that ran well back to the middle of his scalp, the fat fingers with a lodge ring that remained braced on the table as he talked as though he feared if he let go of them they would fly up—did she know him from someplace?" (WET 352).

Among Connie's wrenching losses is the loss of her niece, Dolly, who resorts to prostitution to survive and to drugs to survive prostitution. To be able to survive mentally, Dolly, alternately spunky and spineless, must con herself into believing that she is on top, able to get "nice clothes, pretty things for my baby" (WET 219); but unlike Lewis, whose signature keeps Connie in the asylum, Dolly is powerless. Unable to explore or express her real self—"I say I'm of a Spanish mother and an Irish father. Sometimes I say my mother was a contessa" (WET 220)—she must give up keeping her daughter during the weeks, has to stay slim, dye her hair, and, as her letter to Connie indicates (169), has little opportunity for education. She, too, has had to adapt to 'Anglo' ideals: "The money is with the Anglos and they like you skinny and American-looking. It pays more if you look Anglo, you know" (WET 218). Yet, her true sentiments about her life as a prostitute are revealed in her comment to Connie: "Who can stand those assholes? They drive me crazy. They're all pigs" (WET 218). A patriarchal perspective has polluted Dolly's own and indeed made her go crazy, if that word can be used to designate her state of psychological confusion and delusion. Society has locked up Connie and declared her insane but considers Dolly sane.

Dolly's opposite is the equally appropriately named Sybil, a woman who refuses to give up her perspective and to collaborate in her own oppression. For Sybil, this has come to mean renouncing intimacy with men on the conditions offered. Feeling like "a dumb hole" (WET 85), sex is for her "futile" and "sordid," and she wishes to transcend the whole sad business: "I think we're taught we want sex when we feel unhappy or lacking something. But often what we want is something higher." Since Sybil is "telling women how to heal themselves and encouraging them to leave their husbands" (WET 84), she is perceived as dangerous and must be locked up in the asylum where Connie meets her.

For Connie, for whom groups of men impart a "sense of menace" (WET 67) and who instead "had taken to dreaming about young boys" (WET 37), the first meeting with Luciente is strange. Prima facie, Luciente appears to be a man, and Connie is apprehensive but also curious. "The face of the young Indio smiling, beckoning, curiously gentle. He lacked the macho presence of men in her own family, nor did he have Claud's massive strength, or Eddie's edgy combativeness" (WET 36). Luciente turns out to be a woman, Connie's guide to the future community of Mattapoisett (at Buzzard's Bay) in the year of 2137. Connie has been singled out as a "catcher," one of the persons who can mind-link with other times and places. Appearing first before Connie's hospitalization, Luciente then regularly aids her to escape her dreary days in the asylum. Whereas Patricia Marks finds that Luciente, "at least on one level, represents the speaking voice of Connie's own repressed unconscious" (110), and on another, "the site of a different female subject position" (151), Rachel

Blau du Plessis argues that "Luciente is a character who functions like a manifesto" (1979 1), as "Connie's double, an image of her enlightenment" (3).

In a series of visits to Mattapoisett, Connie is familiarized with the ideals and aspirations of its inhabitants. However, without being a hallucination, this future scenario is not yet a certainty; it is a possible alternative society where different values have been pursued. In depicting three types of societies, Piercy holds up three ideological choices for Connie, and the reader, to consider; and as Natalie Rosinsky comments, "the possibility of narratological unreliability does not invalidate the text's insights. Instead, it is further evidence of their affective authenticity" (188). The values and ideas governing the future communities can be traced back to the present time, the 'edge of time,' in which important choices must be made, and Luciente urges Connie to join their fight for the right choices. According to Barbara Hill Rigney,

> Piercy's intention in *Woman on the Edge of Time* is perhaps not so much to create Eden as to mourn the lack of it. Her utopian vision, while more practical and politically viable than many depicted in contemporary literature, is nonetheless a vision, a nostalgic trip through the values of the 1960s, a kind of summer camp for adults where the entertainment includes hallucinogens and free sex, neither of which entails responsibility or consequence. Piercy's emphasis, then, is a criticism of the real and present world. We must know and experience its fallen state before we can create a garden. (78-79)

In this alternate future, reached through psychism—the existence of which Piercy grew up taking for granted because of her mother's psychism (PCBQ 104)—it is the ideas of feminism, at a height at the time when *Woman on the Edge of Time* was written, that are realized. Ecological concerns are also paramount. "In a technological age in which women are still not trained in technology, correctly regarding it as a male domain, nature as female principle becomes an even more prominent and vital literary image" (Rigney 72). In Mattapoisett technology is used, but with discrimination; people live together within the community but each person has 'per' own space; everybody lives in close communion with nature and contributes to the prosperity of the village. Possessiveness, both in terms of material belongings and in terms of relationships, is considered negative and is something one consciously works to diminish. The elderly are respected, as are children. Most people are part artists, and every seven years they get a sabbatical to pursue whatever interests they like—programmatic, collective, institutionalized arrangements that may seem offputting, but which are none the less part of a serious attempt to transgress contemporary cultural boundaries and envision something different.

The most important change accomplished in Mattapoisett is a transformation in terms of power, a key issue in all of Piercy's work and linked to her vision of balance. In Mattapoisett, both men and women have given up a certain kind of power they alone had, and traditional parental power has been done away with. In the women's house in *Small Changes*, the children have five mothers who share in raising them. In *Woman on the Edge of Time*, children have three mothers, and upon reaching their teens the children go through a process of self-definition and of self-naming. While people strive to be spiritual and pure in heart, it is no longer a patriarchal god that is revered (WET 104). Racism has ceased to exist even though they do "hold on to separate cultural identities"—a multicultural and pluralist utopian ideal. For Connie, the most outlandish, almost repulsive, idea is the "brooder." There, the embryos of the next generation are floating, "like fish in the aquarium at Coney Island" (WET 102). This extrauterine production of babies is more than Connie can stomach, but her friendly guides proffer rational explanations:

> It was part of women's long revolution. When we were breaking all the old hierarchies. Finally there was that one thing we had to give up too, the only power we ever had, in return for no more power for anyone. The original production: the power to give birth. Cause as long as we were biologically enchained, we'd never be equal. And males never would be humanized to be loving and tender. So we all became mothers. (WET 105)

The similarities to Shulamith Firestone's 1970 critique of motherhood within the nuclear family are obvious, but with decisive divergences, since reproduction is actually presented as a privilege women have surrendered in order to allow men to participate on absolutely equal terms. In Firestone's discussion children are burdens, not bonuses, and she even doubts if there is any innate maternal instinct. Since Firestone sees children as a burden, this burden should be shared to avoid one person having to shoulder it by herself.

In Mattapoisett, by contrast, the maternal is an entirely positive force. "Romance, sex, birth, children—that's what you fasten on," Luciente tells Connie. "Yet that isn't women's business anymore. It's everybody's" (WET 251). By making men more maternal, women are freed for a wider range of pursuits and no longer seek their identities solely in motherhood. Comparing Margaret Atwood's *Surfacing* and Piercy's *Woman on the Edge of Time*, Ann Snitow finds that "In *Surfacing*, for example, Margaret Atwood sacrifices sexual pleasure to motherhood as the more profound experience and source of female identity. In *Woman on the Edge of Time*, Marge Piercy examines the opposite choice, showing a society of the future in which mothering has been diffused into the life of the community freeing sexuality to become an area of both play and profound feeling" (718; for a further discussion of the brooder see also Keinhorst, *Utopien von Frauen* 99-101).

In Mattapoisett, the binary hierarchy of Connie's capitalist patriarchal world is in the process of being reversed. The imbuing of life into the embryos in the brooder corresponds to the instilling of a female principle of maternal, life-enhancing, and life-giving properties throughout the culture. In the minds of Mattapoisett's denizens this is the infusion of a healing impulse to counteract earlier destructive divisions of mind/body and to erase the distinctions between power and powerlessness. To realize this ideal, it is men who must change the most, having had more power than women in the earlier society, that is, Connie's present, and therefore more responsibility, as the following quotation suggests:

> "Our history isn't a set of axioms." Bolivar spoke slowly, firmly. "I guess I see the original division of labor, that first dichotomy, as enabling later divvies into haves and have-nots, powerful and powerless, enjoyers and workers, rapists and victims. The patriarchal mind/body split turned the body to machine and the rest of the universe into booty on which the will could run rampant, using, discarding, destroying."
> Luciente nodded. "Yet I can't see male and female as equally to blame, for one had power and the other was property." (WET 211)

Piercy's scenario critiques the slotting of women into either tainted bodily flesh or pure madonna-like spirituality, both of which negate female sexuality. In Mattapoisett, this dichotomy has been transcended. Motherhood, a source of joy and power, is everyone's prerogative. Celibacy, in Connie's culture despised since a woman's value comes through a man, is entirely respected (WET 137). Whether mothers or not, whether part of a couple or celibate, women in Mattapoisett are both spiritual and sexual beings. Their philosophy, a realization of feminist ideals, could be seen as an echo of the feminist debate from the 1960s and onward, one focus of which has been the study of women's alienation from their bodies. Feminist theologians have examined a division of body and soul that dates back to Plato, a division that has been particularly harmful to women, but in extension also to society as a whole. The devaluation of the body has been linked to a problematic stance towards nature, in which dominance and exploitation are creating a disharmony ultimately dangerous to human survival.

Concepts of masculinity and femininity, spirituality and sexuality, are thus being transfigured in Mattapoisett. Delaney finds that "Piercy's new society is surely one of the more attractive and sophisticated in imaginative literature, a heady blend of late 1960s and early 1970s countercultures"—"deurbanized," "decentralized," "nonhierarchical and classless, multiracial and multicultural, industrial, agricultural, highly aesthetic, and sexually liberated" (175). But the values of Mattapoisett are still being struggled for, victory being far from certain. There is another, far less enchanting possibility of a conflicting future version, and a war is raging between these two worlds. This could be seen as a reenactment of a primordial, mythical battle between God and Satan, or between matriarchal and patriarchal principles (a battle in fact posited by some radical feminists who contend that, historically, the outcome of this battle was the ousting of matriarchy and the defeat of a feminine principle), or, as a battle between an impulse of connection and repair and an impulse of division and hierarchy.

According to C. G. Jung, "Knowledge rests not upon truth only, but upon error also" (163). In chapter 15, Connie time travels to the wrong future. In this tableau of terror, New York is a megacity not unlike that created in the film *Brazil*, a nightmare version where all the negative elements of corporate America have been grotesquely reinforced. Connie meets Gildina, a silicone-sculpted prostitute on a contract to Cash, isolated in a windowless apartment where she never sees the sun. As Cranny-Francis has observed, both Luciente and Gildina have names that associate to light, "but with Gildina it is a garish, tinsel light" (136). It can also be noted that Luciente is light producing while Gildina is light reflecting.

A claustrophobic, compartmentalized, artificial world is divided into strictly separated classes of people, defended by men like Cash—"a fighting machine" (WET 298), a "supercop" (WET 299) who has "been through mind control" and can switch off annoying human feelings or needs like "fear and pain and fatigue and sleep" (WET 297). Like everybody else, he belongs to a "multi" (the governing class, a concept that occurs again in *He, She and It*) (WET 300). Freedom and equality do not exist here, old people are sent to "Geri" (WET 290), and nature is out of Gildina's touch. Food comes from "big corporate factory-farms" (WET 296). Gildina's special powers—her ability to physically connect with Connie—are denied and invisible even to herself. Cash, immediately assuming an authoritarian stance, asserts that "There is no such thing as time travel" (WET 299). From his perspective, Connie is a puzzling anomaly that he is unable to classify.

While the dystopian 'error' world is thus constructed upon extreme hierarchical polarizations between men and women, between rich and poor, between old and young, between city and nature, the world Luciente takes Connie to is, at first glance, an androgynous one, where polarizations between men and women as well as between humans and nature have collapsed. In Thielmann's evaluation, "people are androgynous, biologically as well as psychologically. But this androgyny is not an 'elevating' of woman to the level of man, but rather a meeting of former 'female' and 'male' characteristics. Women are no longer 'feminine' in its (present) social implications. Men are not machos but are as nurturant as women" (126). Critics such as Kathryn Seidel, Natalie R. Rosinsky, Pamela Annas, Libby Falk Jones, and Jocye R. Ladenson see Piercy as an advocate of androgyny. Piercy herself sees her vision in *Woman on the Edge of Time* as "truly an androgynous society—one in which women's values and what women

represent are respected as much as the more traditional patriarchal ideas"
(PCBQ 103).   In this instance, I think that Piercy's own assessment is
somewhat misleading. As I interpret *Woman on the Edge of Time*, women's
values are in fact valued more. The trend is *toward* androgyny, a term which
is far from unproblematic for feminists, as Patricia Marks points out (107-09),
but, during the particular time stretch described in the novel, a war is raging
between a patriarchal and a feminine or maternal impulse. Mattapoisett is
"Utopia in transition" (Delaney 176), and traditional patriarchal ideas are not
valued as much as women's values. Men are actually changing more than
women, and they are adopting feminine characteristics, even physically, if they
are mothers. Dorothy Berkson finds that in *Woman on the Edge of Time* "the
most fundamental structural change that must take place is in the
'maternalizing' of men" (111), and in Patrocinio Schweickart's view, "It is
noteworthy that the Mattapoisettian mode of reproduction nullifies the role of
the father as it universalizes that of the mother" (328). Assessing the male
characters, Schweickart is "tempted to call them male women, except that they
are marked more by the absence of masculinity than the positive presence of
femininity" (341). Moreover, as Schweickart points out, not only is Piercy's
protagonist a woman, but "the primary model for human fellowship is female-
bonding" (338), or, as Libby Falk Jones puts it: "Piercy creates fusion through
the web of character relationships radiating from Connie" (123). The operating
principle might be called 'gynandric' rather than gynocentric or androgynous,
if such a morphological switch can suggest the prevailing ideological priority.
As Lyman Tower Sargent points out, "while Marge Piercy wants both women
and men closer to nature, she stresses the special role of women in healing"
(31). From a gynandric impulse of nurturing and healing comes the repair of
a war-torn, dichotomous world.

Consider, for example, the infusion of a maternal impulse in the extension
of mothering to include men.   Contrary to Firestone's proposal of
extracorporeal reproduction, motherhood is here exulted, a privilege to be
shared. On a physical level, men even assume female characteristics such as
being able to nurse, as in this passage, in which nursing is rendered in images
of liquified, free-floating spatiality: "He had breasts. Not large ones. Small
breasts, like a flat-chested woman temporarily swollen with milk. Then with
his red beard, his face of a sunburnt forty-five-year-old man, stern-visaged,
long-nosed, thin-lipped, he began to nurse. The baby stopped wailing and
began to suck greedily.   An expression of serene enjoyment spread over
Barbarossa's intellectual schoolmaster's face. He let go of the room, of
everything, and floated" (WET 134).

Language, rather than characterization, is at the heart of *Woman on the
Edge of Time*, according to Kathryn Seidel (1976 101). The deconstruction of
power structures is continued on a linguistic level, where Piercy deletes the

dimorphism of the objective and possessive pronouns 'his' and 'her,' which have been replaced with the unisex 'per.' The single personal pronoun is 'person.' Phonematically, however, 'per' sounds more like 'her' than 'his.' In Cranny-Francis's view, "The initial clumsiness of these neologisms is an indication to the reader of the pervasiveness of the gender ideologies which structure our society. Again their function is not predictive or a blueprint for the future, but an analysis of contemporary constructions of gender" (135). Integral to the novel's impetus (and far from being just a "lingo," as Roger Sale glosses it in his review), Piercy's neologism is her contribution to a counteracting of what H. Lee Gershuny has called "linguistic sexism" (191): Piercy's neologisms, in this novel and in *He, She and It*, are not only there to dismantle sexist language, but to argue for an overhaul of society. This is underlined in stanza seven of Piercy's poem "Doing it differently" (*Circles on the Water*):

> We will be equal, we say, new man and new woman.
> But what man am I equal to before the law of court or custom?
> The state owns my womb and hangs a man's name on me
> like the tags hung on dogs, my name is, property of.
> The language betrays us and rots in the mouth
> with its aftertaste of monastic sewers on the palate.
> Even the pronouns tear my tongue with their metal plates.

Nancy Walker, who finds "a re-ordering of the relationship to language itself" a pervasive force in contemporary literature by women, writes that

> Recognizing the power of language to confine and define, to claim power, to coerce and subjugate, these novelists suggest not merely the need for a non-sexist language, but more importantly women's full participation in the determination of meaning. And it is here that the devices of irony and fantasy come into full play, for it is the purpose of irony to cast doubt on assumed meaning and of fantasy to reformulate meaning in accordance with a new reality—an alternate world which, once imagined, becomes a possible, a potential place to live. (190)

Linked to the linguistic considerations are the politics of naming. While "Consuelo Camacho Alvarez Ramos trails a string of irrelevant father's and husband's surnames," writes Rosinsky, people in Mattapoisett only have one name, and one which is subject to change—a "sense of evolving selfhood, mirrored and reinforced by culturally accepted, fluid name change" (202). (For a further discussion of the importance of language in *Woman on the Edge of Time* see Patricia Hartman's "Politics of Language in Feminist Utopias.")

Furthermore, that patriarchal ideas are less valued in *Woman on the Edge of Time* is also suggested by Piercy's use of time—the "nearly continuous shifting of time and place that is close to stream-of-consciousness technique" (Khanna 132). Thielmann argues, in my view correctly, that time can be seen as a patriarchal concept, and she refers to *Small Changes*, where it is explained that 'doing time' means being locked up in jail and deprived of one's personal freedom, as Phil experienced it, and to *Dance the Eagle to Sleep*, in which the Indians perceive time as a threat because of the time they are expected to serve the state (114-15). Connie might as well be in prison, Thielmann continues, since her "time in the hospital is strictly regulated as a means to discipline her and make her aware of her powerlessness" (115); but Connie's time-traveling is actually a way to get out of "the system time of the present" and to enter a place where "time has a different content. In Mattapoisett time is an organic process as opposed to being divided into artificial units" (116). Moreover, as Thielmann observes, "On the structural level, the use of time reflects Connie's personal development through the novel" (117). C. R., Connie Ramos's initials, as Rachel Blau du Plessis has pointed out (1985 185), could stand for Consciousness Raising, but "Her consciousness does not flower yet, as her last name, Ramos, indicates in Spanish" (Thielmann 118). *Ramos* means a branch or bouquet of flowers, at the same time as it could, I think, associate to Spanish *ramera*, meaning 'whore,' and thus allude to Piercy's collapsing of the dichotomy between 'good' and 'bad' women, madonnas and whores. Rachel Blau du Plessis has commented on Piercy's choice of a name for her protagonist: "words from knowing and learning (*canny*, *conning*, *consciousness*, *kenning*), words that suggest victimization (*conned*) and critique (*con*—oppositional—and *cunning*). Indeed, Connie Ramos's initials, CR, offer almost as fine a hint of possibilities as Charlotte Brontë's JE" (1985 185).

The structuring of different time levels of the novel thus mirrors Connie's own development and her expanding comprehension of Mattapoisett's ideology. Piercy's use of time in *Woman on the Edge of Time* could be compared to Julia Kristeva's discussion of concepts of time. Kristeva's "future perfect" is, in Alice Jardine's words,

> a modality that implies neither that we are helpless before some inevitable destiny nor that we can somehow, given enough time and thought, engineer an ultimately perfect future. She often uses this term herself, particularly in reference to the poetic text; a literary text is always before or after its time (because of the negativity forcing the rejection of all thesis) but also of its own time to the extent that it represents a certain linguistic and ideological configuration. (5)

In "Women's time," Kristeva situates the development within the women's movement in different concepts of time: the earlier generations of feminists "aspired to gain a place in linear time" which meant a "rejection, when necessary, of the attributes traditionally considered feminine or maternal insofar as they are deemed incompatible with insertion in that history"; after 1968, "linear temporality has been almost totally refused" for a type of time seen as linked with female subjectivity, the 'cyclical' and the 'monumental,' the former being linked with "cycles, gestation, the eternal recurrence of a biological rhythm" and the latter "All-encompassing and infinite like imaginary space" (18-19, 16).

Libby Falk Jones remarks that "Rather than establish past, present and future as a logical continuum, the novel blends them in Connie's consciousness. The movement is not linear, but spiraling; the novel rounds through memory (what has been), fantasy (what might be), and dream (blending both past and future) to suggest that wholeness can be achieved only when all times of the self are integrated" (123). Piercy herself has conceded that "to [her] time seems not entirely linear, so that at moments different times touch and you feel something now gone" ("The Dark Thread in the Weave" 188). The time in Connie's mind-linking episodes subverts the linear time and world of the hospital, where Connie is "caught in a moment that had fallen out of time" (WET 20), to the point that the reader sometimes wonders whether the protagonist is hallucinating. A patriarchal concept of time is being sabotaged by a kind of 'women's time' (see also Franziska Gygax 52).

Frances Bartkowski has compared the use of time in Joanna Russ' *The Female Man* with *Woman on the Edge of Time*, and she writes: "Rather than Russ' version of a multiplicity of time frames colliding and coinciding, Piercy's rougher but simpler rhythm moves the reader back and forth, increasingly disturbed by the dystopian present, and, with Connie, soon preferring the unfamiliarity of the future" (1982 69). She adds: "Russ' twisted braid is a more treacherous and more exhilarating form of time travel, and further estranges the reader" (70).

Also along the lines of a kind of "women's time" is the displacement of normative, institutionalized heterosexuality. If Adrienne Rich is right in her view that heterosexuality can be termed "a *political institution*" that constitutes an oppressive force in patriarchy—"a beach-head of male dominance" that obscures a strong female tradition or, what Rich calls a "lesbian continuum" by which she means a "range—through each woman's life and throughout history—of woman-identified experience; not simply the fact that a woman has had or consciously desired genital sexual experience with another woman" (Rich 637, 633, 648). The bisexuality of Mattapoisett could, from this perspective, be viewed as a transgression of the heterosexual paradigm.

Meaning "shining, brilliant, full of light" (WET 36), the name Luciente associates to light as well as to daybreak, *la madrugada*. Herself associated with birds at first, Connie, moreover, calls Luciente a "crazy loon," but is reminded that loons only *sound* crazy and that they are graceful water birds who "swim low" just like turtles (WET 43). In *Small Changes*, Beth is associated with a turtle. Associated with low levels rather than with heights and with water, the turtle and the loon are part of a significant bird imagery in Piercy's work that is integral to the maternal impulse of healing and connection, while the eagle, as in *Dance the Eagle to Sleep*, is linked to an opposing, oppressive patriarchal principle. It is also significant that a woman is chosen to visit Mattapoisett. Her guide into the future is also a woman, even in the 'wrong' future. This suggests that women are a vanguard worth listening to, that insights from women—in particular from Third World and working class women now struggling on a present frontier for a concept of freedom and equality that includes them—must be incorporated into any true vision of democracy, and society, if dedicated to progress, would do well to follow a gynandric impulse of healing and repair during "crux-time." Despite the predictable drawbacks of utopian fables, "The moral intent of such fables," in Margaret Atwood's view, "is to point out to us that our own undesirable conditions are not necessary: if things can be imagined differently, they can be done differently" (274). Critics have noted the similarities between Connie and Luciente; in a better society, Connie might have a better script; the contrasts between them are, in Cranny-Francis's opinion, "a terrible indictment of Connie's world, which is contemporary US society" (130).

An androcentric culture's bias suppresses and distorts the female perspective, as shown in the impersonal, 'objective,' medical reports on Connie with which her story is closed, "Excerpts from the Official History of Consuelo Ramos," which, as pointed out by Nancy Walker, resembles the "Historical Notes" that conclude Margaret Atwood's *The Handmaid's Tale* (1985), and which "[present the heroine] as a problem in historical verification rather than an actual person" (Walker 156). As Patricia Marks observes, Connie is objectified as Other (148). But her story is impossible to dismiss. After the dual-level narrative in *Woman on the Edge of Time*, the reader is led to perceive this distortion and to question the validity or 'objectivity' of the authoritative-sounding reports. The reports "*require* evaluative choice from the reader," argues Rosinsky, and the fact that they contain actual errors suggests "that 'official' observers [*sic*] may be as biased, as narratorially unreliable as a potentially insane woman's" (194). The subversion of the male-dominated and male-oriented perspective prevalent in Connie's story prepares the reader to see what *is missing* in the clinical summary. Connie's invisibility has become visibility. On the surface, her rebellion is squelched, but, subversively, it continues beyond the ending. As Bee advises Connie: "There's always a thing you can deny an oppressor, if only your allegiance. Your belief. Your co-opting. Often even with vastly unequal power, you can find or force an opening back. In your time many without power found ways to fight. Till that became a power" (WET 328).

In Nancy Walker's view, "The central activity of reading speculative fiction is constant comparison between two sets of realities, and feminist fantasies, by refusing to be confined to the reader's observable world, force a revision of that world through the medium of ironic drama" (184). *Woman on the Edge of Time* could be placed within a genre of feminist utopian fiction or science fiction (with links back to earlier utopias such as Charlotte Perkins Gilman's *Herland*) built on shared ideological assumptions and with similar building blocks, which illumine what the authors find glaringly missing in contemporary society. As Joanna Russ has pointed out, in this sense all utopias are reactive. A fear and dislike of big cities, for example, can be transformed into pastoral dreams. Russ argues that "perhaps the dislike of urban environments realistically reflects women's experience of such places—women do not own city streets, not even in fantasy. Nor do they have much say in the kind of business that makes, sustains and goes on in cities" (81). Visions of a different female sexuality are also reactive to contemporary aspects of sexual codes. As a reaction to women's sense of confinement there is a vision of freedom and mobility in the feminist utopia, with physical mobility being "a direct comment on the physical and psychological threats that bar women from physical mobility in the real world" (82). As a part of this "reactive" writing one often finds didactic elements, which can signify pitfalls leading to the "slightly sanctimonious and preachy," tedious tones that harken back to Thomas More (Atwood 275).

Despite differences in political opinions, most of us are united in a wish for a world where peace and stability reign, where there are no more wars, no unsettling discord, no violence or oppression. But in order to eradicate suffering, do we have to erase passion as well? In Aldous Huxley's *Brave New World*, for example, the Savage's expostulations seem to imply that if we retain passion, suffering will be unavoidable. Some other utopias or dystopias seem to follow this pattern. In *Gulliver's Travels*, Lemuel Gulliver finds a rational and harmonious utopia in the land of the horses, a society that resembles *Brave New World* in its lack of passion. The horses are eminently but boringly practical and even-tempered. Charlotte Perkins Gilman's *Herland* (1915) depicts another rational and rather passionless society, this time consisting of women only. Jean-Luc Godard's film *Alphaville: Une étrange aventure de Lemmy Caution* (1965) features a future society in which emotions and passions have been done away with; the atmosphere here is one of nightmarish oppression, and as in *Brave New World*, the citizens are kept going on drugs. The question that arises from a reading of many of these utopias and dystopias, then, is whether a world of peace and harmony has to be stagnated, boring, and passionless. To be sure, Atwood opines, "all utopias suffer from the reader's secret conviction that a perfect world would be dull" (275). Chris Ferns comments that "because the traditional utopia imposes a perfect pattern on society, the possibility of growth and change is virtually eliminated" (459).

In *Woman on the Edge of Time*, Marge Piercy has attempted to counteract dullness by introducing conflict and passion, even criminality and madness (see Thielmann 133-39). Piercy's novel, moreover, differs from traditional utopia in its "dialectic between the ideal and the actual which generates a very different narrative dynamic from that found in traditional utopian fiction" (Ferns 462). For Piercy, it suffices to point to the *process* toward harmony, equality, balance between humans and nature, union without unity: a process that entails struggle and effort. As Patricia Waugh observes, "the novel throughout emphasizes the importance of human struggle, will, agency, and establishment of relationship as *acts in the world*, in order that the utopian vision may be achieved through the release of repressed desire" (211). In Piercy's view,

> Fiction works no miracles of conversion, but I guess I believe any white reader who spends a reasonable proportion of time consuming Black novels and poetry is less likely to be as comfortably racist in large and small ways; and any man who reads enough of current women's literature is less likely to be ignorant of what women want and need and don't want and don't need, and what patriarchy costs us in blood and energy day and night. (PCBQ 169)

Even though *Woman on the Edge of Time* may not work "miracles of conversion," Piercy's contraposition of three different types of social arrangements does encourage the reader to ponder problems and possibilities inherent in contemporary American society, with the glimpses into the future societies being a way of (to use du Plessis' phrase) "writing beyond the ending."

Chapter 5

The High Cost of Living

> In another
> life, dear sister, I too would bear six fat
> children. In another life, my sister, I too
> would love another woman and raise one child
> together as if that pushed from both our wombs.
> In another life, sister, I too would dwell
> solitary and splendid as a lighthouse on the rocks
> or be born to mate for life like the faithful goose.
> Praise all our choices. Praise any woman
> who chooses, and make safe her choice.
>
> Marge Piercy, "The sabbath of mutual respect," *The Moon Is Always Female*

In *The High Cost of Living*, Piercy "wanted to deal with some of the observations [she] had made of students and of young people generally, of the changing pressures of class, of the confusion between morality and politics so common in our culture" (*Contemporary Authors* 278). In the words of Karen Lindsey, this novel is "a sophisticated, finely crafted portrayal of three misfits—a lesbian separatist, a gay man, and a heterosexual teenage woman—whose souls have been destroyed by social forces they partly understand but ultimately are not strong enough to resist" (31). Piercy has created a somewhat androgynous heroine, appropriately named Leslie. A young graduate student of twenty-three, Leslie McGivers straddles traditional gender roles and moves in both muted and dominant worlds. Bisexual, although primarily a lesbian, at the same time sensitive and tough as well as open and principled, she practices karate, owns a motorcycle, and is an opportunistic academic careful not to alienate her (male) mentor. In the male-dominated field of historical inquiry, she upholds standards of excellence. In the muted or 'alternative' world of women, she works a rape hot line, teaches karate at a newly started women's school, and remains the confidante of the wife of her mentor. Extolling the female body, she also cultivates a link to lesbian communities.

The dynamics of the female world are not idyllic in *The High Cost of Living*. Sue Walker writes of this novel that it "is a book that deals specifically with the dead-end desperation of some lesbian relationships, and it may be classed as Piercy's least successful novel" (139). Honor, an ironically named, affected, precocious high school student Leslie is unaccountably attracted to, fails her for an affair with George Sanderson, Leslie's mentor. Leslie's sister, Cam, moves in with an obnoxious, promiscuous, lesbian-hating man (Mark). Choosing a rich sugar mommy, Leslie's lover, Val, finally abandons her. None the less, in *The High Cost of Living* it is a maternal impulse that points the way to the repair of the world. Women characters farm ecologically, live simply, are portrayed as sensual and in touch with their own selves, they raise the children and pursue alternative forms of knowledge, questioning the 'masculine' world of traditional learning. The female body is a figure of hope, and Leslie is moved as she looks at the women's bodies during their efforts to learn something new, to make something of themselves, during her first class (HCL 283). Low in aggressiveness, women's thrust forward is a quiet rivulet outside mainstream society. Women are depicted as victims of this society in general and of male violence in particular. "Oh, she met women; bleeding, lacerated, vomiting, catatonic. Even the women who worked the hot line seemed to shrink from each other, as if each held too much pain to care to deal with any woman similarly brimming over" (HCL 24). As elsewhere in Piercy's fiction, there are innumerable allusions to women's fear of male attacks or rape, to wifebattering, to husbands' philandering (which seems to surpass that of women). In terms of power, women are poised against men in *The High Cost of Living*, most obviously in Sue's role as the faculty wife of George and in Cam's relationship to Mark.

It may seem surprising in a novel extolling a maternal impulse that a mother is siding with the oppressive side: Honor Rogers, the nineteen-year-old, is suffering under a domineering mother. What Piercy is emphasizing with this portrait, however, is that it is not necessarily individual men who oppress women, but individuals, be they men or women, who have donned what could be called patriarchal values. In *The High Cost of Living*, everyone wishes to dominate Honor. The battle over Honor thus turns into a symbolic battle over male versus female values in American culture. Honor's mother fulfills a role similar to that of Beth's mother in *Small Changes*, through the voice of whom, as Patricia Marks observes, the inflections of an ascendant male culture can be heard, requesting that older women pilot the younger generation of women to proper positions in what can be seen as a double 'reproduction' service (38).

Men's goals and their methods to reach them are depicted as sick and damaging. Leslie's crusade to free Honor from the grip of her repressed mother could be seen as a metaphor for freeing women from men's excessive power.

Honor, an inexperienced virgin and a "stultifyingly silly" character in Anatole Broyard's review (14), is nevertheless the one over whom the main battle in *The High Cost of Living* is waged; she represents the prefeminist woman. Believing his declarations of love, Honor enters a most unequal relationship with Leslie's mentor, George, twice as old as Honor and a powerful university professor, an "academic fucker with a mustache and a rich wife," as Leslie characterizes him (HCL 275). Leslie tells Honor: "You're in the relationship of being exploited" (HCL 274), something that Honor fails to see, construing instead a case in which George is "trapped in a life that frustrates him, with a rich redneck of a wife like a millstone around his neck" (HCL 275). But while Honor is reiterating her culture's clichés about romantic love, thinking that what she has been hit by is a *coup de foudre* based on "real attraction," "overwhelming" and "unmistakable" (HCL 274), this attraction is quite mistakable; it is Honor who is trapped, not George, as she was first by her mother. Even though she is attracted to Honor, Leslie's aim is to help Honor find her own identity, and she reminds herself that her purpose is a noble one of solidarity with another woman (HCL 146, 212). Another character, Bernie Guizot, avowedly desires the same things for Honor, although his methods are more aggressive. Bernie in Broyard's view "becomes a tool for tightening the nuts and bolts of the author's sociology of sex" (14). A lower-class white homosexual damaged by the trauma of his incestuously loved sister's death as a preadolescent, his homosexuality may be psychological in origin rather than genetically determined. His methods of seduction and persuasion are depicted as masculine. Planning to seduce Leslie on his deserted childhood island, he gets carried away and nearly rapes her. Leslie's unfeminine answer is a fist in the solar plexus. Both Bernie and Leslie want Honor, but they go about it in different ways. Obsessed, Bernie pursues Honor at school and waits for her outside her house.

Certainly influenced by the women's movement, the descriptions of male-female sexuality (HCL 92-93) and the long and explicit accounts of lesbian and heterosexual pleasures (or the absence thereof) tend toward the didactic. The dalliance of Bernie and Leslie is an unusual one, in which two homosexuals seek a closer connection through sex. At least that is Leslie's motivation. What matters more for Bernie is the added bonus of feeling like a 'real' male, one who is in control, powerfully on top. Society has emasculated him, as has his class background, and his promiscuous life has apparently meant passively serving other men rather than pursuing his own pleasure, then being humiliated as a 'homosexual' after being exploited.

Pushed into a female role of submission, he feels most at home with women; yet, believing that control is necessary, he attempts to control both Leslie and Honor. When his attempts fail, he cannot accept *their* conditions, and leaves without a word.

The sexual encounter between Leslie and Bernie might be construed as a metaphor for male-female relations in patriarchy. For Bernie, it is a matter of proving that he is male after all and that he is not impotent, as he has previously been with women. That his triumph is taken almost violently, certainly oppressively, without consideration for Leslie's response, evades him. As a homosexual with little experience of women he is, moreover, fairly ignorant of female sexuality and only willing to learn up to a point: he is surprised that their union was not enjoyable for Leslie. "She felt confused. She did not like the way he was holding her, her back to him with her hands lying open and useless before her. This was a position which gave him all the initiative and control and there was an edge to that control, a slight stain of sadism in his excitement. . . . She could not move at all in this position but only lie and be pierced and hammered in" (HCL 190). Leslie feels "claustrophobic," "pinned down" and "too powerless, too contained . . . Even if the thumping inside had aroused her, the complete passivity would have stolen the excitement away again" (HCL 191). Rather than increasing their intimacy, this sadly unequal and unbalanced encounter puts an end first to their communication, then to their friendship. In an article from 1984 in which Piercy candidly discusses her own sexual fantasies and sexual reality, she states unequivocally: "To be afraid of a partner, unable to speak my mind or lose my temper or express my will, would dampen my sexuality. Under the gross inequality that has existed between almost all men and women, I think few women can flourish sexually" ("The Turn-on of Intimacy" 48).

At one point in the novel, Leslie muses: "She was only at ease with gay women, really, and she was less ill at ease with straight women than with the gayest of men. After all, they were still men" (HCL 38). In Anatole Broyard's opinion, there is a prejudice against men in this novel, since besides Bernie, "three other men in the novel are exposed as compulsive lechers" (14). It is true that one can detect a desire to triumph over men or male behavior in some passages of *The High Cost of Living*. Karate and other self-defense methods are held up as beneficial practices for women. In Piercy's plot, Bernie is made into a sad failure while Leslie is advancing at her department and is able to kick Mark out (as a less accomplished scholar, who is also prejudiced and ungenerous toward homosexuals). Sue, the faculty wife of George, begins to practice an open marriage herself—previously her husband's prerogative—a change that leads to the novel's most comic, intensely alive, and revealing marital quarrel, in which George's adherence to a double standard and his notion of the responsibility of a wife and mother are uncovered, while "for the first time in one of their fights Sue felt herself to be in a winning position" (HCL 280).

However, in *The High Cost of Living*, women are depicted as not yet powerful enough to strike out independently, without male protection. In Sue Walker's view, "Society wins in this novel as Piercy lapses into an unprecedented cynicism" (115). Leslie needs George, her "powerful protector and friend" (HCL 287), even though he acts like her owner. "Almost she expected him to summon her to take notes while he was sitting on the toilet. He did not have her sense of privacy. Sometimes that made her feel like a servant, a real domestic" (HCL 215). Paralleling early choices of liberal feminism, Leslie chooses a 'male' road in order to optimize her chances in a male-dominated field of work. At the same time, she is drawn to women's values and quite aware of the power struggles inherent in contemporary male-female dynamics, as illustrated in a dialogue between her and Mark at a party at the beginning of the novel. Embodying negative male values, manners and methods, Mark is primarily interested in 'scoring,' uninterested in Leslie's *own* definition of herself and insensitive to her wants and even openly hostile once he realizes that she is a lesbian. With this dialogue, Piercy illustrates the male prestige of conquering women and male inability to communicate in ways not sexual-aggressive as well as a male belief that women are made to please men: if they do not wear bras, for example, it is to be sexually provocative. Mark attempts to seduce Leslie through a preening, sexually swaggering style, descanting on his past outrageous sexual exploits and on his irresistible attractiveness. The portrait of Mark—"the lower half of his face seemed trapped in sulky early adolescence" (HCL 7) intimates a person who is only partially mature. Mark represents a type of man whose attitudes help fan the flames of women's anger and makes the women's movement seem necessary. Piercy, moreover, has created a highly symbolic setting for the dialogue between Mark and Leslie, a living room visually dominated by "an ashtray in the shape of a woman . . . artful, sort of African, and therefore all the more shocking, as it was supposed to be. The butts ground out on the woman's hollowed belly jarred Leslie" (HCL 9). Metaphorically speaking, the women at the party are indeed putting up with men's grinding, self-important ways and with a male-dominated sexuality obsessed with penetration. Male sexuality takes forms that are less than enjoyable; Leslie wonders, "How can you let this society make you feel ashamed that you don't get your pleasure from raping women in hallways or buying them on streetcorners or marrying one and keeping her in a box and going pump, pump, pump on top of her the correct two point four times a week?" (HCL 89). While male behavior is fraught with violence, and men are so threatened by women who choose to love women as to beat up Leslie and her lover, Leslie says, "I've never been attacked by a woman" (HCL 39). Not surprisingly, Leslie dislikes jewelry, which she sees as "signs of bondage, decorative brands of ownership" (HCL 77).

In *The High Cost of Living*, women gossip (HCL 261-62); they do not distrust words, as does a previous, close-mouthed lover of Leslie's, but exchange information between themselves that help them survive as women. Of course, Piercy's novels in sheer length often attest to their author's faith in words.   Within the novels, references to what books have meant for the characters are abundant.   For Leslie in *The High Cost of Living*, they have meant a new world (HCL 36).   As in *Vida*, social mobility is often advocated through these literary references, although not in traditional, career-climbing ways, but on alternative paths.   A gift from Leslie to Honor, a selection of women's journals, an enchanted cache "selected as at least carrying some quiet freight of content with it, the unlocking of a door or two in the imagination" (HCL 99), can also be seen as a symbolical gift from Piercy to her readers, since "books retain a special power: tickets to elsewhere" (HCL 36). Throughout Piercy's fiction, books have the "special power" of destabilizing the patriarchal discourse and allowing women to construct their own, different narrative perspective, and, departing from what Teresa de Lauretis has called "a view from 'elsewhere'" (25), to interject a subversive production of meaning in the 'abysmal' sites between subjectivity and the dominant culture. This "view from 'elsewhere,'" as de Lauretis defines it, "is not some mythic distant past or some utopian future history: it is the elsewhere of discourse here and now, the blind spots, or the space-off, of its representations.   I think of it as spaces in the margins of hegemonic discourses, social spaces carved in the interstices of institutions and in the chinks and cracks of the power-knowledge apparati."   Similarly, Piercy writes about "wriggling through the cracks, surviving in the unguarded interstices" ("Through the Cracks" 205). Leslie's mission to liberate Honor, then, parallels the author's mission for her readers as well as that of the feminist movement on behalf of all women: "It's good for her to know different kinds of women who've made different choices—work choices, living choices, sexual choices" (HCL 212). This belief in the empowering of reading parallels the belief in the very letters of the alphabet evinced by medieval Jewish mysticists, ideas also of relevance in my chapter on *He, She and It*.

Chapter 6

Vida

I was a weapon. I brandished myself, I was used in the air.
We rushed in waves at the Tower and were hurtled back.
Because we were right, should we not win?

. . . .

Run, keep running, don't look sideways.
The blood is raining down all of the time, how can we rest?
How can we pause to think, how can we argue with you,
how can we pause to reason and win you over?
Conscience is the sword we wield,
conscience is the sword that runs us through.

Marge Piercy, "The Knight of Swords," Circles on the Water

Structured in twenty-five chapters alternating between an autumnal 'present' and a 'past' (October 1967, May 1970, February 1974), Marge Piercy's fifth novel presents an overtly political theme concerning the struggle between 'past' and 'present' ideas, complexly illumined throughout the narrative. The eponymous heroine, Vida (Davida) Ash, whose name signals either an impugnable synthesis of opposites or irresoluble contradiction/paradox, began as one of the many students against the Vietnam war and then became a heroic revolutionary or a threatening terrorist—depending on how one sees it. Unrepentant after participating in a bombing of a building in Manhattan, she is forced underground in a metaphorical assertion of Piercy's message that what is repressed will return—with a vengeance. Piercy has said of her novel:

> *Vida* has as protagonist a political fugitive, a woman who has been living underground since 1970. On one level it is about the sixties and the seventies. On another level it is about two sisters, both politically committed, and some of the inner and outer forces that make one woman a feminist and another

> more oriented toward the male Left. On another level it is a love story about
> two people trying to build love and truth on the margin of danger and
> desperation. On another level it is a study of the destructive effects of male
> jealousy. (PCBQ 215)

Together with other fugitives, Vida continues to produce political pamphlets
and to sabotage selected sites condemned by her Network. As likable as she
is offputting, the character of Vida has been interpreted by Pia Thielmann
(168-73) and others as based on Bernardine Dohrn (who surfaced after ten
years underground) and the Network on the Weathermen, but this was not
Piercy's intention (personal letter from Marge Piercy, October 8, 1993). There
are many other real life stories of 1960s radicals gone underground.   In
September 1993, Katherine Ann Power surfaced after living underground since
1970, when she robbed a bank in her struggle against the Vietnam War (see
"After 23 Years, Double Life Is Over" A-1, A-13). Vida chooses to persevere
in her unremitting and thankless pursuit of what she visualizes as political
justice, driven by the conviction that she is a tool in the 'right' cause. The
deracinated days of Vida, the underground, persecuted revolutionary working
to subvert capitalist patriarchy could be seen also as a metaphor for women's
condition.   In an interview, Piercy comments: "It seems to be one very
common dream of women to dream about being hunted, chased, pursued,
harried" (Betsky 1976 38). Piercy also states:

> The experience of being a political fugitive, after all, is the experience of
> being an invisible woman, instead of a token woman. [Vida] was much less
> open to feminism when she was a token woman, a charismatic woman sharing
> the stage with men. As a fugitive, invisible and necessarily anonymous, she
> has none of that—her experiences are much closer to the experiences of
> ordinary women, and she becomes much more open to the ideas of feminism,
> though I would never call her a feminist. (PCBQ 178)

That Vida is not a feminist or a female-oriented woman is the cause of her
rather sad end. Doggedly following a destructive masculine impulse, Vida
becomes linked to the very system she aims to overthrow. She perseveres as
a combative, male-oriented woman, even when it is to her own disadvantage.
Exposed to the ideas of feminism through her half-sister Natalie, but never
fully embracing them, she remains ambivalent in her view of masculinity and
male roles, as her relationship with Joel shows. At the same time, ironically,
in the view of Virginia Tiger, Vida's helpful cooking and caring "recalls Beth
in Louisa May Alcott's *Little Women* happily sweeping dust—from dawn to
dusk, day after day—in Marmee March's house" (11). This is how Tiger
describes Vida:

> Marge Piercy's *Vida*, a heroine of the 60's radical underground, provides
> another variation in self-punitive martyrdom. Her fanaticism . . . expresses
> itself—puzzling as this may seem at first—in traditional ways, underscoring
> the concept of the female as one who ministers to the welfare of others. In
> the guise of madonna, mother, muse or 'Angel in the House' (Virginia
> Woolf's phrase), this idealized feminine type has given virgin birth, in both
> life and literature, to countless daughters. (11)

In her first marriage to Vasos, Vida indeed settles for a submissive, serving
role. Piercy shows how it is Vida's 'unraised' consciousness that leads her
into marriage to a man who continually rapes her, something he and Vida
(rightfully) believe to be his conjugal right (V 228). In the staunchly
patriarchal setting of the Mediterranean, Vida is forced into a role of wifely
submission.

Her second marriage is situated in America in the heady atmosphere of the
'liberated' 1960s and 1970s, where an illusion of equality reigns. Vida and
Leigh live in an open marriage or, with a term from Ann Rhodes, a
"multigamy" (see Cheatham and Powell 23), as for about fifteen years, Marge
Piercy herself lived in multiple relationships, a lifestyle of the 1960s and 1970s
(*Daughters of de Beauvoir* 16). Leigh appears to be obviously different from
most men in the leftist movement to which they belong, and for this Vida feels
deep gratitude:

> Leigh was the only man she knew who did not diminish the woman he was
> with, who did not think because they fucked that he owned her or she was his
> little garbage bag . . . She was fiercely grateful to Leigh . . . for their way of
> being open, trusting and above all respectful. She could love other men
> briefly, affectionately, as friends, as lovers, but only Leigh could be trusted in
> the center of her life. No other man could ever love her and let her survive
> intact, her appetites, her abilities, her will, her intellect not diminished or
> pruned but encouraged. (V 124-25)

Revealingly, Vida's praise of Leigh is simultaneously an indictment of
most of the other men in the leftist movement. Refusing to be boxed in, Leigh
himself is fortunate in being able to openly indulge in extramarital affairs
without stern looks from a clinging wife or from a condemnatory culture.
Even in this 'liberated' relationship, however, Vida assumes a role of
obeisance, in adapting her sexuality to fit his (V 116) and in renouncing
motherhood since Leigh fears that children would cramp their lifestyle, a belief
held by many counterculture youths at that time. Later Leigh accepts the
pregnancy of a new girlfriend, much to Vida's chagrin. Much later, she is able
to see their marriage more clearly: "His nose stood out like a request, and the
request worked on her as guilt: she should be feeding him, she should be
making him happy. One of the foundations of their marriage had surely been

that both of them believed strongly that Leigh had a right to whatever he needed to make him happy and functional, so that he could get on with his important political work" (V 348).

Unadvisedly, Vida also gets involved with a roustabout ex-con named Kevin, a brutish, macho, vulgar character not above threatening her at knife-point after their relationship is over. His violence extending into the bedroom, as is the case also with some other men Vida meets, Kevin recalls the brutality of Vida's father toward her mother. In Leigh's opinion, Vida's initial dismay at Kevin's being a robber who has gone to prison is 'bourgeois,' thoughts that echo Norman Mailer's 1957 "The White Negro," which proposes that being criminal may be one way of being a rebel. Vida's last lover, Joel, by contrast, comes close to being an ideal. For the first time Vida experiences a more fundamental sense of equality based on shared situations and shared interests as fugitives. A sense of freedom and equality is one of the first things Vida, delighted, relishes in their interaction (V 76). Joel is a much younger man, presumably part of a more aware, younger generation and perhaps more open to a female perspective. Apparently ascribing to a feminine/maternal principle, Joel is caring, empathetic, adroit, lacks the violently aggressive style used by other men in this novel, and is even able to cook and sew—but Vida is not ready for this new man. Addled, she views his uncommon traits with ambivalence and suspicion, thinking, somewhat condescendingly, when he has made coffee, "A real domestic type," and contemptuously, when he decides to chop wood, "Don't tell me even this one is going to try to play macho!" (V 78). Nonplussed, "she felt as if she had come upon a truly new breed of human being, a man untouched by old macho roles, vulnerable and open, gentle and emotional as a woman" (V 89). Vida's dedication to her underground subversive activities and her insistence on "multigamy" undermine the relationship in the end. Their roles are reversed, with the home-oriented Joel wanting to 'surface' so that they can lead a normal life together whereas Vida remains stubbornly loyal to her cause even while suffering from the sacrifices that entails. On the run, Vida has been living in her head, not in her body. Her desire for Joel makes her fear that she will lose her rational, political commitment. While patriarchal principles—represented by the destructive values and behavior of patriarchs like Daniel (Natalie's husband) and Leigh (because of whom Joel gets caught) and by those who feel contempt for women in the movement as well as by the rapists and wifeabusers mentioned in the novel—are shown to be inimical to life, growth, development, change, society is not yet ready for either a new type of man or for an era governed by a maternal impulse—and Joel, the man of the future ambiguously sketched as both beautiful lover and inept, inexperienced klutz, haplessly walks into a trap.

Like several other Piercy heroines, Vida also has sexual relationships with women. In Pia Thielmann's view, Vida "uses sex as a means to get something with men as well as with women. While she flirts habitually with men, to ease tension or direct them where she wants them, she manipulates women sexually" (177). This is what Ann Snitow has called "Sex to Get Something Else" or "instrumental sex," other examples of which Snitow detects in Alix Kates Shulman's *Memoirs of an Ex-Prom Queen* ("instrumental sex exchanged for a man's protection and support for childbearing and rearing") and in Marilyn French's *The Women's Room* (710). Relationships with women, then, do not necessarily represent the impulse of connection exalted in Piercy's work.

Vida's half-sister, Natalie, on the other hand, is a female-oriented woman who sets up consciousness-raising groups, something that Vida feels somewhat alienated from. Not wishing to come to terms with her memories of the violent Vasos, Vida—echoing the views expressed in Eldridge Cleaver's *Soul on Ice* (1968), which actually deems it defensible, because politically rebellious, for a black man to rape white women—defends the man who raped her sister—only because he was black: "My god, Natty, I hope you don't go around saying in your women's groups that a Black man raped you. He was probably incredibly oppressed. That's like putting down Blacks because there's a high crime rate in the ghetto" (V 229). In her politically 'correct' but twisted logic, which also dismisses protests against nuclear power as bourgeois, Vida remonstrates her sister for sounding "like some Southern-belle racist." But in Natalie's analysis, based upon her experience of marriage and after other postmarital relationships, there is not "much in most men besides privilege and arrogance, or privilege and self-pity" (V 347). For Vida, Natalie represents a feminine or maternal impulse of caring and nurturing that she desperately needs, as well as a connection with her mother, into which category Joel, too, falls: "She realized with a little queasiness that part of her passion for Joel was rooted in some subliminal identification of his warmth, his impulsiveness, his earthiness—even his testiness, his quickness of response—with Ruby [her mother]. Well, why not? Why not seek in a lover the best traits of your first love?" (V 471).

Prevalent in the relationships in *Vida*, then, is the battle between the longing for union and the decision to stand justly apart, between a masculine impulse of rational, at times aggressive and violent struggle and a maternal impulse of identification and sharing. On one level, this battle could be drawn up along lines of the Apollonian and the Dionysian. Vida's extrusion of the traits of empathy and caring in herself that she cherishes in Natalie, Joel or her mother, leads to the novel's rather depressing conclusion; her 'heroic' rational decision is once again to strike out alone and live like an army on constant alert, with the denial of the web of connections and the love and intimacy she desperately needs as a viaticum. One might, like Pia Thielmann (176), see

Joel's jealousy as leading to ruin, but Vida's complicity must also be examined.

Vida has received mixed reviews from critics who perceive the characterization as underdeveloped and the narrative as too packed with political or counterculture aspects. In a front-page review in the *New York Times Book Review*, for example, Elinor Langer deplores the "insular presentation of life in the movement," but concedes that this "is a political more than a literary matter, a deliberate decision, a product of the subordination of the novelist's detachment to the radical's allegiance" (Langer, "After the Movement" 36). Still, Langer finds, this novel "evokes life in the radical movement so realistically that it seems at times more literal than imagined," in "a fully controlled, tightly structured dramatic narrative of such artful intensity that it leads the reader on at almost every page" (1). In the view of Norma B. Hawes in *National Review*, "*Vida* is worth reading because it looks at [the anti-war movement of the 1960s] from a feminine viewpoint —a viewpoint that deals with people and their relationships rather than ideas and ideals—without the angry rhetoric that is the mark of so many feminist books today" (675). As Jennifer Uglow, finally, writes in the *Times Literary Supplement*: "*Vida* may not have the force or coherence of a persuasive argument but it deserves attention, even from those who don't agree, as a powerful novel, written with insight, wit and remorseless energy" (56).

Chapter 7

Braided Lives

Pieced quilts, patchwork from best gowns,
winter woolens, linens, blankets, worked jigsaw
of the memories of braided lives, precious
scraps: women were buried but their clothing wore on.
> Marge Piercy, "Looking at Quilts," *Circles on the Water*

A *Bildungsroman* reflecting on what it was like to grow up in America in the 1950s, *Braided Lives* focuses on how its heroine suffers from the straitjacket of the sexual hypocrisy of that era. The main bulk of this 550-page novel depicts the college years and the loves and the poetic and political development of the narrator-protagonist. Set in italics, the immediate present is interpolated into the flashbacks to the near and the distant past (from 1953 to circa 1959), which is set in standard type. The temporal point of departure is thus roughly the same as in Sylvia Plath's *The Bell Jar* (1963), with the Korean War, the Eisenhower presidency, and the Rosenbergs in prison awaiting execution as background. While Plath's heroine and alter ego spends the summer in New York City, Piercy's protagonist moves in innercity Detroit in a Black-Irish-Polish-Appalachian-Jewish neighborhood.

Jewish and of a working-class background, the first-person narrator develops into an independent woman, a successful poet and lecturer living in a harmonious marriage, at the end of the novel forty-three years old. In these particulars, she resembles Piercy herself, and Piercy has indeed stated that *Braided Lives* is her most autobiographical novel, although with some caveats: "Characters in fiction are never people, but the moving simulacra of what we are content to think people are inside a narrative structure. . . . Autobiography also demands that you believe in the self as a discrete entity, which I do not. I am many selves" (essay on "Autobiography" in *Cream City Review* 1990 3).

Betsy Israel writes in *Ms* magazine that "Piercy, with her keen ear for the rumblings of prefeminist America, takes familiar fifties' horror stories out of the realm of feminist cliché to inspire renewed rage" (18). Already as a teenager, Jill, the heroine, notices the narrower scope of women's lives. As a seventeen-year-old, she compiles a long list of admirable men, but on her list of women to admire are only four names. A passionate student of literature, she wonders (echoing Miriam in *Small Changes*) where the heroic roles for women are to be found: "I spend a lot of time adjusting novels and biographies I read to invent roles for myself, which takes ingenuity for a female Hamlet or a female Count of Monte Cristo taxes my inventiveness" (BL 21). Interestingly, however, as Marks observes, the seeds for Jill's rebellion against the limitations of her mother's life and her assertion of her own transgression are found in the seemingly bland childhood lecture of *Rebecca of Sunnybrook Farm* (1903), since Rebecca is a girl who writes poetry. Girls are brought up not to be heroic, but to please:

> Girls when they talk to boys become different. The voice, the expression, the way of laughing and talking and standing of my girlfriends alter; they express different ideas and even their gait changes. I do not know if I cannot or will not do that; I only know I am afraid. Marriage does not figure in the tales I tell myself. I see it daily and it looks like doom rather than a prize. Mother is always saying Riva was a dancer, but then she got married; Charlotte was a buyer for Crowleys, but then she got married. Glory and adventure are the prizes. And love. I despise my hunger for affection. (BL 21-22)

An ideal version of treacly 1950s femininity is depicted in Stephanie:

> For Stephanie the real work she does is Howie. Her classes are secondary. She piles up incompletes. Her friendships fit into the small accidental cracks of the day. She has no politics. I do not know if she holds any opinions she would not change for him aside from those she has evolved on how to attract, get, keep and manage men. Her love for Howie provides her with a massive and intense purpose. Of every event and possibility that rises she asks herself, Is it good for the Relationship? (BL 401)

Girls of the fifties, in this novel, learn how to manipulate men and how to catch a future husband (preferably before senior year in college). Still in college, where *Twelfth Night* is her "favorite Shakespeare comedy with its mutable sex roles" (BL 227), Jill wonders, "Is there nothing more between women and men than the secret war of marriage, sex the economic counter or submission to the alley world of smut? . . . If sex is a war I am a conscientious objector: I will not play" (BL 79). Very early, she sees the sacrifices women of her generation have to make—including that of her mother: "All women are misfits, I think; we do not fit into this world without amputations" (BL 108). The female body becomes an enemy to achievements. Mike Loesser, Jill's first lover and poet friend, explains to her what it means to be a woman: "Inevitably, you're a woman first" (BL 205). The sexual hypocrisy of the 1950s is manifested in the doctor who fits only married women with diaphragms (BL 228) and in the farcical sequence in which Jill's guileful mother, bluffing, claims to have hired a detective to check on the goings-on in the back seat of Mike's car and gets the couple to confess that their relations are, in fact, sexual, whereupon she proceeds to try to force them to marry.

During her teens, Jill's sanctuary, her room of her own, is the attic, recalling the 'attic of her own' of Willa Cather and her early artist heroine in *The Song of the Lark*. This is where Jill is on her own, where she reads, where her self develops. When her mother paints it yellow, almost to spite her daughter, Jill knows it is time to leave home. From the time of her puberty and onward, her relation to her mother is problematic. She refuses to give up her identity the way her mother has. In that marriage, her father "has the real power. It's his money. Mother asks before she spends, but he never does. . . . Why should she lie to him and wheedle and plead?" (BL 36). Jill desires a different life. "I don't know a girl who does not say, I don't want to live like my mother. I don't want to be like my mother. Is it our mothers, ourselves or our men who mold us?" (BL 196).

As previously pointed out, feminist psychologists have found that many women view their mothers and their own prospects of motherhood with ambivalence. Jill Lewis, for example, proposes that "the dilemma of the daughters is that in our blood is the conflict *and* resolution of our mothers' journey" (138), adding that "Our starting point is an unviable choice between acceptance and rejection" (142). In Lewis's words:

> The heritage of our mother-daughter interaction is simultaneously many things: a celebration of similarity and continuity; a process of overidentification with its risks of overimplicating each other in one's needs and dreams; a reliving for the mother of her reactions and ambivalences concerning her own mother, whose life also embodied all the unresolved contradictions patriarchal society produced in her; anger, frustration, and irritability connected to the experience of powerlessness, which is projected onto the baby girl. (136)

"The marriage contract was never, and is still not, an imagining of equal partnership," Lewis writes. "It institutionalized, at one level among many, a gender-based division of powers and responsibilities where women were always—immediately and ultimately—oppressed, excluded, and dependent" (131). Lewis quotes a study by Ann Oakley which "found that regardless of their class background, the women she interviewed recurrently expressed a

sense of enforced loss of control and increased dependency as they became
mothers" (135).

The overidentification and overimplication inherent in the mother-daughter
relationship is well captured in Piercy's poem "Crescent moon like a canoe"
(from *The Moon Is Always Female*):

> You did not want the daughter you got.
> You wanted a girl to flirt as you did
> and marry as you had and chew the same
> sour coughed up cud, yet you wanted too
> to birth a witch, a revenger, a sword
>
> of hearts who would do all the things
> you feared. Don't do it, they'll kill
> you, you're bad, you said, slapping me down
> hard but always you whispered, I could have!
> Only rebellion flashes like lightning.

In Piercy's elegiac but robust poem "My mother's body" (in the collection
with the same name), the fourth section begins with two stanzas depicting the
push and pull of the mother-daughter relationship:

> What is it we turn from, what is it we fear?
> Did I truly think you could put me back inside?
> Did I think I would fall into you as into a molten
> furnace and be recast, that I would become you?
>
> What did you fear in me, the child who wore
> your hair, the woman who let that black hair
> grow long as a banner of darkness, when you
> a proper flapper wore yours cropped?

These lines illumine the similarities between and the lack of boundaries
between mother and daughter, mirrored in having the same hair but whose
rebellions make their hair take on different shapes, being "cropped" or "long
as a banner of darkness." The daughter's fear of merging into the mother in
the first stanza is a fear of being recast to fit into the mold of her mother or
even being returned into nonexistence. In stanzas four and five of the same
section, the separation from the mother and the daughter's individuation are
rendered in a sharply punning knife metaphor associating both to the cutting
off of bonds and to cat-like, stealthy conniving, and to attempts to cut out from
the enclosed box-life of a "good woman":

> I became willful, private as a cat.
> You never knew what alleys I had wandered.

You called me bad and I posed like a gutter
queen in a dress sewn of knives.

All I feared was being stuck in a box
with a lid. A good woman appeared to me
indistinguishable from a dead one
except that she worked all the time.

Similarly locked in combat with her daughter, the mother in *Braided Lives* is
a feisty and sometimes funny character who simultaneously undercuts Jill's
striving toward independence and teaches her market economy sex, that is,
how to best handle men and how to survive as a woman in patriarchy. The
father, on the other hand, is not sharply delineated; Jill's communication with
him is neither intimate nor hostile. When Jill finds herself pregnant, her
mother instructs her in how to induce an abortion—a gruesome experience for
Jill, who thinks, during the ordeal of the abortion: "I could imagine myself a
Hamlet, a Trotsky, a Donne. I thought I was projects, accomplishments, tastes:
I am only an envelope of guts. This is what it is to be female, to be trapped"
(BL 211). After which Jill is forced to sign a promise of chastity for one year,
sexuality being far too costly and dangerous for young women. When Jill
much later is planning to marry Howie, her mother's ambivalent messages
about womanhood surface again. "What makes me feel betrayed are the little
comments that reveal she too imagines that I will buckle down to the boring
routine she calls being a woman and give up everything I want to do. 'You
can always write an evening now and then. Once the children are in school
you'll get a little time for hobbies again'" (BL 527). The portrait of Jill's
mother recalls the shrewish Mrs. Giddens in Lillian Hellman's drama, *The
Little Foxes*. Apparently materialistic, this southern matriarch is also a highly
spiritual woman whose quest for independence has been distorted by
frustratingly limited opportunities. Unexpectedly, however, she *has* been a
role model for her daughter, whose burgeoning spiritedness she applauds and
whose exit she makes no attempt to curb.

A narrative of resistance is interwoven into Jill's interactions with a series
of men. The gallery of men in this novel consists of several, varied and
nuanced, portraits. As in other novels by Piercy, men, too, are victims of
prevailing gender roles and of their particular class backgrounds, thus fitting
into larger structures in society. Mike, for example, has no real understanding
of women's situations and refuses to lend money for an abortion (BL 160).
This "dark, willful, brilliant and moody idol of [her] dreams, [her] own
Heathcliff-Hamlet-Byron-Count of Monte Cristo" (BL 200) ignores the feeling
of entrapment women experience. Lamenting that "[her] type is not yet in
production" (BL 252), Jill is briefly involved in two relationships, thus
combining whatever she needs from two different men, becoming emotionally
involved with her admired professor, Donaldson, a man of high-minded

integrity and strong political passions, while finding in his opposite, the small-time criminal, Kemp, a handsome lover and an excellent cook. Jill's Cartesian solution is to "have Kemp for [her] body and Gerrit for [her] mind" (BL 394). Her relationship with Gerrit Donaldson remains a platonic one infused with a love of books and art movies, but "his coldness holds [her] back. [She] cannot find the fire in the private man that moves [her] in his public self. [Her] hands reach out and come back empty" (BL 394).

Jill's relationship with the rich and problematic Peter Crecy, a young man who is undergoing Freudian psychoanalysis, is a disappointing one, never engaging her fully. His love-making style bears a strong resemblance to Bernie's in *The High Cost of Living* in its unilaterality and brutality: "I let him pull me roughly down on the bed. His face grim, determined, he acts out a scene of brute mastery. I am something soft he is conquering. Holding my wrists in one hand over my head he pokes at me, thrusts in finally. I don't think he knows a lot about exciting a woman" (BL 272). Moreover, Jill resents his cowardice: instead of telling her that he has been seeing her best friend, Donna, Peter leaves a letter from Donna out on the kitchen table for Jill to find. Influenced by the tenets of his generation, Peter is not a believer in ambition in women. As he explains to Jill: "it's obvious those absurd ambitions and intellectualizing are compensation mechanisms you've picked up because [your mother has] made you insecure as a woman" (BL 246). Sigmund Freud's doctrines also dominate his observations of their sexual relations: "He has learned that certain things you do in bed are healthy and certain things are forbidden because unhealthy under his Freudian code. I don't know who assigned all the point values but they have nothing to do with what feels good to me" (BL 283). The most admirable man in her acquaintance, as Jill sees it, is Howard Dahlberg, Howie, her loyal friend from Detroit. Only too late does she realize that she is sexually attracted to him, after her roommate Stephanie has managed to seduce him. Still, when Jill and Howie are alone in New York after college, they initiate an intense erotic relationship, lasting until Stephanie arrives on the scene. For a while, a ménage-à-trois limps awkwardly along, until Howie proposes to Jill. They are planning to get married when Donna dies. The interruption in their romance that ensues is aggravated by the fact that Jill, bisexually inclined since her teens, has tried to seduce Stephanie, at which prospect Howie is less than thrilled. Neither does he approve of Jill's involvement in illegal abortions; rather, he expects her to give up this work, which is crucial to the core of her self-respect. Howie says, "You can't marry me and do all these things" to which Jill retorts: "I told you I didn't want any marriage I'd ever seen. I thought we could invent our own . . . I can't kill myself to become your wife. You have to want what I really am" (BL 547).

Refusing to 'amputate' herself in any way in order to accommodate a husband, Jill demands to be accepted entirely as she is, including "the me inside" (BL 547), and she adheres to the credo expressed earlier in the book: "I believe in being honest with men . . . I'm not going to pretend I'm somebody else with him. I think if you're straight with men, they'll be straight with you" (BL 128). At one point, she reflects: "The core of falsity in the search for love: a woman gives herself to a man as if that got rid of the problem of making an identity, with a most personal god to reward, pardon or damn" (BL 349). Jill's intransigence makes her lose Howie, but she does retain her self-respect.

Obviously, although Jill's relationships with men are both challenging and satisfying, they are also generally lacking in encouragement of her writing. Patricia Marks has commented on Mike's dismissive and trivializing response to the alledged subjectivity, "All that I business" (BL 86), of Jill's poetry. Relying upon Emile Benveniste's analysis of the pronoun 'I' as a requisite for entry into discourse and the symbolic order, Marks finds that "All that I business" of Jill's work is an assertion of her own specific subject position (173). Marks also points to the misogyny inherent in the critique of Jill's poetry after a poetry reading, with Mike arguing that her poetry is "formless and silly. It isn't art, naturally" (BL 153, see also Sue Walker 116). "Her poem is 'silly,'" comments Marks, "because it focuses on the issue of the female body and its sexual pleasure which requires not separation between self and Other, but the 'single wire' connection between self and Other that is made possible through female sexual pleasure. The young female artist, giving voice to the muted discourse of female sexuality, resists the dominant discourse's ideology of separation—for to be male is to be separate" (176). Focusing on the female body and sexuality, Jill's poetry challenges the traditions of literature as taught at her university, which shies away from issues of race, class or gender, teaching students "to explicate poems and analyze novels and locate Christ figures and creation myths and Fisher Kings and imagery of the Mass" (BL 274-75). In the poem "In the men's room(s)" (from *Circles on the Water*), a female voice laments the egg-walking that seems necessary around male intellectuals and poets:

Eventually of course I learned how their eyes perceived me:
when I bore to them cupped in my hands a new poem to nibble,
when I brought my aerial maps of Sartre or Marx,
they said, she is trying to attract our attention,
she is offering up her breasts and thighs.
I walked on eggs, their tremulous equal:
they saw a fish peddler hawking in the street.

Refusing to truckle to the regnant white, male, universalist canon, Jill critiques New Criticism's division of art and experience in terms that resemble Kate Millett's in *Sexual Politics* (1970). Like Millett, Jill—and Piercy herself—rebelliously mixes literature and politics and interrogates the ideological assumptions hiding in the selected canonical literature, a stance continued in Jill's career as a poet. Throughout her writing career, she will get reviews that reveal the traducing antagonism of what the feminist critic Mary Ellman has termed phallic criticism, which reviles what it decries as a separate and unbalanced category of women poetasters, as demonstrated in this sample:

> Miss Stuart's seventh volume of poetry is crammed with reductionist simplistic snippets of women's lib cant. In describing a series of male/female encounters in which women are injured, raped, maimed, Stuart is unsympathetic to male needs. Individual poems stress only the woman's role and anguish, instead of taking a balanced view. . . . Her poetry is uterine and devoid of thrust. Her volume is wet, menstruates, and carries a purse in which it can't find anything. (BL 500)

This review is quite in line with Jurij M. Lotman's plot typology as discussed by Teresa de Lauretis, which visualizes the space of the Other "as 'a cave', 'the grave', 'a house', 'woman'" (and, correspondingly, allotted the features of darkness, warmth, dampness) . . ." (as quoted by de Lauretis 43). Patricia Marks comments: "That which is damp or wet, that which is closed-space, in other words, that which is connected to the 'uterine,' is outside the realm of active agency and therefore outside the realm of the universal" (Marks 184-85). Ironically, Piercy's satirizing of phallic critics' reviewing of texts by women is not too far removed from an actual review of *Braided Lives* itself. Roger Scruton writes in the *Times Literary Supplement*, in a review entitled "Bodily Tracts": "The book is written in a chatty, cluttered style, too reminiscent of a woman's magazine to sustain the feminist ideology of the text; at the same time the succession of mundane episodes so lacks urgency that only a kept woman would have the time and curiosity to read with interest beyond the first twenty pages," and he adds later that "the book ends as plotlessly and as pointlessly as it begins" (807). In the introduction to the anthology of women's poetry Piercy has edited, *Early Ripening: American Women's Poetry Now* (1987), Piercy comments: "Those of us who began to create a consciously female poetry and those of us who began to create a consciously feminist poetry are the target for male and female critics who resent us and review our work in terms of politics they disagree with, or who simply ignore our accomplishments" (4). As if responding, half tongue-in-cheek and half seriously, to the fictionalized parody of a review above, Piercy's poem "It ain't heavy, it's my purse" (from *Mars and Her Children*), explains that

We have marsupial instinct, women
who lug purses as big as garbage igloos,
women who hang leather hippos from their shoulders:

we are hiding the helpless greedy naked worms
of our intentions shivering in chaos.
In bags the size of Manhattan studio apartments

we carry . . .

. . . .

maps, a notebook in case, addresses of friends

estranged. So we go lopsided, women
like kangaroos with huge purses bearing hidden
our own helplessness and its fancied cures.

Braided Lives resembles *Small Changes* in its contraposition and intertwining of the fates of two female characters. A weighty factor in Jill's becoming a feminist is the destiny of Donna Stuart, her cousin, roommate and best friend. For Donna, blond, beautiful and promiscuous, contemporary notions of female sexuality prove costly, and ultimately, deathly. Donna has a series of more or less turbulent affairs, and, during one of them, experiences a pregnancy scare that interferes with her studying for her exams. On a later occasion, she dates a "towny," an unknown local boy, and is raped. Coming home bleeding and bruised, she is too ashamed to report the rape or seek medical care: "Everybody makes jokes about it. Everybody thinks that's what you really want. I didn't want it. I was scared of him. I was terrified lying there. I was terrified he'd do something even worse and cut me up or kill me. I was sure he was going to kill me and leave my body there" (BL 339). In "Rape poem" (from *Circles on the Water*), Piercy depicts, starkly, the terror, panic, and helplessness caused by rape:

Fear of rape is a cold wind blowing
all of the time on a woman's hunched back.
Never to stroll alone on a sand road through pine woods,
never to climb a trail across a bald
without that aluminum in the mouth
when I see a man climbing toward me.

Never to open the door to a knock
without that razor just grazing the throat.
The fear of the dark side of hedges,
the back seat of the car, the empty house
rattling keys like a snake's warning.
The fear of the smiling man
in whose pocket is a knife.

> The fear of the serious man
> in whose fist is locked hatred.

Unfortunately, Donna gets pregnant from the encounter and has to go through
an illegal and prohibitively expensive abortion. Less secure in her identity
than Jill, Donna needs a narcissistic identification with a man. Marrying Peter
Crecy, she says: "He is everything I try to be and can't quite bring off" (BL
359). Unlike Jill, she does not challenge Peter's notions of women's roles; she
downplays the feeling of accomplishment and stimulation she enjoys at her
work for CBS. The second time Donna gets pregnant, she has the money
herself for an abortion. However, no aftercare is provided, and Donna bleeds
to death after the operation.

Abortion is an issue that politicized Marge Piercy herself. As a teenager,
she had to undergo a dangerous, self-induced abortion that nearly cost her life.
With pathos, she has since struggled for women's right to choose—as in her
poem "The Right to Life" (from *The Moon is Always Female*), the sixth stanza
of which declares that

> We are all born of woman, in the rose
> of the womb we suckled our mother's blood
> and every baby born has a right to love
> like a seedling to sun. Every baby born
> unloved, unwanted is a bill that will come
> due in twenty years with interest, an anger
> that must find a target, a pain that will
> beget pain. A decade downstream a child
> screams, a woman falls, a synagogue is torched,
> a firing squad is summoned, a button
> is pushed and the world burns.

In her nonfiction, too, Piercy has expressed her sadness and anger at women's
fates of suffering and even death after illegal abortions. In an article from
1979, "A Touching Detective Story: Who Really Killed Rosie at 27," Piercy
reviews a work on the death of Rosie Jiménez in 1977 from an illegal
abortion, and in a foreword to *Back Rooms: Voices from the Illegal Abortion
Era* (1988), Piercy warns against the consequences of women being forced to
resort to the savagery of back-street abortions: Whether abortion is legal or
not, Piercy writes, women will resort to it "until or unless we can absolutely
control our fertility" (*Back Rooms* x). The difference if it is illegal is that on
top of a woman's inner conflicts around her pregnancy will be added stigma,
pain and danger. Only since 1973 and the Roe v. Wade decision has abortion
been legal, which is not to say that it has always been easily available for all
women; with rigorous accuracy, Ellen Messer's and Kathryn E. May's
Introduction to *Back Rooms* reminds us that "in the short time since then, we

have developed a cultural amnesia so complete that young people appear to have no real knowledge about the shame and illegality which haunted the lives of their mothers and grandmothers for more than one hundred years in America" (xi).

After the sum total of her own experiences as a woman, and those of her friends—her mother's life of submission and dependence, her own painful abortion, almost being raped (BL 30), Donna being a victim of rape, illegal abortions, and beatings by her husband (BL 510), another friend being sexually exploited by a therapist (BL 107)—Jill ends up fighting for a better situation for women. *Braided Lives* is a passionate plea for women to control their own lives and their own sexuality. In Donna's words: "Female sexuality bugs people. We're supposed to produce babies on request and not otherwise and orgasms on request and only in both cases with our proper wedded husbands" (BL 302).

Jill moves away from being defined by a man and toward a desire for self-definition: "Once I was Mike's lover and that defined my world. When I was Peter's lover, that defined only the content of certain evenings and what I did for sex. What I do with the men I see now is even more peripheral. I don't know if that's good or bad. My society tells me it's wrong, my relationships are promiscuous and I am a bad woman who will come to an early and quite nasty end" (BL 401).

In *Braided Lives*, however, the heroine is rewarded for her principled integrity, a fact that, in Marks's words, "represents what du Plessis calls a 'transgressive' narrative strategy of twentieth-century women writers" (193). Jill's stormy odyssey in love and in work finally brings her to a harmonious haven. If her type was not yet in production in the 1950s, in the 1980s she strikes the perfect match. Josh is a man she is deeply in love with, as well as a man she can respect on all levels. Far removed from the Freudianisms of the 1950s, he encourages her work as a poet no matter what happens to the relationship, and is not a man to applaud *"burning witches and women's clinics"* (BL 549). He fully understands how important Jill's work is and recognizes her sharing the economic burden: *"No matter how much you love me or whatever happens between us, you aren't going to give up. You've written for years. And what would pay the electric bill? Together we just make it"* (BL 549). Josh's support is of utmost importance to Jill.

As Katha Pollitt writes in a review of *Braided Lives*: "Too many heroines of feminist novels are privileged, fragile innocents. A discouraging professor, a patronizing boyfriend, a pushy parent are enough to make them resign their ambitions and sleepwalk into obedient housekeeping for a husband the reader can see from the start is a creep" ("A Complete Catalogue of Female Suffering" 7). Jill, however, triumphs over "society," gaining both an ideal husband and admirable achievements. Spatially speaking, she has journeyed through a terrifying terrain, "across the wasteland around factories and down unmarked city streets without a map and I both know and do not know where I have been" (BL 2). The message of *Braided Lives* to women is that it is possible to win both love and work without compromising one's beliefs. One question remains, however: Jill and Josh have no children. If they had had children, would Jill then have fallen into women's classical either-or dilemma of having to supplant their careers for a family or vice versa? That question falls outside of the framework of the story. Let it suffice that Piercy, with fluency and persuasiveness, has created an unusual, strong, intelligent female character as well as several other credible and engaging characters, male and female, and raised a number of important and urgent questions. I would agree with Katha Pollitt's assessment that "*Braided Lives* won't win any literary prizes, but it will make its readers pay more attention to the current attack on legal abortion, and make them more eager to defend the imperiled gains of the women's movement. For a novelist whose aim is didactic, that's no small compliment" (32).

Chapter 8

Fly Away Home

All over America women are burning
food they're supposed to bring with calico
smile on platters glittering like wax.
Anger sputters in her brainpan, confined
but spewing out missiles of hot fat.
Carbonized despair presses like a clinker
from a barbecue against the back of her eyes.
If she wants to grill anything, it's
her husband spitted over a slow fire.

          Marge Piercy, "What's the Smell in the Kitchen?" *Stone, Paper, Knife*

Piercy's oxymoronically entitled eighth novel, *Fly Away Home* (its title, from a children's rhyme, also appears, verbatim, in *Small Changes*), describes the flight of a forty-three-year old woman, Daria Walker, away from her marriage and idyllic life in a 'historical' home to a new home and a new purpose in life. A "divorce thriller" (personal letter from Marge Piercy, October 8, 1993), this novel works as a detective story that exposes the shady dealings of Ross Walker and his mafiosos, in a critique, resembling that in *Going Down Fast*, of the kind of corrupt and ruthless urban renewal that hits the less powerful.

Initially, Ross Walker was, in his wife's view, "raw, bright, idealistic and entirely unsure of himself, spiny as a sea urchin, shy as a feral cat" (FAH 2). As a young man, Ross worked for the Johnson antipoverty program where he found a "level of corruption in the state and county and city government he simply could not believe" (FAH 25). Daria "had always trusted Ross; she picked him out for his rectitude" (FAH 28). But since then, Ross's career has evolved, changing him more than Daria at first realizes. When Ross is becoming increasingly critical and withdrawn, Daria assumes that he is merely going through a passing crisis. His criticism of her avoirdupois, for example, she refuses to take seriously: "Men were silly to attach importance to the momentary shape or style of a female body, when inside and outside everyone was always changing" (FAH 3). Countless of Piercy's poems express an earthy, sensual love of good food and wine, and some voice a disdain for the dictates of fashion "to look like undernourished fourteen year/ old boys" ("Cats like angels," in *The Moon is Always Female*). However, in the context of Daria's expansion on more levels than one, Ross's resistance to her expanding body makes perfect sense. Later on, Daria will reassert her femaleness in her discussions with Sandra María Vargas about how they experienced being pregnant, contumaciously questioning the culturally prescribed institutionalization of pregnancy and motherhood, an image from which both Daria and Sandra María have deviated, one of them glorying in an unwonted sense of power while pregnant, the other revolting against her sense of an invasion of her body.

Daria persists in holding on to her image of Ross, her idea that he is "a good and faithful husband" (FAH 1), that he "exemplified every virtue her wandering father had lacked. She adored his solidity, his straightness, his rectitude, his tenderness, his capacity for feeling about the domestic . . . He never needed to play macho" (FAH 16). However, Daria will discover that she is wrong. The marital crevasse widens, her attempts at being suitably submissive, constantly apologetic, or willing to diet for Ross's sake notwithstanding. She is beginning to feel "like a servant waiting on him" (FAH 79). In the midst of a midlife crisis, Ross wants to disburden himself of family responsibility and start over again: "Too many years of compromise and habit are choking us. Gritting my teeth and buckling down. Fulfilling my responsibilities and commitments, again and again and again and again!" (FAH 113) Ross's development has, however, been to ally himself with destructive forces and to disparage the values Daria stands for; for example, he calls the cookbooks she writes "fat books" (FAH 82). But the cookbooks are highly significant. Patricia Marks argues that "Piercy's inscription of Daria's production of cookbook literature encodes the historical marginalization of women's writing in general and female domestic labor in particular" (250).

As Ross withdraws, communication between them breaks down completely. That is when Daria's detective work begins. She allies herself with a neighborhood organization that fights the corruption and arson that plague buildings owned by Ross Walker, in Daria's name, unbeknownst to her. What she really begins to investigate are power structures, both in her own marriage and in American culture, and she realizes that she has been abdicating all her financial responsibilities to Ross, to the point of not knowing her own income, much less what their joint economic enterprises are worth.

Placed within the conurbation of Boston, *Fly Away Home* posits a moneyed upper class against the working class, the concinnity of a suburban lifestyle against the congestion of slum neighborhoods. It is feminist in its affirmation of the importance of women's autonomy and of equality in marriage, and also in affirming a woman-oriented perspective and imagery. I would therefore disagree with Pia Thielmann's assessment that "Daria's ability to leave her husband has nothing to do with political insights or processes of struggle within herself" (199). I see Daria's process of leaving her husband as both personal and political, since she discovers that power structures in her marriage also apply in society and vice versa. Daria's life changes substantially. Thielmann concedes that Daria "develops friendships with women, and becomes able to have friendships with men without a sexual connotation" but deplores that this change occurs out of a basically liberal consciousness, rather than "out of social or even feminist considerations" (205).

Daria, however, is not an ideologue, but a cook, who does not aspire to the theoretical sophistication of some of Piercy's other heroines. Still, her actions speak louder than words; her siding with a slum neighborhood organization, after two decades of comfortable suburban life, is fairly revolutionary, as is her engaging in research concerning the buildings: an act of taking charge of her own life and of scrutinizing her own part as well. That the buildings are in her name could be seen as women's own complicity in their situations, a complicity that is invisible until investigated (see also Eugenie Lambert Hamner 94). Daria is making a conscious choice about the people she lives with, different from the kind of people she and Ross would see socially. She is looking for different qualities in her new lover. "He didn't save me, this one, she thought, not even from a burning house. I saved myself" (FAH 423). Of primary importance is equality—"Never with Ross had she felt equal. Why would the sense of equality with Tom free up her sexuality?" (FAH 353), and autonomy—"not to live in the relationship as if in a house; not to refer whatever she did to him for approval or disapproval" (FAH 353)—but picturing a food metaphor, she also wants a "new whole": "In some recipes before cooking is commenced, the disparate ingredients must sit together for a time: it is called the marrying of the herbs, the spices. At a certain point the flavor is different than the sum of its parts. That is happening, she thought, we are changing each other, we are making a new whole" (FAH 330).

The most apparently mundane details, such as the descriptions of food, are endowed with a kind of agency throughout Piercy's writings. Impatient with left-wing rhetoric, in "In the men's room(s)" in *Circles on the Water*, Piercy writes: "Now I get coarse when the abstract nouns start flashing./ I go out to the kitchen to talk cabbages and habits" (8). In her introduction to *Early Ripening: American Women's Poetry Now*, she likens the selection of poems to the organization of a dinner party with the guests subscribing to a plethora of contemporary diets from vegan to macrobiotic to sufi or being aficionados of rare beef or suffering from a host of allergies, and with the resulting menu coalescing "only in the mind of the Ideal Eater" (1). Piercy's fragments of dietary delight and her canticle to the growing, harvesting, and preparing of vegetables (as in *Gone to Soldiers* and *Summer People*), I see as linked to the earthy maternal metaphor of caring and nurturing prevalent in Piercy's writings. By contrast, the oppressively patriarchal institution that is the mental hospital in *Woman on the Edge of Time* is associated with a barely edible fare of flavorless food, and in *Small Changes* traditional marriage is heralded by a tasteless "store-bought sawdust white cake" (SC 22). In a review of Margaret Atwood's poetry, Piercy has written that "women have been forced to be closer to food, to know more of where it comes from and what it looks like raw . . . and where the garbage goes afterward" (42). In an autobiographical essay, moreover, Piercy reveals that "food is important to me. I am a proud cook, snappish overlord of my kitchen. I find cooking like gardening a physical joy after the intense detail work of writing" (*Contemporary Authors* 278). Innumerable, highly evocative references to the growing, cooking, and tasting of food recur throughout Piercy's poetry. One example is her invocation to the onion in "Bite into the onion" (from *Mars and Her Children*):

> Onion, I undress you in your wardrobe of veils,
> I enter you room upon room inside each other
> like Russian dolls. You sizzle in my nose,
> healthy, obstinate, loud as a peasant uncle
> coming in with his boots dirty and a chicken
> with its neck wrung clutched in his fist.
> What soup or stew is not empty without you?

In the quotation above, redolent of the delicious aromas of "the marrying of the herbs" one might thus see a reference to a recipe around which much of Piercy's fiction revolves: the sexual metaphor of balancing, marrying, or re-pairing dual forces, and thus creating a new whole. The food imagery, moreover, articulates a female hunger left unquenched in the American patriarchy: it is a hunger for something not yet articulated, as in the case of Jill's mother in *Braided Lives*. In "What's the Smell in the Kitchen?" (*Stone, Paper, Knife*), quoted in the epigraph to this chapter, a female anger at male expectations of servile domesticity has become explosive. (For a further analysis of the food imagery in *Fly Away Home*, see also Eugenie Lambert Hamner 96-98).

With its cookbook writer heroine, *Fly Away Home* could be seen as a more lightweight novel than Piercy's other fictions, as a "domestic novel" as Thielmann terms it (199), or, as Ellen Sweet has put it, a novel "about a 'small' subject all too familiar in recent novels: a conventional woman coming to awareness because of divorce" (32), and in a review in the *Times Literary Supplement* John Clute deplores the "trashy plot" (658). But Sweet finds that Piercy "manages to turn this hackneyed theme into something new and appealing . . . Although her novel has a strong subplot dealing with social change through political action, at its heart is Piercy's faith in the transforming value of love and intimacy" (32). In Thielmann's view, the characterization is stereotyped and the ending, too (201), the effect of which on readers she compares to that of romance reading.

Fly Away Home differs from romances in its affirmation of a muted female principle and a female world, and in its critique of patriarchy not through manifestoes but via characters choosing to adhere to a life-enhancing maternal principle and to struggle against destructive male rationality and profit-mindedness. Its title implies women's arising and flying out of old enclosures, finding their way to a more real home on the level of intrapsychic and relational contexts. Ellen Sweet has noticed all the "images of ashes and rebirth, death and life, parking lots and gardens, destruction and rehabilitation, fire and earth" (32), an imagery that I see as part of the structural subtext counterpositing masculine and feminine principles that runs through Piercy's other novels. Adhering to a masculine principle are, apart from Ross, also his and Daria's daughter, Robin, who is a male/father-identified, anorexic, competitive MBA student oriented toward corporate capitalism, and also Daria's insensitive brothers and her egotistical father. On the other side of the spectrum, adhering to a feminine/maternal principle, are Ross and Daria's daughter, Tracy (Teresa), the grandmother, Nina, and Daria's sister, Gussie. Real estate corruption, governed by flagitious profit motives, is posed against nurturing, life-enhancing values or pursuits such as motherhood, gardening, cooking, cooperation and communication with other people, with animals, and with nature. "There are few contemporary novelists," writes Susan Mernit, "who so inextricably interweave such large and small concerns" (18).

The well-kept house is a prime symbol of the maternal principle. Daria "loved the subliminal contact with the many women who had lived in this house over the last hundred and forty years as she went about cleaning, as she sat looking out on her garden, as she cooked, as she worked" (FAH 82). The Walker family has been based on a false unity, hiding the polarization and division smoldering underneath. Initially an idealistic young man, Ross is transformed into a villain who even attempts murder in setting fire to Daria's house in order to secure his ill-gotten prosperity. He leaves Daria for a younger and richer woman who carries his son and who breeds dogs, while Daria becomes involved with Tom Silver, a hero reminiscent of Joel in *Vida* in being a more feminized, although not effeminate, male. With him, her two daughters, Tom's two daughters, another woman friend and her daughter, Daria creates a woman-oriented house that could be called 'Daughters of the Revolution,' a house where equality reigns, "a community that redefines the structure of the family" (Marks 234). As Louise Kahan in *Gone to Soldiers* rearranges the spaces of her apartment to fit her own needs after her divorce, Daria moves her work area from the room on top of the garage, "commonly referred to as the maid's room" (Hamner 99), to Ross's old study; she uncovers the hardwood floors Ross had covered with wall-to-wall carpeting and plants a kitchen garden. An entirely transmuted realm, the house even smells different. "In *Fly Away Home*," writes Christine Sizemore, "Piercy shows in her portrayal of contemporary Boston that women, if they work together, can actually gain power in the city and help to construct a new kind of urban space, a space based on female values, an urban realization of psychoanalyst Benjamin's intersubjective space" (101).

However, this is a transformation that threatens the patriarchal principle governing Ross's transactions. By proxy, Ross sets fire to the house in order to collect insurance money. Comparing this fire to the one that occurs in *Jane Eyre*, Patricia Marks sees it not as a representation of repressed female anger as is the case in Charlotte Brontë's novel, but rather as male fury at women's self-definitions, the burned-down house being an image of the destructive authority of a dominant discourse (239). Ambiguously symbolic, fire, which both destroys and safeguards life, can be interpreted both positively and negatively. Foreshadowed earlier in the novel, however, the conflagration that occurs at the end should perhaps primarily be seen as the purifying fire that precedes justice and regeneration, recalling how paradise regained was circled by walls of fire and angels with burning swords. Perceiving *Fly Away Home* as "scaled-down utopia—Piercy's mellowed vision of family and home," Sweet finds that "it may even prove to be more revolutionary than her more obviously radical novels" (32).

Chapter 9

Gone to Soldiers

I am pregnant with certain deaths
of women who choked before they
could speak their names
could know their names
before they had names to know.

Marge Piercy, "They inhabit me," *My Mother's Body*

"To write a good *big* novel," according to John Casey, "you must make your story intimate with the solitary hearts of characters but also with a community, even a country; you must give the illusion not just of someone's life but of *everything* about a complexity of lives, and still have the story move within the limits of a reader's memory and interest" (1). According to these criteria, *Gone to Soldiers* is indeed a "good *big* novel." It is even "a huge novel in every sense of the word," as Margaret Atwood has expressed it in a blurb on the book cover. Based on extensive research on World War II, including hundreds of memoirs and interviews and on travel to sites in Europe (as, for example, to Drancy, about which trip Piercy has written the quiet-voiced but powerful poem "The Housing Project at Drancy"), Piercy's historical novel took seven years to complete. Originally around 1,100 pages long, the final version was abridged to 850 pages.

Confronting a subject she had always known she would have to approach, in *Gone to Soldiers*, Piercy enters the perspectives of ten different, convincingly realized, and vital major and minor characters whom she moves through a shifting set of sites such as Detroit, New York, and Washington, places of combat in Europe and in the Pacific, the underground struggle in France and the deathly concentration camps of Auschwitz, Bergen-Belsen and Dora-Nordhausen. Unflinchingly, Piercy depicts the dehumanization of the war, the barely survivable conditions on tankers and in armed struggle, and dredges up the dark memories of the ideology and methods of Nazism in its unfathomable horror. *Gone to Soldiers* is a realistic novel, and in an afterword Piercy states: "This is a novel conceived in the imagination, but I wanted nothing to happen in it that had not happened somewhere in the time and place I was working with" (GTS 773). Marleen Barr points out that in *Gone to Soldiers*, a battle is fought on two fronts: "The world order American men fought to retain depended upon defeating both the Axis powers' political expectations and women's personal expectations regarding power" (68). In her discussion of this novel, Marleen Barr observes that "Piercy juxtaposes the officially accepted (patriarchal) version of what happened to women during World War II with a dissimilar, feminist version of the world. She revises the patriarchal historical record's content. She refuses to mirror non-feminist postmodern historical novels which juxtapose the patriarchal real with the patriarchal unreal" (70-71).

Gone to Soldiers combines several disparate strands into a thematic tour de force. "Rather than spinning out from a center," writes Mary Biggs in the *Women's Review of Books*, "the stories seem to converge willy-nilly from peripheries" (23). Marge Piercy herself "[thinks] of it as a cantata" (Eugenie Hamner and Sue Walker, "Interview with Marge Piercy" 151). Divided into ninety-four parts, it maps the trajectories of ten major characters, weaving a tapestry of interlocking fates which sometimes thread into each other in fortuitous ways. The pattern of links and parallels indicates how Piercy views humanity as invisibly interconnected across the boundaries of race or religion—that we are all family, "almost mishpocheh," as she has entitled one of her chapters. It is first helpful to take an overview to briefly untangle these intermingled journeys. Then, the motif of doubleness and duplicity of the characterization and plot become evident, along with the ways in which this doubleness metaphor, moreover, is connected to a birth imagery that is ultimately an affirmation of a maternal, healing impulse and a celebration of the survival of the Jewish people.

The novel opens with the perspective of Louise Kahan, a journalist and writer, who is divorced from Oscar Kahan, a Columbia professor, and who lives with her teenage daughter, Kay. With the war raging in Europe, she is wondering about the fate of her American-Jewish sister-in-law, Gloria, who lives in France. Oscar begins work with Abra, a graduate student, and they enter a relationship with each other while stationed in Washington, then leave for London. In Washington, Abra has met Daniel Balaban, who is in love with her but who, in her absence, begins an affair with Louise, when she ends up living in Abra's old apartment. Among other trajectories that intersect are Louise's trip to write about women pilots, during which journey she meets the aviatrix Bernice Coates, "Piercy's fictional carbon-copy of a real-world

WASP" (Barr 66). Bernice's brother, Jeff, goes to Europe to aid the resistence movement.

In France, we see the development of the war from the perspective of Jacqueline Lévy-Monot, whose family is shattered during the Nazi persecution of the Jews: her mother and a sister, Rivka, are arrested and sent to a series of concentration camps, her father leaves to become a fighter in the Jewish *résistance*, and her second sister, Nadine/Naomi, Rivka's twin, is sent to relatives in America (the family of Ruthie) while that is still possible. When Jacqueline herself becomes a member of the *résistance*, she meets Jeff Coates.

Through the viewpoints of the less central characters of Ruthie's brother, Duvey, and her fiancé, Murray, Piercy depicts gruesome combat from inside. Duvey dies, but Murray returns after years of living and witnessing the horrors of killing and death. In her portrayal of Murray, Piercy conveys the difficulties both of separating and of reconnecting, first being away and then coming home, changed for life by the war. The sense of estrangement between Murray and Ruthie as they try to find each other again and discover that their old selves are gone is convincingly rendered.

As reviewers have pointed out, the most engaging fate is that of Jacqueline, a vividly drawn portrait conveyed through the first person narrative of Jacqueline's diary, which, as Hilma Wolitzer has observed, recalls the diary of Anne Frank (11), although, significantly, the voice of the first person is wrenched from her in the eleventh section, "Arbeitsjuden Verbraucht," in which Jacqueline has become a nameless inmate in Auschwitz. Piercy has managed to show Jacqueline's development from a self-absorbed and immature, principled but haughty young Parisian intellectual into a selfless, mature and courageous (although not saintly) woman who risks her life in helping to save the lives of Jewish children. It is through the fate of Jacqueline that Piercy's credo is illuminated, unequivocally affirming the necessity for political awareness and struggle. The kind of New Age philosophies that stress that our own thoughts create our exterior world are severely challenged in Piercy's depiction of the fate of Jews during World War II. While a crucial point of departure, one's thoughts alone cannot keep evil back: organized, collective action is required to fight the invasive Nazi politics. Initially, Jacqueline's Jewishness means very little to her; rather, it seems "absurd" as a religion and its stipulations about diet "archaic" (GTS 19). Identifying with "the universal" (GTS 20), she "[believes] in attaining an inner tranquillity . . . . To grow angry is to give power to those who attack" (GTS 21). Jacqueline is both French and Jewish, a startling mixture in Jeff's view: "She was so rational a creature, she seemed to him quintessentially French, a female Voltaire, and yet she carried around her religion like a pet porcupine, he thought, caressing its quills and addressing it in passionate tones. It was a paradox he could not resolve" (GTS 466). Step by step, however,

Jacqueline, who at the beginning of the novel correctly perceives a "romantic weakness" in herself (GTS 16), grows to face the limitations of relying on "inner tranquillity" when faced with the horrendous "outer" force of Nazism. At the end, Jacqueline's romantic weaknesses have been swept away.

Through the eyes of Jacqueline, we witness the growing stranglehold of the Nazis in Paris, how the Jews are gradually pushed to the margins of society, closed out from cafés, libraries, and confined to the last car of the Métro, increasingly being viewed as not quite human, thus adding to the distance and disconnection which will pave the way for the atrocities that, ironically, make the Nazis themselves less than human, an irony, since in line with Hitler's *Mein Kampf*, the Jews are seen as not quite human but as vermin that the New Europe needs to be purged of. Here, it is an impulse of total disconnection and distancing that is followed, which Jacqueline sees quite clearly in Auschwitz in a passage in which we enter Jacqueline's thoughts directly, while the rest of the chapter is in the third person:

> Why do they do this to us? First, they intend to treat us as beasts, they try to make us beasts. We have no names, no clothing, nothing individual. We are forced to live in terror as if it were the air we take into our lungs. The skinnier, the uglier, the more scabrous, the filthier we are, the greater superiority they can feel. They rub our faces in our dirt so we may stink to them, and to ourselves. (GTS 622)

Through spatial imagery, the sense of limitation, of being cramped, is rendered, of not having the space of quiet, of cleanliness, of rest (GTS 623): they lie "on filthy straw without room to stretch out a leg or an arm" (GTS 621).

Jacqueline has no twin, but in terms of courage and strength she is subtly linked to Bernice, since she is associated with Jean Racine's *Bérénice*, and she also has the same first name as Jacqueline Cochran, a real-life pioneer in aviation pushing for female pilots to have the same benefits and opportunities as male pilots (GTS 583). Initially, Jacqueline follows an impulse of separation and superiority, as in her feeling different and somewhat apart from the rest of her family, and in her relation to her first lover, Henri, a relationship ruled more by the mind than by the senses and in which she observes her own reactions during her first experience of sexual intercourse with comically cool and crisp detachment: "I wanted particularly to examine his penis carefully, but while he wanted me to handle it, he did not seem to feel comfortable about my wish to explore it as an unfamiliar object" (GTS 146-47). But Jacqueline discovers a real sense of connectedness with her friend Daniela, whom she loves the way "the twins loved each other, as if she is my sister, my other self" (GTS 228), and at the end of the novel, connectedness has become Jacqueline's guiding star, both in terms of her primary family and in terms of caring for her larger family of fellow Jews. A survivor, Jacqueline resurfaces in the end after almost dying from the inhuman brutalities of Auschwitz and Bergen-Belsen, places depicted in stark, monochromatic coloration as ashy sites of death-in-life. Her coming back to life is an affirmation of the unquenchable Jewish people. In the end, she is reunited with her pregnant teenage sister, Naomi, who has been sent to relatives in the United States during an early stage of the war; Jacqueline brings Naomi with her to pioneer a new life in Palestine. For Jacqueline, the black clouds of death over Europe are not so easily dispelled; she cannot bear to wonder always which side people she meets were on during the war. Going to Eretz Yisroel will obviously open a new chapter of struggle; of this Jacqueline is well aware, yet that is where her hope resides.

In *Gone to Soldiers*, Piercy uses images of doubleness, division and duplicity to construct several often interrelated themes. Most fundamentally, the images of distance and division relate to the lacerating disintegration of war, to the severing from their roots of families, cultures, and races. Naomi thinks, "All these wars cut up the world into bleeding pieces and nobody could cross over" (GTS 70). In "The Dark Thread in the Weave," Piercy states that "We as a species are capable of such I/Them dichotomizing, such civilized savagery, such organized sadism, and as a writer, I have to enter and embody that death-loving part of our collective and individual psyches" (190-91). The duality imagery in this novel is double-edged: most obviously, Piercy contrasts an impulse of duplicity and falseness with a principle of truth and insight. However, the duplicity can also be a cloak disguising insight, working underground as a connecting principle, as when the *Kulturbund* in Berlin set up plays that convey the truth obliquely, indirectly (GTS 92). That these double images of falsity and truth flow into one another in imagery and characterization suggests how humanity harbors both creative and destructive impulses and how dependent these are on each other, continuously engaged in a shape-shifting, dialectical dynamic. One can never eradicate a principle of destruction, necessary for the recreation of life. But the destructive impulse, too, has two sides, and here is where human choice enters: over the natural processes of decay and destruction we can have no control other than the acceptance before the inevitable. But human-engendered, conscious evil is not inevitable. While a principle of distance and division makes us see our other 'halves' as inimical, embracing an impulse of connection will abridge the distance between individuals and between peoples.

Water, a life-giving symbol and an image of connection, is part of the duality motif in this novel. Waters that are tainted or stagnant breed trouble and death. Piercy renders the putrefaction of the war in her description of Jeff's depression: "His life appeared a series of stagnant lagoons connected by barely moving sewers" (GTS 135), and in Murray's experience of the island of Guadalcanal where "everything he [touches is] spongy, rotten, moldy" (GTS 215). On the other hand, when Bernice is in the process of realizing her dreams of being a pilot, her exhilaration is expressed through a water metaphor: "She felt that her love for [her brother] had cleared like a stream no longer contaminated, without the taint of envy for his freedom, his opportunities" (GTS 354).

In line with Piercy's doubleness motif, many of the characters in *Gone to Soldiers* have doubles or parallels in friends or relatives, they are "doubled" in being divided or duplicitous, in leading dual lives, or in "seeing double." Murray, for example, develops a strong friendship with Jack, and Duvey is saved by his friend Ziggy during an attack on their ship. Jeff sees the doubleness of the war, how the war can be seen as a battle between good and evil, but finds that it really is more complex than that: Jeff's sense of the war, before he got into it, was "as a crusade of good versus evil. But now I see our side in action, I don't know. I see fortunes being made. I see business as usual. I see us as shoring up the corrupt and the rich" (GTS 238). His interlocutor reminds him, however, that it is not necessary to be 100 percent good in order to fight evil in shape of the Nazis, who are "the shit of the earth" (GTS 238). Daniel Balaban is double in being bicultural, growing up as an American in China and later, as a cryptanalyst, becoming fluent in Japanese. Daniel's doubleness illustrates the artificial and limiting boundaries set up between different cultures, with the Americans in China being isolated from the Chinese culture surrounding them, barriers which Daniel refuses to accept. Oscar's sister, Gloria, is also double with her dual French-American citizenship and in also being American-Jewish, and in her duplicitous repair of the world: helping to hide members of the Jewish underground movement.

With the female characters, a doubleness underlines their public and private roles as well as the duplicity sometimes necessary to follow one's own path (as in the case of Bernice). Like Bernice, Abra has a brother whom she resembles, as a friend tells her, "In fact you even look exceptionally alike" (GTS 155). Duality is a particularly prominent feature in the portrait of Louise Kahan, who is also Annette Hollander Sinclair, author of women's romances. In order to be able to sell her stories, Louise has taken on a nonJewish pen name that also implies that she is married. Since implementing this duality, she has lived with being divided into two and with a certain duplicity: "Annette Hollander Sinclair" has a separate wardrobe and even speaks in a different voice. The adoption of the Annette Hollander Sinclair persona is a survival strategy chosen to enable the family to survive financially, but she is a fake, an impersonator that Louise Kahan, the serious writer, cannot wholly embrace. The division Annette/Louise is a division between the conventionally feminine and a gut-level female impulse, something deeper and more real that wins out in the end, but the boundaries between Louise and Annette are not always firm. Louise, supposedly, is in charge of Annette, but Annette has a way of infiltrating Louise's visions and language, as when Louise regrets not falling for her ex-husband: "Louise felt as if she had been reprieved from probable folly at the very last second, a Victorian damsel saved from the smooth villain, but she regretted her salvation" (GTS 65).

An interesting form of duplicity develops when Louise is called upon to write propaganda to encourage women to work outside the home during the war. Louise, whose mother and grandmother "always worked," finds the propaganda "neither novel nor shocking" and "[prefers] the new line to the old one: she was much closer to believing in working women as loving, responsible, even exciting citizens, than the line that had been pushed since she began publishing that the working woman was manipulative, selfish, dangerous to her family and society" (GTS 112). Working women like Louise herself may, however, find themselves in a dilemma when hiring a housekeeper—another working woman, but one who is less well paid, and "Louise summed up the contradictions of her life in a phrase she had once heard herself say: 'Just tell Mrs. Shaunessy to put the *Daily Worker* on the coffee table'" (GTS 115). Ironically, thanks to the war time government propaganda in part created by Louise, her housekeeper quits in order to take a better-paid factory job (GTS 266). Louise's life is divided into compartments: while as Louise Kahan she writes "serious" articles on strikes and on women factory workers, as a romance writer, she calculates what fantasies or plots might sell best. As the war continues, she does not relinquish the latter identity completely (sometimes coming up with ideas for a new romantic story), but she does increasingly find a new line of work first as a propaganda writer and later as a war correspondent. Louise's destiny and her writings illustrate the shifting demands that pushed many American women out into new occupations during the war. Well aware of the backlash against the effects of government propaganda to engage women in the war effort, she notices how "all kinds of experts and officials are terrified because so many women are working. They really think that women have to be coerced into having babies and raising kids" (GTS 317). Oscar's explanation for this feeling could hold true even for the 1990s backlash against women's independence: "If women demand jobs, there's a real fear that there will be unemployment for men. If women want money, who's to pay? Those who have. It's the same fear that gripped the nobles when the peasants revolted." Oscar adds another thought: "Maybe as men, we suspect women wouldn't bother with us if they didn't have to" (GTS 317). The campaign to get women to work was not based on the real incentives of money, but on women's traditional role as helpmate and support to husbands or brothers, a role sheathed in glamour in the government propaganda. Louise notes that the Nazi ideology is unable to accommodate the idea of working mothers, "that although there was a far more acute shortage of laborers in Nazi Germany than in the United States, the Germans were using foreign workers, slave labor, anything rather than their women. . . . Even in wartime, maintaining sex roles could be felt as more important than victory" (GTS 368). After the war, women must return to the kitchen: "Not only were women being laid off en masse, but entry jobs were being redefined to involve heavy lifting, to exclude women from the factories. In a Flint auto plant, all the women were put on the graveyard shift in violation of seniority, and the UAW, which continued to address members as sirs and brothers, refused to fight for its women members" (GTS 733).

The developments in the work force in terms of women's public roles also make Louise ponder the possibilities and limits of romance writing: how far can one go in depicting independent women? Reading Mary McCarthy's *The Company She Keeps*, there is a "matter-of-factness about sex in ways that intrigued and fascinated Louise as a new level of discourse about women's lives," and she has "a vision of women writing about sex as openly as male writers, but quite, quite differently. Some women would treat sex much as men did, as conquest, as adventure—in a way as McCarthy had. Other women would treat female sexuality far less romantically than men who did not consider themselves romantics, like Hemingway, were wont to" (GTS 419-20). Louise concludes that "as a woman there were still far more things that could not be said than could be said; if they were said, they could not be heard" (GTS 420).

Louise's rebirth is expressed in spatial terms. Her territory is expanded after the divorce—as she tells Oscar, "I have expanded to fill the entire apartment" (GTS 693). Louise's journey is also toward (re)connection in her remarrying Oscar: "She had a sense of roots deep in soil groping together. She was being healed to their common history, her life was coming back together" (GTS 732).

Another character who similarly illustrates the demand for women to go out and work in previously all-male work places is Ruthie (a portrait perhaps inspired by Piercy's own Aunt Ruth), who goes to work in a factory and who like the other women is laid off after the war. A chapter entitled "Of Good Girls and Bad Girls" depicts the hazards of becoming a working girl during a time when that, despite the propaganda efforts, equals being a bad girl. Through the eyes of Ruthie we see the harassment male workers hurl at the newly employed female coworkers: "She was pinched, she was handled, she was stared at until she felt as if she were a mass of raw bloody tissue. She still could not cross the floor without forty men making lowing noises like besotted cattle or whistling. Some men were always trying to sabotage the women's work. They seemed terrified that women would take jobs permanently" (GTS 197). More significantly, Ruthie is a "bad girl" for agreeing to premarital sex with Murray before he leaves for the war. With this portrait, however, Piercy shows how false the good girl/bad girl dichotomy is: Ruthie, ambitious and hard-working, is in reality a good girl, while Mrs. Rosenthal, traditional wife and mother, could be seen as "bad" when she spitefully reports that Ruthie's mother has set up an unlicensed child-care center. In her portrait of another minor character, Mrs. Augustine, furthermore, Piercy blurs the dividing lines, when this traditional housewife unexpectedly encourages Bernice to "Get out while you can" (GTS 211).

After years of confinement in her father's house, Bernice becomes a "bad" girl when she learns to fly, literally and metaphorically. As a WASP (Women's Air Force Service Pilots), Bernice is part of "an experimental arm of the Air Force that recruited women pilots in 1942 to relieve the overtaxed ranks of male flyers and free them for combat" (Brown 6). Always close to her brother, Jeff—they have always been "halves of some unreconcilable whole" (GTS 639)—Bernice attains a sense of belonging and becomes whole at the same time as she is doubled and duplicitous in coming to the insight that she is a lesbian. She thinks: "It was not that she felt like a man, even in male clothes. With Flo, she sensed her own female power flowing out and returning to her. She felt her mother in herself, Viola's warm strength; she knew herself loved and gathered into female tenderness that she had missed and lacked and always, always wanted. She felt more of a woman, not less" (GTS 717). "Double" in being bisexual, Bernice allows her lesbian relationship to take precedence toward the end of the novel. Duplicitously, in order to be allowed to keep flying when this is no longer open to women after the war, she decides to appropriate a fake male identity, something that Marleen Barr analyzes along the lines of Louis Althusser's concept of 'interpellation,' since Bernice "absorbs an imaginary male identity, creates this identity as her own representation, and, hence, causes it to become real" (71).

The doubleness motif continues in Bernice being so close to her brother "that when Jeff and she were together, they were interested in nobody else" (GTS 362). A mutual friend comments: "Your closeness was unusual and fascinating. It seemed at times to border on incest" (GTS 359). Jeff and Bernice are like twins—and from the point of view of Zach Taylor, their friend and lover, they are interchangeable. In terms of gender roles, they are, of course, not interchangeable: "[Jeff] had freedom in abundance and she was starving for a crumb of it" (GTS 41). Bernice is duplicitous in her avoidance of the straitjacket of women's traditional roles, and thinks, "She did not feel female; she did not feel male either, certainly not. What was she?" (GTS 300). She escapes the drudgery of being the dutiful stay-at-home daughter of Professor Coates, a grumpy, demanding man who considers his own needs to be uppermost and who refuses to let her work outside the home (GTS 48). Between Bernice and her father there is a seemingly unbridgeable distance and division of interests, well captured in Piercy's spatial imagery: "The Professor erected the fence of *Christian Science Monitor* before his face" (GTS 210). Behind that "fence" is utter disapproval at his daughter's growing competence as a pilot. The distance between them is also vertical: "They simply could not communicate in any other way than by his issuing commands de haut en bas" (GTS 213). In spatial terms, moreover, Piercy conveys the sense of liberation Bernice experiences as she is becoming increasingly in charge of her own life, as shown in her dreams: "She was crawling down a long tunnel. Sometimes it was a drainpipe or a sewage pipe: other times it appeared to be a culvert for runoff. Sometimes it was one of the steam tunnels that connected the older buildings at St. Thomas. Suddenly she reached an exit and struggled out. The dream always ended with her standing at her full height in a field and feeling as if she were soaring, free" (GTS 300). Unlike Jill/Joanna in *Dance the Eagle to Sleep*, who tries to hide in a tunnel but who gets caught there, Bernice exits her tunnel and finds herself "standing *at her full height* in a field" (GTS 300, my italics). Literally and metaphorically, thus, Bernice learns to fly, in a story which Barr sees as a "[deconstruction of] the typical patriarchal story about the superior, winged flying phallus" (92). She flies away home, to paraphrase the title of Piercy's previous novel. Immersed in the rigors of training to become a pilot, she thinks, "Home? She was far more at home here than she had ever felt in The Professor's house, after [her mother] died" (GTS 298). In her wish to transgress enclosures, Bernice resembles the goddess Diana: "if she still lived mostly in a cocoon, at least she knew what she wanted to be, like the moon herself, a huntress roaming free through the mountains of the clouds and the rivers of the wind" (GTS 102).

Piercy's construction of doubles is perhaps most pertinent in the portrait of Naomi/Nadine, the twin sister of Rivka, who is still in Paris with their mother while Naomi is in America. Naomi is so close to her sister that in her dreams she is with her back in Europe, and in this sense she is a double, or doubled. Naomi is also doubled in becoming bicultural and bilingual during her time in America, and at the end, she is literally double in being pregnant (there is also duplicity involved in her being pregnant by a married man). Both in her pregnancy and in her connectedness to other women in her family Naomi represents a maternal impulse. "Naomi loved to persuade Aunt Rose to talk about [her] sisters. It made the connections real, that she was still in the same family however scattered they were across Europe and America" (GTS 123). When Naomi stops dreaming about her sister and mother, nightmares that tell her the truth about their fates, she misses her dreams and feels disconnected (GTS 652). The relationship between Ruthie and Naomi, who comes to live with Ruthie, resonates with references to the biblical tale of Ruth and Naomi, although with considerable deviations from that tale. In the Bible, Naomi is the older woman, and Ruth her daughter-in-law, who is determined to follow Naomi back to Bethlehem after her husband, Naomi's son, is dead. According to Anita Goldman, Ruth is one of the most radical women in the Bible, a woman who truly follows her own inner voice (88). Goldman observes that the Book of Ruth depicts not only women's relationships to each other and to society, but also to their own fertility and that of the earth. In the Book of Ruth, male and female cultures are sharply delineated, the male world obsessed with a safeguarding of patriarchal names and genealogies, while the depiction of the female world, writes Goldman, shows that love between women is possible and valuable (99). Moreover, she points out that the bond between Naomi and Ruth is a chosen one and that their relationship is marked by love and cooperation rather than, as in some other relationships between women in the Bible, by competition and bitterness (89). Naomi has lost her husband and her two sons; this has left Naomi "empty," while having her family made her "full," as the original text in Hebrew puts it (90). Initially, she is not grateful for the friendship Ruth offers. Ruth insists on following Naomi back to her country, where she (in Goldman's interpretation) seduces Boas at the site of the harvest and bears a son who will grow up to take care of Naomi. Ruth gives the child to Naomi, since her relationship with Naomi, a mother-daughter relationship, is much more important to her than that to Boas. In *Gone to Soldiers*, Naomi's relationships first with Ruthie, and later with Jacqueline, are far more important than her relationship with the father of the child she is carrying, a theme elaborated also in Piercy's poem "The book of Ruth and Naomi" (in *Mars and Her Children*):

> Show me a woman who does not dream
> a double, heart's twin, a sister
> of the mind in whose ear she can whisper,
> whose hair she can braid as her life
> twists its pleasure and pain and shame.

Two other novels by Piercy end with pregnancies symbolically celebrating life: *Dance the Eagle to Sleep* and *Summer People*. In Piercy's poetry, metaphors of conception, gestation, and birth abound, as in the lines concluding "Sand roads" (from *Circles in the Water*):

> Flow out to the ancient cold
> mothering embrace, cold
> and weightless yourself
> as a fish, over the buried
> wrecks. Then with respect
> let the breakers drive you
> up and out into
> the heavy air, your heart
> pounding. The warm scratchy sand

like a receiving blanket
hold you up gasping with life.

In *Gone to Soldiers* and *Summer People* the pregnancy metaphor is both a celebration of a maternal principle and an affirmation of Jewish identity and the continuation of Jewish life. It also ties in with the image of women giving birth to themselves.

Figuratively speaking, Jacqueline finally gives birth to herself as she escapes from a prison cell. Thrown on the floor of this cell, she is smeared with body fluids, blood, urine, and semen from having been raped. Her vagina is bleeding. She is enclosed in the small space of the cell, with the door "firmly locked," but finds an opening in the window bars and "thought of the space a baby is born through, and [she] thought it was worth trying" (GTS 544). Aided by the arrival of planes coming to bomb Toulouse, which make the ground shake (almost like labor pains), she "forced [her] head through . . . continued forcing [herself] through" despite the pain, and finally falls on the ground outside seeing "vast zinnias of flame, red and gold and incandescent white, the clusters of rockets from the anti-aircraft batteries" (GTS 545-46). Like a baby, she is emerging from the darkness within to the explosively strong light outside. She is like a newborn: "Lying there in the dirt and my blood, naked and filthy and torn, I felt like some small fierce creature of the night, a weasel, a stoat, something tiny and lithe and close to the ground with sharp teeth and an immense will to live" (GTS 546). Jacqueline has been born to her own strength.

Analogously, Abra, too, is giving birth to herself: alone in the strange and eerie landscape of Dartmoor, England, she comes upon an ancient double row of stones, passing between which gives her "a sense of strangeness, of power." Looking down, "she could see circles of stone, pits and boundaries of something ancient." One stone speaks to her: it is a "massive stone . . . roughly diamond with a hole through it . . . big enough to pass a package through, or a baby, or a head." Abra feels that "The stone loomed over her, squat, female, a wise woman mocking her folly" (GTS 614). Entering into a dialogue with this mysterious, wise, female stone, she exits the site with the long overdue insight that she will never be Oscar's wife, that she must let go of the illusions that have imprisoned her. Her communion with the stone is almost an act of pagan worship, of sacrifice and renunciation, and it is a ritual of being born to true knowledge about herself: "she kissed the stone and pushed her head briefly through the hole" (GTS 615). The religious undertones of sacrifice are continued as Abra arrives to the manor house where the antifascist members are gathered to a "last supper" (GTS 615).

In the course of the novel, Jacqueline and Abra thus give birth to themselves, liberating themselves from inner and outer prisons and emerging into new light, literally and metaphorically. Ruthie, too, could be seen as giving birth to her self, through her long and arduous labor, and Naomi, finally, is actually pregnant at the end. The maternal metaphor extends to Duvey, who, drowning in the sea, is returning to something maternal, dark, wet, a black pit. He calls out for Mother, who is talking to him, welcoming him as he dies. The journey toward the Mother takes many shapes and different meanings, but on a fundamental level, Piercy's maternal metaphor indicates a direction toward an embracing of a celebration of life and a healing, nurturing impulse that is necessary for humanity to survive. Under Nazism, and in the war, the journey towards the Mother is distorted or blocked, as illustrated in one of the most wrenching passages in *Gone to Soldiers*, when Tovah, an inmate at a concentration camp, is giving birth. Both her pregnancy and the birth must be hidden, and the newborn little boy must be left to die outside in the cold.

In a review of "Marge Piercy's Big War Novel" in the *Washington Post*, Jonathan Yardley deplores the "leaden prose and lifeless dialogue," finds that "nothing in it is surprising or revealing" since "Piercy has nothing new or arresting to say about a subject that has already been written into the ground" (3). In "Me and My Novel," Piercy counters: "I would have to say that war is too important in our time to leave only to men to write about, especially in the limited ways that men have often thought about and felt about war" (19). Other reviewers have been less disparaging, Mary Biggs, for example, finding *Gone to Soldiers* "so ambitious that it seems petty to find fault with it" (23). Lynn Rosen in *New Directions for Women* construes Piercy's aim to be a "[striving] to recreate an entire period for her readers, a large percentage of whom were born after World War II. She is excavating history, and by focusing in large part on the issues, the work and the suffering of women, she is reclaiming the war for feminist history" (14). In the portrait of Louise, Rosen sees "the roots of the women's movement: issues buried in the 40s would resurface later. Without understanding this period in women's history, today's dialogue loses its meaning."

World War II may be "written into the ground" by male writers who have addressed the subject from their (male) perspectives that largely left out women's wartime experiences. As Lynn Rosen has emphasized, Piercy audaciously invades male territory but deviates from a male point of view in bringing a feminist consciousness to bear on her subject. Sue Walker contends that "*Gone to Soldiers* should establish Piercy as one of the leading novelists of our time" (146). Through her intricate motifs of doubleness and division and through her birth imagery, on her huge canvas, Piercy contrasts an impulse toward division and destruction against an impulse of healing and repair, thus connecting the themes in *Gone to Soldiers* to the themes in her other novels. In addition, however, *Gone to Soldiers*, more somber than anything else Piercy has written, has another mission: to make us remember that lost world, "a *ganzeh velt*, an entire world vanished forever" ("The Dark Thread in the Weave" 177), a mission that seems all the more urgent today, when recent polls "[indicate] that as many as 40 million American adults—1 in 6 Americans—hold strongly antisemitic views" (Chesnoff 64). In "The Dark Thread in the Weave," Piercy writes: "Knowledge of the Holocaust is knowledge of the darkest secret, the worst obscenity about being human. It is a sore that cannot heal, a pit that swallows light. Yet survivors triumphed by surviving, and Jews exist. In survival and in resistance, I find strength I stretch to imagine" (191).

Chapter 10

Summer People

Jagged Susan, enamel Susan,
Susan of sullen sleeps and jabbing elbows,
of lists and frenetic starts,
of the hiss of compressed air and the doors slide shut,
you can't hang in the air like a rainbow.
We are making the revolution out of each other.
> Marge Piercy, "Trajectory of the traveling Susan," *Hard Loving*

In Marge Piercy's multisymbolically entitled tenth novel, the complexity of relationships is a central concern. One major thrust of the narrative, which is structurally divided into fifty-five sections alternating between the different points of view of its main characters, is the movement toward the exposure of the hidden or denied shadow sides in the relationships depicted as well as in the characters' self-illusions, aptly symbolized by the view of a truck getting stuck in a septic tank they are installing on the lot, falling through the septic tank, "its front wheels held up like the paws of a dinosaur, a Tyrannosaurus rex in its dotage" (SP 241). Another major thrust is the need to believe in the sacredness of love and life, in the survival of humanity, of the Jewish faith, as well as in some concept of continuity and meaning. In a review entitled "Red-Hot Pastorale," Stephen Schiff makes a somewhat facile summary of Piercy's aims with *Summer People*: "Ms. Piercy seems to have recognized that her timeworn polemic can't enter the 90's blowing the same old steam, so she's not waving banners and fomenting revolt here; she's not even pitting male values against female. The battle lines 'Summer People' draws are between the urban and the exurban, between the frozen-souled glamour of '80's New York and the earthy nurturance only Mother Nature can provide" (26).

Placed within Piercy's oeuvre in its entirety, however, the major thrusts of *Summer People* can be seen as related to the two fundamental impulses I see in Piercy's previous novels—an impulse of separation or cutting off versus an impulse of connection and continuity. These impulses are depicted in an interesting way in Piercy's constellations of relationships with a particular focus on the woman-to-woman relationship. Piercy excels at showing the unreliability of the perceptions of her characters. From a limited omniscient point of view, she shows her main characters, unable to distinguish between fantasy and reality, constantly misinterpreting each other's actions since they see them through the filter of their own emotional states and temporary and shifting desires. Subtly, she shows how her characters' fears or fantasies create various inner scenarios, sometimes far from realistic, even when they congratulate themselves, as does Susan, that "She was the only person who saw the situation clearly, and no one would listen to her" (SP 225). In the interpretation of Sue Walker, "*Summer People* is a study of codependency. It does not intend to address itself to how a happy bisexual triangle might work—for if such a relationship works and is happy, why explore it further? A primary psychological issue in 1989 is codependency, and Piercy is right on target in showing how addictive relationships destroy the love they intend to nurture" (147).

In Marge Piercy's own view a comedy or an operetta (personal letter from Marge Piercy, October 8, 1993), *Summer People* focuses on the unusual ménage à trois of three artists living on Cape Cod: Dinah, an avant-garde composer; Willy, a politically engaged sculptor; and Susan, a fabric designer and Willy's wife. Dinah and Susan are best friends and lovers, and Dinah is also involved in a relationship with Willy. Willy is a somewhat self-satisfied but also open and engaged character. His dreams of his mother (SP 74), around the memory of whom there is a sense of loss, foreshadow the coming loss of the maternal halo in which he has been basking, that is, the love of Susan and Dinah. After that breakup, the triangle collapses, and Willy does not do much to prop it up again. Different from other men in his need for the womanly or maternal, "he was a man who must have a woman" (SP 153). At the end of the novel, he has entered a new relationship (with his neighbor, Candida McIvor), as has Dinah (with the flutist Itzak Raab).

The harmony and stability that has marked the triad for a decade is jarred from the beginning of the novel, with the sound and the fury erupting in the novel's opening passages pointing toward interior and exterior battles to come. Sounds are central in *Summer People*: noise, silence, and music are metaphors of relativity, applicable also to the battle between the women in the novel, marring the harmonious visions of total, sisterly intimacy. The development of the relationship between Dinah and Susan is left devoid of any final hopefulness. Produced in friction between groups of people, the natives of

Cape Cod, the washed-ashores, and the summer people, then, noise is a double-edged metaphor of relativity, applicable to personalities and relationships as well as to art: what is noise to one person is another's music.

Inextricably linked to the novel's fundamental themes, the narrative moves toward dissolution and separation and then toward reconstruction and rearrangements of the relationships depicted. There are dividing lines in the narrative, such as the passage in which a blizzard almost kills Susan, after which the friendship between her and Dinah is killed, and Susan demands that Willy, too, give up his relationship with Dinah. Another turning point is Susan's suicide by drowning, which occurs after the revelation that Willy and Dinah are still having a relationship after the rupture between Susan and Dinah. It is Johnny, Susan's daughter (who has renamed herself and become an avant-garde artist, settling as far away from her mother as she can), who will explode that unwelcome truth to her mother. Susan's illusions about a gracious relationship of genuine caring and equality with Tyrone Burdock, her rich neighbor, have also been shattered.

Susan, at the age of forty-six, is haunted by ennui. At an earlier point in her life, she had gotten out of an emotional low by getting involved with Dinah. Susan shares neither Willy's political engagement nor Dinah's battle for equality. In Susan's view, "Dinah had a strong sense of what was due her. She was forever cutting a pie into fanatically equal slices, counting chocolates in a box to make sure each got his or her entitled share" (SP 163). But Susan's condescending assessment masks a lack of self-esteem: "She knew that hidden within was a jagged wound Dinah had given her self-esteem, not in one blow but in hundreds of small contemptuous lessons in how to be a good person like Dinah, rather than a flighty butterfly like herself" (SP 164). Fundamentally, Susan's malaise is also an escalating existential crisis and a sense of orphanage in the world: "who will ever love me the way I want to be loved? I'll die and it will never happen" (SP 165). And she asks: "Was her life done at forty-six? Was there nothing to look forward to but slowly dying?" (SP 166). She spins an illusion about her relationship to Tyrone, whom she makes into a representative of a refined lifestyle and about whose engagement in herself or the share she has in his life she is sadly mistaken, believing that "she and Tyrone shared that high civilized discussion of feelings and intentions and relationships that made life interesting and which for her defined the true best province of human interaction" (SP 65).

Susan deludes herself that she and Tyrone are practically family, having been neighbors for such a long time, while for Tyrone she is a convenience, a local person looking after his property in his absence or a stand-in mother to his daughter Laurie. When Susan finally realizes this, during her swim out to the raft where she discovers Tyrone and Candida McIvor making love, something in her shatters. Susan's drowning could be seen as a negation of birth and a regression to the amniotic waters of the womb.

Like her cats, Dinah, on the other hand, is an extremely independent woman who has little interest in the fluctuations and strictures of feminine fashions. At once an earth mother and sturdy and masculine, Dinah "[acts] with her the way men traditionally act with women" (SP 103), according to Susan's (angry) view. Dinah is, however, rather androgynous. Not only is feminine and masculine in some respects blended in this character, in Dinah, mind and body are also harmoniously fused. As she roams the country, the dunes, along the ocean, her music starts spinning out in her head. Singularly devoted to her music, almost like a priestess guarding something holy—and music *is* holy for Dinah, she is also an extremely physical and sensual woman and a bon vivant. What to value in a relationship is expressed by Dinah: "real love was much rarer than people liked to think. The remainder was friendship, sensuality, affection, domesticity. However, she had come to value that portion highly" (SP 24).

Dinah has also come to desire motherhood. Her desire to have a child is an affirmation of a maternal principle. Fearing a conflict between work and motherhood, she has delayed childbearing to her late thirties. Her work is of monumental importance and shape, sometimes she feels "as if she were moving mountains and seas around in her head" (SP 37). There is something almost mythical about Dinah, recalling ancient mother goddesses. This is how Laurie sees her: "Dinah was always a presence like a Buddha, squat, full-bodied, a broad, slightly flattened face with piercing, glittering eyes . . . She also had the capacity for sitting without saying a word for endless amounts of time, not fidgeting, not moving, like a woman turned to warm stone" (SP 48). She is a "simple, a true peasant, a dim earthy soul" (SP 49), associated with the primeval, the ancient, wordless, mythical, and imperturbably earthy. Despite being described as "chunky, zaftig, an earth mother" (SP 54), however, Dinah has not adopted any traditional female role: "She had no housekeeping skills, no preparation for what she thought of as the daddy/mommy roles" (SP 59).

While gender roles are a more prevalent issue in some of Piercy's earlier fiction, there is also in *Summer People* an awareness of the difficulties women still encounter in the workplace. Dinah finds that, on top of the difficulties of being a conductor, "as a woman, it was always a matter of having to storm around and demonstrate her grasp of what she should not need to prove at all, her own score" (SP 216). Piercy demonstrates that the maternal metaphor does not necessarily mean acquiring a traditional feminine gender role. Further, while exuding femaleness, Dinah is not particularly feminine. If anything, the *recherché* feminine is derided in *Summer People*, as in the portrait of the ingeniously named Candida McIvor, a doctor's wife and a summer person who is a hyperbolic image of masculine desire. In her high-cut bathing suit and oiled, hairless legs, Candida is a modern version of Alexander Pope's Belinda in *The Rape of the Lock*, a moving doll resembling an American icon, the ubiquitous Barbie doll, about which Piercy has written a poem (in *Circles on the Water*, and included also in the multiauthored 1993 collection of stories and poems *Mondo Barbie*, edited by Lucinda Ebersole and Richard Peabody). Susan perceives Candida thus: "Her blond hair was up on top of her head in a knot, except for a lock on either side curling along her cheek. The effect was artful, flirtatious. Susan noted that Candida moved rather carefully, not nodding, turning her body rather than her head, so as not to dislodge the hairdo" (SP 189). This is a type of imposed feminine immobility that Piercy has deplored in her essays.

At the outset, the friendship between Dinah and Susan is lyrically described. Here is Dinah's point of view: "She had female friendship laid on like pure water from the well, something precious and daily and comforting as milk, something as intoxicating and joyful as wine" (SP 19). Dinah is emotionally closer to Susan than she is to Willy. Ideals of sisterhood have formed the background of the lesbian aspect of their relationship: "it was out of loyalty to sisterly ideals from the period each had decided to try a relationship with a woman" (SP 154).

Ostensibly, it is over Tyrone and what he stands for that the quarrel between Susan and Dinah erupts after Susan has ventured out in a blizzard to check on Tyrone's house, jeopardizing her own life and having to be rescued from a truck on which a huge pine tree has fallen. It is really thanks to Dinah's perseverance that Susan is rescued, since Willy, who never wears a watch, has no idea of how long Susan has been gone. But Susan downplays Dinah's part in the rescue, reinterpreting Dinah's anger at Susan's foolhardiness as an irritating wish for control. When Dinah observes that Tyrone is a "self-important ass" (SP 93) and that "his relationship to [Susan] only differs from his relationship to that Haitian maid in that he doesn't pay [Susan] a salary, but [she] does it for nothing!" (SP 94), that is the end of her relationship to Susan, who flings a vase at her. Since vases, and the liquid that goes in them, often are symbols of the female or the maternal, Susan's shattering of the vase could be seen both as the shattering of a link to Dinah and to a maternal principle. After this, she will be fiercely oriented toward the patriarchal-capitalist world of Tyrone and will go through a stage of silence and of displacing Tyrone's power and control onto Dinah as well as projecting her own anger onto Dinah: "She was beginning to realize Dinah had masses of unresolved anger floating loose in her—poisonous envy, possessiveness, jealousy—which had been allowed to grow so strong that now Dinah was unable to perceive Susan clearly" (SP 95). Susan reconstructs Dinah's criticism of Tyrone's feudal ways into the jealousy of an eclipsed egomaniac and construes her own refusal to analyze her own perspective as the righteous refusal of the gentle to be stepped on by the roughshod. Neither of the two women feel they have anything to apologize for, and, when it becomes obvious to Susan that Willy has continued to see Dinah against Susan's wishes, the breach is cemented and does not heal. Between them "was now a desert, a wasteland, an industrial zone studded with tools and piles of lumber and cement blocks" (SP 227-28). If women's friendships are idealized, the unforgivingness when they are betrayed might be that much greater. As Jimmy expresses it about his mother, Susan: "She's much less forgiving with women. She has different standards for women" (SP 247).

Dinah's reaction to the breach is incomprehension and a sense of loss. In a friendship like hers and Susan's, she feels she had no reason to "soft-pedal" Susan's opinions. Withdrawing into a world of projections and imagining that Dinah is somehow punishing her when she is having a conversation with Susan's son, Susan assumes an insultingly and haughtily cheerful manner whenever she runs into Dinah. Alternating between her characters' different perspectives, Piercy manages to show their unexamined assumptions about each other and their displaced jealousies. Susan, for example, is aghast at Dinah's wish to bear a child with Willy or with anybody, attributing her own angry reaction to her sense of being through with those stages of childbearing and rearing. Discounting Dinah as a mother (SP 120), she does not relish the role of grandmother herself, a role she visualizes as passivity and withdrawal from the real world into a stultifying armchair world of television game shows.

Before the second wave of feminism, women's friendships were seldom extolled in literature. Rather, women's relationships were often supposed to mask or to be marred by competitiveness and rivalry for men's favors. In the renewed feminist fervor, women's sisterly solidarity came foremost, and all the strength and supportiveness, the intimacy and inspiration of women's friendships were praised, whereas relationships with men, not infrequently, came under cross-fire, at least by radical feminists. The shadow sides of women's friendships were, on the other hand, mostly suppressed or ignored. A title such as *Competition: A Feminist Taboo* (ed. Valerie Miner and Helen E. Longino 1987) is revelatory, as is the title of Laura Tracy's 1991 *The Secret Between Us: Competition Among Women*. "Right now," Tracy contends, "competition between women is a taboo subject, much as adultery was only thirty years ago" (xii). That women are indeed competitive is a fact many feminists have preferred to suppress. It seems to be especially difficult to admit to being competitive oneself, even while deploring it in *other* women. The issue of competitiveness between women ties in with Piercy's central themes of separation versus connection. Women's fear of admitting to being competitive arises out of their fear of separation and abandonment: "the desperation we feel when we *do* compete is a response to a deeper feeling of disconnection" (xiii).

Feminist psychotherapists have argued that during the more recent decades of feminist effort, women's anger at each other has been more taboo than that directed at men, with, as a result, suppressed resentments, friendships growing rancid and sisterly affection replaced by silence, denial, and breakups. One reason for this inability to handle conflicts or to express forbidden feelings, it is suggested, is women's lack of clearly defined psychological boundaries. This boundarylessness is from one point of view a strength, a vast, seemingly limitless capacity for sharing that distinguishes many female friendships from those of men. Taken too far, however, identification with another leads to a sense of symbiosis, of not knowing where one life ends and the other begins. Too strong an identification and a lack of psychological boundaries may then produce an unspoken stipulation that the two friends continue to share the same progress and at the same pace. Then, if one shoots off too rapidly, achieving things the other woman has not yet achieved or maybe not even formulated to herself as desirable goals, be it in terms of work, love or motherhood, this may be perceived as a threat and give rise to feelings of inferiority, isolation or betrayal, even despair and a poisonous envy grounded in the conviction that one will never have what the friend has or has achieved. Having experienced a sense of being marginalized as secondary citizens, women may feel that there will never be enough for them to get a share, so if one woman does achieve something desirable, there may not be anything left for her friend.

Even while lauding connectedness, then, each individual's space must be respected. The balance between Dinah and Susan is disrupted, in part also because they have come to embrace opposite impulses. What Piercy seems to suggest is that the impulse to continuity and connection must not mean an obliteration of differences or a symbiotic merging, a motif echoed in the fourth stanza of "The homely war" (in *Circles on the Water*):

> I never want to merge: only to overlap,
> to grow sensitive in the moment so that we move
> together as currents, so that carried
> on that wave we sense skin upon skin
> nerve into nerve with millions of tiny windows
> open to each other's light as we shine
> from the nebulous center like squid
> and then let go.

Initially apparently enigmatic, Piercy's choice of a title, which does not refer immediately to the protagonists, stems from her "taking a walk in Wellfleet and seeing what some rich summer people were having done to an eighteenth-century Cape they had bought—gutted it and turned it into a high-tech New York loft" (as stated in an article on her writing in *The Women's Review of Books* 1989 25). Piercy's protagonists may once have fallen into the category of summer people, but they are now among the washed-ashores, having resided on the island for a long time, and Susan and Willy's son, Jimmy, is counted among the natives. But Piercy's title is symbolically suggestive on several levels, some of which tie in significantly with her most fundamental themes.

Susan, attracted to the lifestyle of Tyrone, a rich tycoon and summer visitor who represents the glamour, power, and material well-being she craves, finds that "pond life was gayer and more civilized in summer" (SP 27). For Susan, moreover, "summer" is a nostalgic vision of herself as the sun within a swirl of warm family intimacy, summer is motherhood, but also the tingling warmth of flirtations—an intense human web of strong connections (SP 28). Seen by the "summer kids" as "the perfect Madonna, Our Lady of the Pond" (SP 210), Susan's own son "used to feel she preferred the summer kids to us" (SP 211). Laurie, Tyrone's flimsy, passive, self-deluding daughter, was one of those summer kids. Laurie's assessment of how startling it is to notice that Jimmy, a "year-round person," has grown while she has been away, metaphorizes the novel's message of how nature is constantly, silently, and invisibly at work, at all times, as opposed to the peaks and flashes of human achievements. The year-round versus the summer imagery thus contrasts "the real world" (SP 47) against the illusory, and the primeval against the man-made.

The summer people metaphor also comprehends another level that could be visualized along the lines of Shirley and Edwin Ardener's double circles of muted and dominant worlds. The natives or the washed-ashores are here a muted group, while the summer visitors, like Laurie and her father, Tyrone, belong to a dominant group of high gloss and high visibility. Tyrone, whose kitchen is remodeled in "ash and glass, black and white marble" (SP 13), imagery associating to death, is a representative of power. His daughter "had never thought of the town as active in the winter, having a life of its own. Obviously they recognized her, but she had not even known they existed, local builders and businessmen" (SP 105). Laurie's perspective is marked by a social snobbery recalling the early stages of Emma's development in Jane Austen's *Emma*, when she is "wondering who on earth Dinah thought she could become involved with, the plumber?" (SP 108). Laurie is a male-oriented, submissive daddy's girl to an even larger extent than she herself realizes. The loss of her mother, who was driven to alcoholism before her divorce from Tyrone, is a dark gap: Laurie is "undernurtured" (SP 11). Incorrectly experiencing herself as powerless, she enjoys a sense of superiority in the relationship with Jimmy, Susan's son.

Associated with the dominant group but in fact part of the muted world, Celeste, Tyrone's maid from Haiti, is a shadow woman who keeps the household running, makes the beds turning down the corner of the coverlet, a woman who is expected to deal with the tasks her employers find distasteful. Almost a feudal servant, Celeste is described as *"grimly* busy in the kitchen" (SP 183, my italics). Piercy's depiction of Celeste is a subtle comment on the dearth of opportunities open to women of color lacking education. The dominant world in *Summer People* as Piercy depicts it adheres to a principle of disconnection, separation, cutting off, and ascribes to a hierarchically organized universe. In part, the summer people act as insensitive, greedy, violent oppressors, as do the hunters spied by Dinah, to whom the muted group remains practically invisible: "the hunters were completely crazy running around spewing beer cans and emptying their shotguns into trees and neighbor's dogs" (SP 23). Within the muted world, hierarchies are not lauded; instead, there is a vision of connectedness, sometimes visualized as a web.

Connected to the description of a muted world, and increasingly important in Piercy's fiction is the celebration of a Jewish heritage, and in particular, aspects of Judaism that can be linked with a maternal, healing principle. Certain Jewish holidays, such as Pesach, are especially important. It is the life-saving and healing aspects of Dinah's Jewish heritage that are central, the commitment her dead husband had "to struggle for justice in the world, to engage in that repair of the world, tikkun, which is commanded to the just" (SP 14), while other, equally important parts are the struggle for freedom and the nurturing of a Jewish identity. In *Summer People*, Dinah's father, Nathan, who had survived Auschwitz, dies when she is only ten, but she has since then lived with his gaze upon her. Part of his heritage is "the sense that music was supremely important and except for human kindness, perhaps the only sure good" (SP 58). When Dinah sees a doe and her fawn at the pond, she visualizes herself as a mother telling her daughter about her grandfather, in a passage emphasizing the sense of connection and continuity, which superimposes and merges images of nature, animals, and humans through images of water, plants and words. Dinah is *among* trees, but *is* also, metaphorically, a tree "[burning] off the energy rising in her spine like sap" (SP 130)—a phrase that may also be an oblique reference to Dionysos, who was associated with fluids in nature such as the sap of trees. A similar fusion of mind and body with nature is achieved in the second stanza of "The queen of pentacles" (in *Circles on the Water*):

I can sink into my body like a mole
and be lost in the tunnels of the nerves, suckling.
I want to push roots deep in my hillside and sag with ripeness,
an apple tree sprawling with fruit.

and in the last stanza of "The window of the woman burning" (*Circles on the Water*):

> You are the icon of woman sexual
> in herself like a great forest tree
> in flower, liriodendron bearing sweet tulips,
> cups of joy and drunkenness.
> You drink strength from your dark fierce roots
> and you hang at the sun's own fiery breast
> and with the green cities of your boughs
> you shelter and celebrate
> woman, with the cauldrons of your energies
> burning red, burning green.

This sense of empathy, identification, and connection with nature and with other humans is an important trait in the portrait of Dinah and a significant feature in the dynamics illustrated in Piercy's fiction, with its central suggestion to "struggle for justice in the world, to engage in that repair of the world, tikkun, which is commanded to the just" (SP 14).

Chapter 11

He, She and It

Cyborg imagery can suggest a way out of the maze of dualisms in which we have explained our bodies and our tools to ourselves. This is a dream not of a common language, but of a powerful infidel heteroglossia.

Donna Haraway 181

. . . Intellectuals
sneer at moviegoers who confuse
Dr. Frankenstein with his monster.

The fans think Frankenstein is the monster.
Isn't he?

Marge Piercy, "Absolute Zero in the Brain," Stone, Paper, Knife

While most of Marge Piercy's earlier fiction can be seen as realistic narratives (although not unproblematically so), in *He, She and It* Piercy pulls out all the stops of fantastic fiction, borrowing freely from cyberpunk and science fiction. If her eleventh novel sometimes strains credulity, it is nevertheless an appealing hybrid of compulsively readable adventure story and thought-provoking rewriting of religious myth. Within a futuristic adventure story, Piercy braids a subtext of deeply philosophical and spiritual questions. This is a novel of great suspense with a religious resonance at the core that ties in with the themes treated in her earlier novels, notably the celebration of a 'maternal' impulse toward connection, caring and continuity, which is crucial to *tikkun olam*, the repair of the world.

Some reviewers have objected to the plot of *He, She and It*, Malcolm Bosse in the *New York Times*, for example, finding it "intermittently frenetic and weird" and "frequently reminiscent of a video game." Conceding that Piercy "confronts large issues in this novel," he dislikes the "heavy symbolism, unrelieved by humor" (22). Robert Chatain, on the other hand, writes in the *Chicago Tribune* that "Readers who don't get caught in technological implausibilities who, in other words, read 'He, She and It' as literature, not science fiction are likely to enjoy her story" (6). In Chatain's interpretation, with which I would agree, "what Piercy gives us is more a philosophical romance, and the story she tells is at once new and old."

Ostensibly, Piercy's eleventh fiction is thus a work of science fiction, a picaresque tale from an ominously exotic land. The sprawling narrative is, or contains, an adventure story, a quest novel, a detective novel, and a highly unusual love story, as well as a kind of inverted travel guide moving at a rapid clip through a blighted landscape that feels like an onslaught. It can also be read as a political novel of an anarcho- or ecofeminist persuasion. Half of it, moreover, resembles a historical novel, relating the persecution and oppression of Jews in Prague and the development of empirical science and astronomy in the early seventeenth century. Through themes, motifs and imagery the storylines mesh, sometimes traveling on parallel tracks and engaging in each other to open up a vaster panorama. Not every passage in *He, She and It* is equally poised, but many of the scenes are so reekingly vivid that the reader feels bodily transplanted into the worlds of the seventeenth and the twentyfirst centuries.

He, She and It is full of a dizzying and defamiliarizing array of futuristic details in terms of housing, clothing, transportation, and technology in general. There are house computers who seem to have minds of their own. The characters' wardrobes contain some bizarre and farfetched items (but who knows what mid-twentyfirst century fashions will be like?). In Y-S, there are moving sidewalks, even an express lane, there are "float cars" and "zips." Most cleaning and maintenance are done by robots. As a replacement for twentieth century cinema there are "stimmies," which recall Huxley's "feelies" (and which recall the "holis" and the "Sense-Alls" in *Woman on the Edge of Time*)—multidimensional chimeras that let one enter into and vicariously experience what is portrayed.

That Piercy has a purpose with this novel—to engage her readers in more serious protection of and thoughtful interaction with the environment in order to avoid a realization of the dystopian scenario she paints and to celebrate fundamental principles of political democracy and connectedness, sharing, maternal nurturing—does not sap the fun from the outrageously unrealistic and fantastic aspects of the adventures of her characters. Intelligently and humorously, Piercy moves her cast through a narrative that could itself be metaphorized as "the Net," Piercy's far-reaching computer space.

He, She and It contains two separate but interconnected stories, one being a flashback to the year 1600, "a tale of kabbalah, of religious magic" (HSI 25) set in Prague around 1600, and the other a future present depicting the world in the middle of the twenty-first century. In both worlds, the Jewish population is relegated to its own, marginal and enclosed worlds: in Prague, Jews live in the ghetto, and in the future scenario they are gathered in the free town of Tikva, on Massachusetts Bay. Prague is ruled by religious and secular hierarchies and by mobs, while the future world is divided into twenty-three "enclaves" ruled by "multis." The earth, Gaia, has revenged herself on her exploitative and careless children after the devastations of war, pollution, destruction of the ozone layer, and so on, which has resulted in the world becoming uninhabitable, exceedingly hot, with lethal levels of ultraviolet radiation and with almost zero possibilities to grow food naturally. Those who survive do so in cave cities or under protective domes (or wraps) extended over the rooftops to shield from a now murderous sun.

Within the multi-owned enclaves, a strict order and hierarchy reign, but there are worlds outside these climate-controlled enclosures: there are the "free towns" along the ocean, and the "Glop" somewhere in between: "the Megalopolis that stretched south from what had been Boston to what had been Atlanta, and a term applied to similar areas all over the continent and the world" (HSI 6). The Glop is a dangerous, hellish, pungent zone of anarchy, gang violence, disease, heat, sheer dreck, a kind of primal bog—but also a place from which "One Lazarus, Two Lazarus" (title of chapter 34) and subterranean rebel groups spring. The Middle East, the 'cradle of civilization,' is entirely uninhabitable. Within Piercy's spatially constructed imagery, rejuvenation and recreation occur outside the enclosed, Apollonian domes of hierarchy; it occurs on the margins, along a still polluted and dangerous but also slowly self-cleansing ocean and within the hot, anarchic, Dionysian chaos of the Glop: "Nili saw the Glop differently than Shira always had. Shira realized she had been trained automatically by her culture, especially by corporate culture, to treat the Glop as an unimportant place where nothing consequential happened. Nothing that mattered to the real, the significant, people could originate there. But Nili turned to the New Gangs for answers. In people living off the garbage of the preceding century, Nili found much to study and admire" (HSI 361). Bridging these worlds is Piercy's protagonist, Shira Shipman, whose point of view we follow in two-thirds of the forty-nine chapters. She has grown up in the free town of Tikva, then married and lived in the Y-S, or Yakamura-Stichen, enclave. When she divorces her husband, she loses custody of her son, who goes to live with his father on a for Shira unreachable space platform. Returning to her grandmother's house in Tikva, she accepts a position with Avram, a scientist who has created a cyborg named Yod, to socialize whom will be Shira's task.

As a parallel story, Shirah's grandmother, Malkah, who is responsible for a third of the programming of Yod, tells him a story of the Jewish ghetto in Prague in 1600. In order to defend this ghetto against a bloodthirsty gentile mob who is planning to attack it on Good Friday, the Rabbi Loew creates a golem, a clay man of superhuman strength, whose function it is to help defend the ghetto. The Rabbi Loew was a historical figure, who, according to Marie-Hélène Huet, "had played an important role in sixteenth-century Prague and had personally intervened with Emperor Rudolf II on behalf of the Jews at a time of heightened persecution" (241). Both stories assume aspects of the detective novel presenting puzzling questions: Where is the young servant the Christians claim the Jews have incarcerated and perhaps murdered? (a task for Joseph, the golem, to solve); why are Y-S trying to infiltrate Tikva, and why are they so interested in Shira? And who has attempted to kill Malkah? The plot takes on a garb of outlandish science fiction adventure with dreamlike, shape-shifting passages as Shira and Yod travel incognito to Y-S to kidnap Shira's son. To respond to Y-S by mastering their own methods in order to reunite with her son and struggle toward comprehension of a complex system—that is Shira's quest. Malkah's pursuit of knowledge and love moves on a parallel track. The two separate narratives are interwoven into each other, forming a multicolored braid (to paraphrase the description of Malkah's life), a rich tapestry of distinct threads but with echoing patterns. Piercy has managed to create two distinct voices, one the slow, painstaking first person who is actually telling her story to Yod, thus imaginatively welding past with the present and the future (Malkah's aim is to program Yod for future action). Shira's story has a different tone, a quicker beat, a slight impatience to it.

In the story of the golem, Piercy draws on a spellbinding Jewish legend that has inspired many writers, notably Isaac Bashevis Singer and Jorge Luis Borges. Early nineteenth-century German Romantics were equally fascinated by this legend and saw in the golem a *doppelgänger*, or double, representing unreason as opposed to the reason of the self. "With the advent of psychoanalysis, the golem, in turn, came to represent the Id" (Huet 243). In Hebrew, golem means "the unformed, amorphous" (Scholem 161). Before he had a soul, Adam, newly created by God from the finest earth, is referred to as a golem. Referred to in the Talmud (and, ambiguously, in Psalm 139:16), the golem legend, "the very essence of Jewish folklore" according to Isaac Bashevis Singer (9), was developed further by German Jews in the Middle Ages, first as an inner, mystic experience and later as an externalization. A late Jewish version is found in a piece by Jacob Grimm in *Journal for Hermits* from 1808, which describes how the Polish Jews created golems, on whose foreheads they inscribed *'emeth* (truth). The golems, however, had a threatening tendency to keep growing after they had been created, whereupon the Jews, out of fear, erased the first letter on the forehead, which left *meth* (dead): this made the golem return to dust. One golem, however, grew so tall that his master, unable to reach up to his forehead, requested that the golem take off his boots so that he would be able to reach. The master managed to erase the letter, unfortunately only to be erased himself as the golem turned clay collapsed on top of him (Scholem 159)—an erasure of the father that is echoed in Piercy's novel.

Piercy's novel could have been called "He, She *or* It," since much of the narrative questions the boundaries between the personal pronouns. Is Yod, a cyborg, a he or an it? As if echoing a passage in Mary Shelley's *Frankenstein*, in the chapter entitled "He, She and It," Shira switches from the use of 'it' to 'he.' Is Nili, an Amazonian superstrong laserwoman, a she or a he? Can we always be sure of where to draw the borders between the two genders? The title also associates to the father, mother, and child triad. On one level, the novel is about constellations of filiation and the abrogation of patriarchal authority. Shira and Josh are involved in a custody suit over their son, Ari, who, in the eyes of Y-S, is simply an 'it,' a mere pawn in an elaborate chess game. Another set of genitors in *He, She and It* consists of Avram, the wizardly scientist who has created the cyborg and Malkah, the bewitching and witch-like computer specialist, "a magician of chimeras" (HSI 160) who helps program him. Yod calls Avram "father," something Avram does not relish. In the Prague story, the Rabbi (Judah Loew) 'fathers' Joseph, the golem, who finds a teacher and mother figure in Chava, the brilliant midwife and Jewish scholar, whom, in an oedipal twist, Joseph comes to wish to marry.

He, She and It also deals with the parent-child relation between God and his created children. The title, finally, could also refer to the relations of Shira and Yod and of Chava and Joseph to the 'it' of the cause they jointly embrace and work for with parental engagement and love: the fight for justice, democracy and religious freedom. "It" could of course also be the huge ethical and philosophical questions these couples grapple with together and individually: What is life? What is consciousness? What does it mean to be human? Where, exactly, is the borderline between human and nonhuman, when the humans at this futuristic point in time already are so artificial, with surgical implants and alterations in body and visage, and when nonorganic objects talk back at people? Further, as regards questions of life and death, of creation and destruction, what "rights" do humans have? Is it ever right or justifiable to kill another human? Do human beings have the right, usually the prerogative of God, to decide which causes should be prioritized? A question that could be leveled not only at totalitarian ideologies but at any political or social convictions and credos is how far one can go, ethically speaking, to ensure the success of one's personal plans or political projects.

The title thus resonates with multiple associations to themes and motifs within the novel: parent-child stances and issues of legitimacy linked to a discussion of biological reproduction and the cultural production of meaning, the construction of gender, male-female relationships, and individual or collective relations to fundamental and intricate matters of ethics and politics. "It" also evokes a component of the unknown or unpredictable, affirming the unknowableness of a Dionysian nature principle, which ties in with the detective novel aspect of *He, She and It*, the puzzle "it" that the He and She are fighting to solve. The impatience for quick answers and resolutions of the adventure aspects is tempered and balanced by deep ponds of sprititual and scholarly reflection, just as youth is tempered by old age and as Shira is tempered by her grandmother, Malkah, the emotional linchpin of the novel, whose very name associates to the life-sustaining and soothing milk of maternal love—as well as to *Malkhuth*, the last *sefirah*, sometimes identified with Shekhinah or God's presence (Scholem 58) into which the kabbalistic system of emanations is joined.

Piercy continues her elaboration of fundamental impulses towards separation, hierarchy, and destruction on the one hand and toward the repair of an ill-used world on the other, impulses depicted in the motifs and imagery in *He, She and It*, as, for example, in the motif of disguises, of the fake/unreal or illusory versus the real, and in the spatial metaphors. Ontological and epistemological queries harking back to Plato and Aristotle hide in the narrative, as do cosmological and existential concerns linked to Jewish mysticism. As to the nature of reality and identity: what is 'real' and what is 'unreal,' fake, or duplicitous? Where do we locate the boundaries? Are the boundaries themselves 'real,' for that matter? Duplicitously, for example, Yod and Joseph assume the personae of real men in their communities. Malkah is duplicitously hiding from Shira her brief love affair with Yod. Everyone assumes garbs of disguise in "the spatial metaphor that [is] the Net" (HSI 388), by donning 'fake' identities. Riva, Shira's mother, arrives in Tikva in disguise, and Shira goes to Y-S disguised as a yard worker in order to kidnap her son. What is identity? The novel plays upon the meanings of the words 'identity' and 'identical,' signifying what is unique and distinguishes one person/object from another on the one hand and identical duplication as in mass reproduction on the other, meanings one might see as analogous to the fundamental principles of separation and connection in Piercy's work. Indeed, Piercy's narrative itself sways between the poles of the unique and the mass-duplicable, between identity and shape-shifting dissolution of identity. One chapter is called "The Shape-Shifters," another "A Sea Change"—the latter a reference to Shakespeare, but perhaps also an oblique reference to Lois Gould's novel *A Sea Change*, which dissolves gender boundaries in an even more far-reaching way than *He, She and It*. The ramifications of this discussion reach out to the nature of literary procreation or production: is literature the unique product of authorial singularity, or is it a multi-authored reproduction of what has gone before?

Josh and Shira are duplicitous in surreptitiously practicing their Judaism at home just like the "marranos," the "Spanish Jews under the Inquisition who had pretended to be Christian to survive" (HSI 2). As an ironic parallel, Shira is teaching Josh to "pass," not as a Christian but as a cyborg trying to pass for human. But what does human mean? As Shira tells Yod, "We're all cyborgs, Yod. You're just a purer form of what we're all tending toward" (HSI 150). Shira is echoing Donna Haraway, who writes that "by the late twentieth century, our time, a mythic time, we are all chimeras, theorized and fabricated hybrids of machine and organism; in short, we are cyborgs" (150). Haraway says further that "the cyborg is a creature in a post-gender world; it has no truck with bisexuality, pre-oedipal symbiosis, unalienated labor, or other seductions to organic wholeness through a final appropriation of all the powers of the parts into a higher unity." Our Western origin stories of the fall from innocence depend on a vision of blissful unity, which is repeated in psychoanalysis' positing of the mother-infant oneness that must end in separation and individuation. A cyborg "skips the steps of original unity, of identification with Nature in the Western sense" (151). Of course, a cyborg is completely cut off from such bonds, abstractly individualized as, in Haraway's words, an "illegitimate offspring of militarism and patriarchal capitalism, not to mention state socialism." Most importantly, however, the "cyborg myth is about transgressed boundaries, potent fusions, and dangerous possibilities which progressive people might explore as one part of needed political work."

In *He, She and It*, the cyborg is associated with Samson, who in the Bible (the Book of Judges) married a Philistine woman who betrayed his confidence and thus incurred his violent wrath. Tempted by another woman, Delilah, he revealed to her that his incredible strength lay in his hair. When he was asleep, his hair was cut, and he was blinded by his enemies. Given the opportunity for revenge somewhat later, he caused a whole building to fall, thereby killing both himself and others—just as the master was crushed under the structure of the golem. In Piercy's Prague story, Joseph, the golem, is insulted by the comparisons of himself to Samson, since he has resisted temptation and since his strength resides not in his hair, but, as he sees it, in himself. Chava, the midwife, responds: "Our strength is in each other and in the eternal one, Joseph" (HSI 202), thus affirming the theme of connectedness in this novel. In spite of Joseph's superhuman strength, it is this sense of connectedness that is the strongest, and even in his defense of the ghetto, the collaboration of everyone else there is needed, even of women and men who cannot, or will not, fight. In the twenty-first century, in Tikva, similarly, every citizen spends a week each year replanting trees in a collective effort to slow down the warming of the globe (HSI 384).

In *He, She and It*, Piercy has inserted a puzzling story within a story, that of Joseph and the pregnant Maria. Why has Piercy brought in a rewriting of the biblical story of Jesus' mother, with some alterations that make it enigmatic? In Malkah's Prague story, a young servant of virtuous reputation, Maria, is rumored to have been kidnapped by Jews and perhaps killed, so that the Jews can get Christian blood for the matzohs. Building on this outrageous myth called the blood libel, this false rumor (again, a motif playing on the real versus the unreal, truth versus lies or illusions) is dangerous to the Jews in the ghetto as a pretext to attack and kill the Jews, to unleash the unprovoked violence of 'self' attacking its 'other.' As the story now assumes the cloak of a detective story, Joseph the clay man turns sleuth and goes searching for Maria in order to clear up the mystery and thus dispel the fabricated myths harmful to the Jewish community. As an inversion of the Blue Beard fairy tale, Joseph surreptitiously enters the knight's house, penetrating through bolted, off-limit spaces until he detects a locked passage at the end of which, and close to the river, he finds the incarcerated Maria, pregnant with her lord, a Blue Beard who indeed plans to kill her. As Joseph liberates Maria, they form yet another version of a "he, she and it"-unit, temporarily and superficially. Ironically, it is Maria who perceives that picture and "laughs mischievously": "Maria and Joseph and little baby in the womb, the son of the lord! Lord Stefan" (HSI 138). In this grotesquely sacrilegious rewriting of the story of what precedes Jesus' birth, Piercy collapses the madonna-whore dichotomy, a Damocles-sword that has been hanging over Judeo-Christian women for two millennia. This Maria is no tender, pious mother figure: she is a misguided teenager who mistook Stefan's attentions for an angel addressing her, she is the deceived and used 'other' woman, discarded rather than revered when she becomes expectant (in both senses of the word). In the stable, she attempts to seduce Joseph, who in this (in)version is the real 'virgin,' who has never 'seen' a woman before. In this temptation scene, Joseph-Samson-Adam remains unmoved, in obeisance to his own lord and maker. Appropriately, Piercy does not let Jesus be born—it is not yet time, since this madonna/whore "has only a slight swelling" (HSI 140). But the world—the Jewish ghetto of Prague—is temporarily saved, and Joseph has fulfilled his mission.

Aside from the religious associations, Piercy plays with the identity/difference or the self/other theme. Joseph, Maria's savior, is not a man at all—he only appears to be. Joseph, furthermore, had to cross the boundaries between Jewish and gentile spaces in this passage, but there is a suggestion that these boundaries are false, illusory, *man*-made. Furthermore, a principle of separation—symbolized by the walls of the ghetto—is posed against a principle of connection: the tenuous unit of Joseph, Maria and the unborn baby. An impulse of destruction—the wrecking of the ghetto and the murdering of the Jews—is posed against an impulse of creation—Maria's "slight swelling," and of saving life: Joseph's liberation of Maria and his saving the ghetto. Underlying the multipartite ramifications of this episode are thus some of Piercy's most fundamental themes.

A principle of connection is uppermost in Malkah's tutelage of Yod. She comments to Shira: "Avram made him male—entirely so. Avram thought that was the ideal: pure reason, pure logic, pure violence. The world has barely survived the males we have running around. I gave him a gentler side. . . . a need for *connection*" (HSI 142, emphasis added). With men being so easily provoked to violence, Shira tells Yod that women learn to avoid staring at men since that can unleash violence. Through her depiction of the cyborg/golem, Piercy brings in a discussion of violence, part of a principle of separation: *can violence be justified? Ever?* If so, what are the criteria for justifying the use of violence? For the right cause? Who decides what is right? For both Joseph and Yod, violence and killing is pleasurable: it is, after all, what they have been programmed to do, and they do it well. Have human males been similarly 'programmed,' genetically or hormonally, to respond with violence when provoked and to enjoy it?

This discussion is linked to the construction of gender in *He, She and It*, in terms of which things have both changed and remained the same. At Y-S, rigid sex roles have been done away with in the work place, for economical reasons: "no one could afford such nonsense" (HSI 100). In all other areas outside work, however, a division between the sexes is maintained and reinforced, as, for example, in dress codes. This is due to notions of hierarchy no longer resting upon maternity as a rationale, since few people are able to procreate because of damaged fertility and have to rely upon reproductive technology. In Tikva, the role of housewife or homemaker has simply been dismantled. If anyone cooks, it is for fun. "No one kept house" (HSI 156). Women's work outside the house is seen as highly meaningful. Both for Shira and for Malkah work is absolutely central, and they are very good at what they do. With everyone in Tikva over fifteen being in the work force, work is in fact central for everyone, and with housework mostly automated, women's old conflicts are reduced or resolved. Children are in day care even if mothers work at home because of the value seen in the socialization that day care offers. The stinging conflicts experienced by countless working mothers in America in the late twentieth century between the demands of and desire for work on the one hand and those of motherhood on the other are thus defanged. No more do articles with titles like "Will Motherhood Cost You Your Job?"—as in *Redbook* May 1993—seem necessary. For Chava, of course, living in Prague in 1600, the conflict is irremediable: "How could she bear and raise children, run a household and also engage in intellectual labor, scholarship, religious thought?" (HSI 370).

In her depiction of Yod through Shira's perspective, Piercy humorously and subtly conveys what Shira considers as shortcomings in human males (in a manner that recalls the comedy film *Making Mr. Right*). Yod, for example, has been programmed for equality. He is confused by the 'old' sex roles, and for him, a princess might just as well be the heroine saving the prince as vice versa. Knowing how hard it is for Yod to articulate his thoughts and feelings, moreover, Shira's appreciation of his efforts reveal how seldom human males make the effort to communicate: "Human males don't often have that habit" (HSI 120). Neither do human males have the habit of being careful not to hurt, as is the case with Yod. Sardonically, Shira comments: "That would make you different indeed from any man I've known" (HSI 168). Pleasingly, Yod, furthermore, lacks the "abrasions, pimples, scars, irregularities" that men "always" have. Sexually, he has many features resembling a woman's (such as placing a premium on intimacy) and many characteristics seemingly made to order to please women, such as his total lack of regard for female beauty stipulations. Shira will never have to worry about her appearance. Also, "He did not require much, unlike a human male. In many respects, he was refreshingly undemanding" (HSI 236-37).

As part of the discussion of the construction of gender one might see Riva, Shira's highly unusual mother, who, much like Vida in Piercy's fifth novel, is an outsider and political fugitive emblematizing the porous and palimpsestically assembled postmodernist subject. Shira has never really known her mother, who gave away her daughter to the grandmother, Malkah. Harking back to Miriam in *Small Changes*, who, as Kathleen Halischak observes, "begins to collect computer access numbers that may help women reach vital information sources" (Halischak 53), Riva is an 'information pirate,' an outspoken crusader and female Robin Hood of the information age who steals, or liberates, information about useful items so that anyone can benefit without paying for it. Like Vida, Riva is constantly on the run, assuming various disguises and making herself into an unsentimental and finely honed instrument for the cause that needs her. Spatially rendered—likened to a mountain (HSI 310)—the freedom-loving Riva has always "hated closed doors" (HSI 80) and miraculously escapes the door of death.

Another character dwelling on dangerous margins is Riva's companion, Nili, "a very well made bomb" (HSI 189), although not exactly a sex bomb. Through room imagery, Piercy weaves together her themes of opposing gender roles and opposing impulses or principles. Hidden in caves in what was the Middle East are a group of superwomanly strong, Amazonian women, one of whom is Nili. They are Israeli and Palestinian women who have survived and who are determined to create a new Yerushalaim in what is still "truly no-man's-land," in both senses of the phrase. Nili likens herself to the dove or raven that flew out, reconnoitering, from Noah's ark (recalling the bird imagery in some of Piercy's earlier novels, with the female guide to the utopian future in *Woman on the Edge of Time* being likened to a loon), to see whether the world is ready for the victory of a healing, repairing principle, for connectedness instead of hierarchy, and for a triumph of the maternal—principles that have enabled these Amazonian women, "the strongest women in the world" (HSI 417) to survive both the political animosity that has killed off their men and the devastation resulting from that war. During a transition period necessary for regeneration, these women have lived the politics of an extreme radical feminism that welcomes no men. To this "womb of religion, the sacred desert, the cave of dancing women" Malkah journeys in the end, as a pilgrimage and in pursuit of health and a healed vision, guided by "a crazy caïque with a female crew" who will "carry [them] off the map" (HSI 419). In connection with the "womb of religion" referred to, it is interesting to note that "the Hebraic conception of compassion and love is grounded in the essentially feminine image of the womb, which holds, nurtures and protects the fetus—be it perfect or malformed, pretty or ugly, worthy or undeserving" (Shkop 43).

Highly relevant in *He, She and It*, spatial metaphors are connected with Piercy's elaboration of Apollonian and Dionysian forces, of sex and gender, and of oppression and liberation, as placed within a freedom-loving Judaic tradition. "Psychologically," writes Yi-Fu Tuan, "space in the Hebraic tradition means escape from danger and freedom from constraint. . . . On the spiritual plane, space connotes deliverance and salvation" (58). Yi-Fu Tuan also observes that "Architectural space reveals and instructs" (114). In her depiction of Y-S, Piercy shows how architectural spaces can be used to oppress and to intimidate. In Y-S, there is a compact sense of enclosure, with the dome sheltering the whole area from the sun. The Hall of Justice, where the novel opens, "[glitters] in black and white marble, higher than wide and engineered to intimidate" (HSI 1). This black and white marble recalls the decorating choices of another dominant world, that of Tyrone Burdock, the rich summer person connected to merciless financial speculation in *Summer People*.

The idea of living under a 'dome' brings to mind an experiment conducted at Oracle, Arizona. For two years (1991-93), a crew of eight people lived in the self-contained 3.15 acres of "Biosphere 2," producing most of their own food and recycling air, water and waste ("'Cabin Fever' Nears End for Crew of Biosphere 2" A-13). Tikva is protected by a "wrap" rather rather than a dome, but, located on the ocean, it is more vulnerable than Y-S. There is a risk of inundation. The ocean has already drowned seaside towns, the high rises of which now eerily lurk in the masses of water like huge, ominous man-made rocks. The proximity to the ocean makes Tikva a more vulnerable but also a freer place. A major spatial metaphor in this novel, the ocean is still dangerously radioactive, yet, as a metaphor for the unlimited, of that which lies outside of regulation and control, it is also an image of freedom. The "unprotected" areas that lie outside of domes and wraps called "the raw" (HSI 99) also appear to be more easily accessible from the free town of Tikva.

If Y-S represents an extreme Apollonianism of order and hierarchy, Tikva is an "unregulated" place where Shira experiences a Dionysian "loosening" (HSI 36)—Piercy's phrase for her own first encounters with the poetry of Whitman ("How I Came to Walt Whitman and Found Myself" 98)—and in Malkah's lyrically described courtyard she finds a "garden of almost Eden" (HSI 37). Malkah's and Shira's lives center around this courtyard house, with many significant conversations taking place in the courtyard—recalling the restorative courtyard where Jill and Howie sit in *Braided Lives*, where the sound of traffic trickles in like the murmur of the ocean.

It is highly significant that Piercy has chosen the image of the courtyard house as an icon of transformative space, an image that deviates considerably from the American prototype of the single-family house sitting on its individual site. In America, the courtyard house has been developed chiefly in southern California, but, as the authors of *Courtyard Housing in Los Angeles: A Typological Analysis* observe, "Despite occasional support from progressive architects" courtyard houses have generally been seen "as modest buildings unworthy of consideration as architecture" (Polyzoides, Sherwood and Tice 9). Linked to Piercy's fundamental themes, the courtyard house could be seen as a symbol for a balanced duality of openness and enclosure and of rural and urban elements, as well as a celebration of a muted zone. As Polyzoides, Sherwood, and Tice rightly remark, "any housing prototype that challenges the American intellectual monopoly of the building in the park deserves careful attention and study." The courtyard house, moreover, emphasizes the horizontal rather than the vertical, endowing it, in the context of Piercy's fiction, with a matriarchal rather than patriarchal luster. Extrovertedly introverted, it stands in sharp contrast both to the claustrophobically introverted high rise in the dystopian future envisaged in *Woman on the Edge of Time*, indeed a nightmare extreme of a principle of separation and hierarchical oppression, and to the home of the heroine of that novel, a New York high-rise with only a narrow air-shaft at its core that does not even give enough light to grow some plants. Even as multifamily units, the California courtyard houses are prototypically low rises. At Tikva, significantly, the high rises of earlier eras have been swallowed up by the ocean. Further, at the same time as it can be "a place of contemplation" (56), the courtyard house can be linked to Piercy's valorizing of an impulse toward connection, since "the emphasis on use of the ground plane minimizes stairs and permits an unusual degree of interaction" among its inhabitants (9). In

California, the courtyard house is associated with an unusual degree of heterogeneity, since "Unlike in most multifamily dwellings in the United States, there was no stigma attached to living in them" (12). In its multisymbolic significance, the courtyard is a highly positive image. As Polyzoides, Sherwood, and Tice state of the buildings they studied: "The courts offered an Edenic sense of well-being, permitting residents to live either indoors or outdoors in natural surroundings, without needing to worry about the weather and its effects" (10).

Piercy's choice of architectural structure recalls Beth's cave of mirrors in the first lines of *Small Changes*, as well as the open and airy yet comfortingly embracing women's house in the same novel. Often completely introverted, with blank, windowless walls to the outside world, a courtyard house gathers all the rooms around an outdoor space. Thus what is in terms of plan the most internal space of the house is in fact exterior space, an image I associate with the inspiring cave symbol analyzed by Sandra Gilbert and Susan Gubar in *The Madwoman in the Attic*: a sheltering, womb-like place which is still open to the outside. As in Mary Shelley's parable, the ocean is nearby, to which Shira escapes for a rejuvenating solitude (or, in her teens, to meet with her lover, Gadi). The waters obliterate all differences and hierarchies, and the ocean is both lifegiving and pleasurable. Indeed, for Shira, sexual bliss brings her into a "medium of her pleasure" that is "like a brilliant pulsating jellyfish" and a "transcendent liquid ecstasy" (HSI 118).

The courtyard house, with its inversion of what is 'inside' and 'outside' can be linked to a philosophical inquiry in *He, She and It* pondering what is outside and inside the walls of 'reality.' The spatial metaphor of the Base, for example, raises ontological and epistemological questions pertaining to the nature of reality and the construction of knowledge as well as referring to writing and literature. In Malkah's view, "energy is mental and physical at once and everything that appears as matter in space is actually immaterial. . . . I cannot always distinguish between myth and reality, because myth forms reality . . . Our minds help create the world we think we inhabit" (HSI 25). Entering the ambit of the Base in pursuit of knowledge and clarification, Shira paradoxically dons a cloak of unreality while confronting illusion. These illusions are mental projections originating in her and the other participants' brains. In the Base, Shira and Yod meet sub rosa in a sensual embrace within the huge petals of a rose, "Rosa Mundi," which, having no scent, is "unreal." Their thoughts become stamina arising separately but connected within the petals of the flower of the text. They are "joining in the Base," but, as Yod observes, that "is only the image. I want the reality" (HSI 167). The Base resembles a platonic world of ideas, with "highly abstracted" objects moving around. But even after stepping out of the Base, is Yod real then? Malkah points out that in Hebrew, the word *davar* means both 'word' and 'thing': "no distinction. A word, an idea, is a thing" (HSI 259). Yod remains a platonic blueprint himself, inhumanly smooth, regular, embodying the idea of himself, an idea that is infinitely duplicable. Or is it? Even though the "genetic" setup would be identical, Piercy indicates that the cultural programming affected by Avram, Malkah, and Shira, as well as Gadi, and their interactions and tensions, have made a difference in Yod's development. While genes/chips constitute a given, perhaps predictable point of departure, the journey of a person or a machine is subsequently shaped by the surrounding environment in unforeseeable ways.

The golem fantasy represents, as Marie-Hélène Huet writes, "the oldest and most successful story of paternal singularity. In this act of procreation, sexuality is erased and replaced by a linguistic pronouncement, first meant to duplicate God's act of creating man, and meant also as an illustration of the magical and cryptic power of words and the mysterious origins of life" (245). Creating the unreal, the unnatural, is an Apollonian fantasy linked to the futile fantasy of being able to control the real. Created by magic and advanced technology, Joseph and Yod are 'unnatural' creations not stemming from a woman's womb but from male minds. They are created to control reality, to protect their creators and their communities. By contrast, Chava and Shira are 'natural,' they are biological mothers, and Chava, moreover, is a midwife who assists other women in giving birth to 'real' offspring. Shira "[is] commonplace, banally human, as natural as seaweed and mud" (HSI 125). She is more 'real' than most of her fellow "techies" at Y-S, who are surgically transformed into an ideal mold, "resculpted by scalpels, implants, gels, to the latest image of radiant beauty." While Shira, one of the very few women who has been able to conceive without heroic efforts, is repeatedly connected with the Dionysian, with nature and fertility, and with natural processes—although she has implants, too—Y-S is Apollonianism driven too far, so removed from "unregulated" life that it approaches the perfect stillness of death.

He, She and It raises questions of cosmology: how we came into existence, how we fit into a universal scheme, and what the relation is between us and our creator: how does the creator feel about us, and what do we need from our creator? Is our creator male or female, both, or neither? Further, what would the implications of any of those alternatives be? Is the cosmological scheme itself a patriarchal or a matriarchal one—and how does it matter which it is? The frequent conceptualization in Judeo-Christian religion of God as a father or an artist figure is not unequivocally consoling, since as an artist God can cut himself off from his work, and even destroy it, if it does not conform to the standards he has set. At the other, matriarchal, pole of religion, a mother goddess represents an image of protective, uncritical warmth and a sense of unquestioned continuity and connection. Creating the stories of the golem and the cyborg, Piercy raises questions that echo those discussed by Carol Ochs in *Behind the Sex of God*: "What is God's creation, the perfect realm of ideas or this material world? Do humans accept as divine the creations of the mind or those of the body?" (7).

Central to the discussion of the real and the unreal is the story of the golem. The golem concept developed from a strand of Jewish mystics who believed that by uttering the word of God's secret name or a combination of Hebrew letters, they could breathe life into the golem. By contrast, another branch of Jewish mysticism, following the Zohar, a thirteenth-century text that comments on the first five books in the Bible, centered on the body, on sexuality and on a loving family life (Ochs 9, 14). In *He, She and It*, these two strands of Jewish mysticism and their view of the flesh are echoed in the dynamics between Rabbi Loew and Chava and between Avram and Malkah, dynamics analogous to the archaic myths of a contract between God and Earth (Scholem 164-65). The natural functions of the body become unimportant if creation is achieved through words or thoughts. As Ochs states: "When the creator creates humans in this external way, they will necessarily be less in God's image than if they had been created from God as parent, that is from the very substance that makes God" (11). External creation may thus give rise to feelings of disconnectedness and impurity in the created. Piercy contrasts a Judeo-Christian, patriarchal cosmology with a matriarchal one, as well as contrasting the word-centered, medieval Jewish golem tradition with the body-centered Zohar-inspired mysticism at the same time as she is comparing two parenting styles: that of the coldly cerebral Avram, who is alienated both from his real and from his artificial sons, and the warm intelligence of Malkah; the chilly disconnectedness of Josh and the ardent connectedness of Shira; Rabbi Loew (who is an eagle, HSI 22) and Chava, the compassionate midwife. (Recalling Corey in *Dance the Eagle to Sleep*, Avram, significantly, chooses the heights, literally ascending to higher places from where he can look down. In situating Avram thus, Piercy associates him with patriarchal values, as high/low is a patriarchal/matriarchal cleft). *He, She and It* illustrates Ochs's thesis that "patriarchal creation 'by word' leads to the serious problems of estrangement and flawed creation without moral responsibility by the creator" (13-14). In the Bible, a patriarchal parenting style often meant judgment and conflict, even infanticide. "In matriarchy," writes Ochs, "God is a mother frantically trying to save her child. In patriarchy, God is a father who is both creator and destroyer" (23). Good works—that which can be judged and evaluated—are contrasted against faith in itself, in which Ochs sees patriarchal versus matriarchal principles.

In the Zohar, traditional Judaism was feminized, according to Carol Ochs, and elements that had been repressed were allowed to resurge. In my view, elements from the Zohar may have a bearing on *He, She and It*. As opposed to rationalistic and legalistic Judaism, the emphasis in the Zohar is more spiritual and emotional. In its analogies between the human body and God, moreover, it underlines the importance of the body, "reclaimed and exalted as a metaphor of the cosmos" (60), in a way that Ochs deems matriarchal. In the intricate pattern of the Zohar, more importantly, the fundamental balance of the scheme rests on a sexual metaphor, with different aspects being either male or female and married to each other, including even the very letters of the Bible. The objection may be raised that these generative pairs are nothing other than the usual hierarchic dichotomies of Western philosophical and theological discourse. But Ochs argues that "a sexual metaphor is matriarchal because it returns to the concept of creation from the body and not 'by word alone'" (61). Furthermore, the Zohar foregrounds the Shekinah, initially an abstract concept of God's presence, as a feminine element which "[fulfilled] the function of goddess for the Jews" (63).

In *He, She and It*, Yod is one in a series of automatons created by Avram and named for Hebrew letters. In this, too, a reference to a Zohar-inspired mysticism may be present. In the prologue to the Zohar, interestingly, there is a parade of letters, each wishing to be singled out by God as the first letter of the Bible, but each one is rejected as imperfect—just as the cyborgs preceding Yod are rejected as imperfect by their creator. The letter *tsadeh*, which is rejected in the prologue to the Zohar, in Hebrew calligraphy consists of the letter *nun*, which is female, and the letter *yod*, which is male, with these two signs turned back to back. God will divide the letter *tsadeh* and place its parts face to face: in God's reply to the letter *tsadeh*, its sign "is the mystery of the creation of the first man, who was created with two faces (male and female combined)" (Ochs 64). Through this reference, Piercy links Yod to both biblical genesis and to platonic tradition, which, as Ochs observes, held the "same view, that man was originally man-woman." According to Esther M. Shkop, "Genesis 1:27 relates that God created *ha-adam betzalmo*, male and female" (43). This image of the letter *tsadeh* brings me back to how two of the couples in Piercy's text are portrayed, explicitly or implicitly: Shira and Gadi mirror Malkah and Avram; this is underlined when both couples are likened to a serpent. Avram and Malkah are identity and difference, the harmony and the pulling apart aptly symbolized in the image of "a snake with two heads, one straining east while the head on the far end pulls west" (HSI 175). Bearing a close resemblance to the letter *tsadeh* as well as to the "holi" in *Woman on the Edge of Time* in which "the image of struggle was a male and female embracing and fighting at the same time, which resolved into an image of two androgynes" (WET 210), this image of the two-headed snake emblematizes the dynamics of Piercy's most central metaphors of separation versus connection.

The snake imagery, moreover, associates to the casting off of old skins, necessary for the connection to, and survival into, a new phase. According to

Donna Haraway, "Cyborg writing is about the power to survive. . . . In retelling origin stories, cyborg authors subvert the central myths of origin of Western culture" (175). Rewriting Mary Shelley's Frankenstein myth, then, Piercy's cyborg fantasy points to a possible resolution of the imbalance caused by the battle of the matriarchal and patriarchal elements depicted in Piercy's fiction. In the Zohar, writes Ochs, evil is "understood to be the result of a cataclysm which separated the male from the female aspects of God" (65-66). In accordance with the kabbalistic impulse that inspires *He, She and It*, "The world is imperfect and requires repair as long as any people is under the rule of any other" (HSI 315). Along with the mystical spirituality of the Zohar, too, Piercy seems to suggest that we need a balanced, double-gendered concept of God, a balanced gender dynamics: we need good works *and* faith, justice *and* mercy, a reconciliation and linking of the larger panorama of collective political action with the compassionate caring of a maternal impulse.

Chapter 12

The Longings of Women

Women's lives particularly were lived in a kind of shadow of inattention. . . .
That was her job perhaps in a sentence: making obvious to people what had
been invisible to them before.

The Longings of Women 66

In the first half of *The Longings of Women,* Piercy weaves together three
separate narrative strands which she then disentangles in the second half.
Enmeshed in intricate and invisible ways, the lives of the three characters
could be seen as what Rachel Blau du Plessis has called a cluster protagonist.
As du Plessis writes, "The collective protagonist in speculative fiction is both
formally and thematically central. These fictions replace individual heroes or
sealed couples with groups, which have a sense of purpose and identity, and
whose growth occurs in mutual collaboration" (1985 179).

The three protagonists are brought together through plot and
characterization as well as through an imagery of marginal or open spaces
juxtaposed with tropes of invisibility, dissimulation, and camouflage, which are
integral to the novel's exploration of women's encapsulation in patriarchal
codes and their methods of actualizing some measure of autonomy and
authenticity.

This novel, Piercy's most recent to date, is centered on women: on the
triple, transgenerational protagonists and their female friends, sisters, and
relatives—in particular, on Leila's mother and sister, her friend Melanie, who
dies early in the novel, her lesbian friend, Jane, and Jane's lover, Emily. This
does not mean that the male characters are insignificant or negatively
portrayed: Zak Stein, for example, with whom Leila enters a relationship, turns
out to be one of Piercy's gracious and honorable male characters. In an
involved and intimate fashion, then, the women characters' lives echo each

other, sustaining the sense of a celebration of the principle of continuity and connection so fundamental in Piercy's earlier work.

In the middle in terms of age, Leila Landsman, a forty-five-year-old writer and professor, is a specialist on battered women and incest survivors and their relationships to their children. Also from the point of view of characterization, she is the most central in Piercy's cluster protagonist. More than the other two main characters, Leila moves the most towards her own center, away from the marginality in which she is placed in her marriage to the monumental Nick Landsman, a charismatic raconteur and iconoclast who is likened to a great hunting cat. A wandering Odysseus, Nick deludes his patient Penelope that his journeys are finished and that he is permanently back in the harbor of marriage, something that in the course of the novel turns out not to be the case.

Mary Burke, the older protagonist, is homeless. Throughout the novel, her daily ordeal of finding someplace to sleep is rendered in fastidious detail. Working as a cleaning woman among whose clients are the Landsmans, she is able to sleep overnight in their houses when her employers are away, on the sly, of course, always on the alert, rehearsing escape routes if her 'hosts' return unexpectedly—which happens. Slipping in and out of houses like a ghost, Mary has to catch her sleep in the most unlikely places. Her other daily struggle is to camouflage her poverty and her homelessness and present an appearance of normality and respectability to the world. A crisis propels her out of her borderland of concealment into a different, but safer, kind of marginality.

The youngest of the trio, Becky Souza Burgess, comes from the perimeters of American society, from a hidden pocket in a neighborhood of the working poor. In the Souzas' overcrowded house in New Bedford it is hard to find solitude, and through spatial metaphors, Piercy conveys Becky's ambition to 'get out' and to find her own space. Among Becky's prized possessions, significantly, "a cigar box of treasures" (LOW 27) stands out, foreshadowing both the condo she will share with her husband, which was "empty, a box to fill with some as yet untried, unlived life" (LOW 182) and the mental, metal box in which she will hoard the pins of class insults received in the course of her tortuous journey. Becky loves her long-suffering and put-upon mother, but has no desire to replicate her fate. From the start, Becky has different plans for herself. What does self-sacrifice bring women? A question Leila answers for herself: "All her sacrificing meant was that she was home, paying the bills, and [Nick] was off in New York with Sheryl" (LOW 81). Becky finds that being "good" does not necessarily make you "a successful modern woman" (LOW 30). Her self-proposed trajectory is toward fame, light, and visibility, but this is a trip society does not want her to make. Becky, moreover, lacks real-life role models to emulate. The only models available are the buffed and fluffed women on TV and the elegant and professional aunt of a friend. When

Becky seeks role models in her men, they take advantage of her and then betray her. Through both psychology and social context, however, internal and external factors dialectically entwined, Becky's journey boomerangs into an even more constricted and enclosed space than the one she issued from.

Despite significant differences in their ages and social backgrounds, Piercy has highlighted the similarities between her three heroines, or anti-heroines, as the case may be, linking them through parallels in temperamental qualities, behavioral reactions and even formal qualifications (for example, all three women have college degrees). In their marriages, all three are deceived and abandoned, literally or mentally. In particular, they are linked through their constant probing of the rules, of how to live in patriarchy, and of how to survive through duplicity, deceit, or manipulation. Just as Mary is hiding her life on the margins behind a mask of conventionality and propriety, Becky is learning to smile even when her real reaction is a grim and cynical one, and both learn to move in the center of the acceptable and suburban in fashions and manners, scrupulously hiding past or present backgrounds of poverty. Camouflaging to the world her role as the primary breadwinner of the family, Leila also conceals to herself the inequality of her marriage. In this interplay between revelation and concealment the three characters all take on the garb of detectives *or* must deal with actual detectives themselves in the course of the novel. They either detect, and confront, the deception in their own lives or go on to create new illusions. Appearances and the hidden, truth and deception, disclosure and confrontation, are aspects of their shifting journeys.

The metaphor of invisibility as linked to the placelessness or homelessness of women is central to *The Longings of Women* and valid in the characterization of all three women. It is epitomized in Mary, who is transparent; as a child, Mary had a favorite comic book character: Invisible Scarlett O'Neill. Scarlett could slip in and out of invisibility, a very appealing state to the child Mary, who wished to slip out of the stifling atmosphere in her family in order to explore "everything hidden" (LOW 16)—like the upper-class matron in Woody Allen's movie *Alice,* who, transcending locked doors without any problems, investigates both a potential lover and her own unfaithful husband, a supernatural voyage sending her to unexpected self-discovery and independence.

An overriding theme in this novel is transgression, expressed both in imagery and narrative and in references to other works (such as *Anna Karenina* and *Oedipus Tyrannus)*. Subtly linked to a violation of boundaries not normally transcended, Mary is also linked to the transgression of Eve in her pursuit of hidden and forbidden knowledge. In the Bible, Mary and Eve are of course revered foremothers, but Eve also represents a subversive disrespect for patriarchal boundaries. Mary's surreptitious movement in and out of spaces thus ties in with the representation of transgression and the

enlargement of women's spaces that is a central theme in this novel. None of
the protagonists respect the usual boundaries limiting women's lives. In order
to realize their dreams or just to survive, they disrespectfully disregard written
or unwritten codes and laws. Apart from trespassing into people's homes
without permission, Mary also resorts to theft—in order to survive. She takes
some food from her employers' refrigerator, and an unused sleeping bag.

As a middle-aged woman, Mary has thus achieved a transgressive
invisibility: "She walked through walls. She came and went without being
seen or heard" (LOW 16). Mary's curiosity to learn about "everything hidden"
is applied toward learning everything she can about her clients, in order to
know when they might be out of town so that she can use their homes. For
purposes of her own survival, she has learned to act like a full-fledged
detective.   Constituting one of several important links between the three
women, this engagement in detective work, authorized or unauthorized, is
something Mary shares with both Leila and Becky. Leila is conducting her
own investigation into Becky and her background in researching her book.
Becky contrives to "study" the men in her life, first her boyfriend, Ted Topper,
to whose every word and intonation she harkens, then her husband-to-be, Terry
Burgess, whom she sees as a course she intends to 'ace'—at the same time as
she is offering a minimum of data about herself, thus participating in the
constitution of herself as invisible. While coveting visibility, Becky works to
cover up the 'unacceptable' aspects of her life and to fabricate a *false*
visibility. Consider, for example, her beating herself to produce an impression
of having been abused by Terry. With her husband, her 'invisibility' later
stands her in good stead when, disguised in a wig and in dark glasses, she
follows him in her car, determined to find out whether he is unfaithful; he is.
She feels like a tough, competent agent onto a major breakthrough.

Feminist psychologists (e.g., Jean Baker Miller) have discussed the
imperative of an oppressed group to study their masters precisely in this
sideways, surreptitious mode. An intimate knowledge of the dominant group
becomes a survival tool, albeit in a somewhat negative, defensive sense, but
one that allows the oppressed to find the cracks in the structures of domination
in which they can best survive. For a dominant group, it is less urgent to
comprehend the deepest fears and desires of a subordinate group. Women's
work, too, for example, is often 'invisible.' Thus, in *The Longings of Women,*
for Terry Burgess as for Nick Landsman, housework is something magically
taken care of by others, that is, by wives or domestics. Without any thoughts
about the laundry, Terry throws his dirty clothes on the floor for Becky to deal
with. Becky herself, in all her complexity, is invisible to Terry, who, when he
finally begins to see her, stares at her as if "he did not like what he saw"
(LOW 338). All of Becky's manipulations and machinations are integral to
her desire to emerge from this opacity and, through the television camera,

radiate outwards in preeminent visibility and fame. Meanwhile, she is stranded in an anteroom to television productions, wondering why no one listens when she speaks, why no one recognizes her qualities and qualifications, why they look *through* her instead of *at* her. Luck and money are the two main factors Becky is able to identify as leading to visiblity. It is Sam Solomon's *attention*, his being completely focused on her, that electrifies Becky sexually, revealing that all along her real desire has been to become visible. Significantly, both from the points of view of spatial metaphors and the invisibility trope, what Becky most of all desires is to be an *anchorwoman*.

In *The Longings of Women,* the female characters study their masters or husbands, speculating about their comportment and motivations in order to be able to plot the most successful strategies. Like the artist Sophie Calle, who took employment as a hotel maid in order to photograph people's intimate articles or rubbish, Mary snoops around her clients' houses in order to be cognizant of the darker secrets of 'her' families, of the shadow fantasies family members keep, even from each other. Prying loose the less presentable angles hidden behind the respectable public personae, she gains an edge of superiority, since she knows vastly more about her masters than they will ever know about her. Purposely aiming to maintain that balance, Mary makes herself seem simpler than she is, and has been so successful in her dissembling that Leila pictures Mary's life as utterly and unimaginatively staid and conventional. Mary is invisible even to her own son and daughter, who have no idea of how their mother is living her life: neither of them has fathomed that she is homeless. Her work, too, is invisible. Nick Landsman, for example, appears both oblivious to the fact that running a household means housework and ignorant of who does that work. Coming upon Mary mopping the kitchen floor, he looks at her in amazement, wondering who she is. Mary, who thinks of Nick Landsman as "the master" (LOW 87), realizes that "she wasn't real to him" (LOW 83).

Tied in with the metaphors of invisibility, homelessness and the clandestine are the spatial metaphors of place and space, of marginality and mobility, all of which are integral to the motif of transgression of accepted codes or boundaries. In *Space and Place: The Perspective of Experience,* Yi Fu Tuan makes a tentative definition of the relationship between place and space: "Place is security, space is freedom: we are attached to the one and long for the other" (3). Whereas place can be experienced in a more literal, concrete way, space is more abstract: "What begins as undifferentiated space becomes place as we get to know it better and endow it with value" (6). For Tuan, place is "a pause in movement" (138). Place is associated with comfort and security, space with the threatening and alluring wastes of the unknown, that which, in Tuan's words, "invites action" and "suggests the future" (54). Interestingly, "A root meaning of the word 'bad' is 'open.' To be open and free is to be exposed and vulnerable." Accordingly, when Becky's life has derailed from its normal ruts, she feels that "she had plunged into open space, dangers, pleasures, the exciting and terrifying sense that she could do anything whatsoever" (LOW 313).

The idea of a place of one's own is important both in Piercy's work and *for* her work, "for it was only after her family moved to a house where the 15-year-old finally had her own room with a door that Piercy wrote her first poem. And it was then that she decided to become a writer" (Fredette 269). Houses are significant symbols in *The Longings of Women,* recalling in particular Piercy's 1984 novel, *Fly Away Home.* In what Christine Sizemore has called Piercy's "two urban novels," Piercy deals specifically with "the question whether women can create feminine spaces, places for themselves within the city" (90). In *The Longings of Women,* women are houses or rooms—as when Becky sums up her place in Ted Topper's life: "She was a rented motel room outside the house of his life" (LOW 301), an image that well captures both the transience and the marginality of her position. The characters' lives are visualized through images of rooms and spaces and the condition of spaces. Mary sees the interiors of her woman clients' houses as barometers of their mental states, and Leila is likened to a caryatid, "a Greek woman holding up a building, a woman in the form of a structural column" (LOW 174). Leila is hence part of a group of stone women with a burden to bear. Leila is, in fact, an imposing woman, towering and buxom: seeing herself on videotape she even feels that she is "[taking] up too much space" (LOW 35). All three women, in fact, are caryatids, female columns supporting their metaphoric entablatures in diverse ways but with an inescapable ambiguity: while the remembrance of the original caryatids, the women from Carya ravished by the Greeks and thrown into captivity as slaves, casts a claustrophobic and oppressive tinge onto Piercy's analogy, in the eighteenth-century, caryatids or *herms* recurred as chimney pieces bracketing the hearth, symbolic guardians of home and warmth—an image associating to Piercy's celebration of a maternal principle of caring and connection.

As reiterated in feminist literary criticism, houses are often extraordinarily meaningful symbols in literature by women. Piercy's rendering of women's lives as houses recalls some passages in Doris Lessing's *A Ripple from the Storm* and *Landlocked,* as discussed by Eleanor Wikborg. In *A Ripple from the Storm,* the heroine perceives the loss of a relationship with a man as producing an "empty space," a space that has been and will be formed by whoever she is involved with (see Wikborg 388). In this passage, the man emerges as an architect, one whose conception 'creates' the woman in making the fragments of her self coalesce, and who thus represents active intelligence and presence, while the woman is *mater,* or materia, passivity and absence. In *Landlocked,* the heroine visualizes herself as a house with many rooms,

rooms that are her different roles or selves. Paralleling the "empty space" image in *A Ripple from the Storm*, here is an "empty lit space," a symbolic center of the symbolic house that is the woman. The man's role is still that of architect, of someone who will "unify her elements" and who "would be like a roof, or like a fire burning in the centre of the empty space" (as quoted by Wikborg 389). The man is thus expected to be both provider and head of the household at the same time as he is the agent in charge of kindling female sexuality.

In the Landsmans' house in *The Longings of Women,* it is not Nick, but Leila who has been the main provider, yet her vision of their marriage resembles Lessing's picture of marriage as a house, confirming the image while inverting it. Leila as house has been structured around Nick, constituting the margins of his center. Contradictorily, her role is "central but partial" (LOW 9). As a supportive wife, Leila deems it her duty to keep Nick in good health and good humor. Much like Vida serving Leigh in Piercy's earlier novel, *Vida,* Leila carefully prepares an enticing breakfast tray for Nick. From the start, their marriage has been constructed upon the unequal premise that Nick needs his freedom and that she can never have all of him. A bonus is, perhaps, that Nick's frequent absences gives Leila the time to pursue close friendships with women, something that many women, in her experience, must relinquish after marrying. Financially, of course, Leila is the main breadwinner, a fact that needs to be concealed for fear of publicly humiliating Nick. As in some of Piercy's earlier fiction, notably *Summer People,* illusion and denial are contrasted against the pursuit of truth and knowledge, whether objectively and solidly or subjectively and precariously assembled. At the beginning of the novel, Leila is diligently constructing reasonable, perfectly plausible explanations for Nick's conduct: for why he has not returned her phone calls while working on a stage production in New York, and for his abrupt termination of a phone call when she steps in the door: she tells herself that he hangs up because he is so impatient to see her! Nick *has* been notoriously unfaithful for years, but recently he and Leila have been striving for a 'new' marriage, excluding out-of-town romances. However, Leila's denial does not persist, and even before overhearing that Nick's actress girlfriend (who is half his age) is pregnant, her presentiment has pointed to the liaison. Their marital crisis leads to the discovery that Leila has built a center in herself after all, a pivot reaching out to her relatives, friends, colleagues, and even her cat, wryly named Vronsky. Toward the end, Leila thinks: "I want to stretch out and fill my own space" (LOW 391). At the end, she has a house of her own, less elegant perhaps than the one she has shared with Nick, and the ground floor of which she has to rent out, yet literally and figuratively a space of her own.

Mary Burke's whole existence revolves around the lack of a home. Haunted by a sense of marginality, of being an outcast bearing a secret but always agonizing stigma of failure, she resembles Vida, who is constantly on the run. According to an interview in *Publishers Weekly,* Piercy wanted her earlier heroine's "experiences as a fugitive to serve as a metaphorical parallel for 'the way all women feel like fugitives'" (Dong 19). Like a fugitive, Mary dwells in borrowed spaces, in basements, in sites of transience such as Logan Airport or the malls. As a teenager, Becky, too, seeks the peace and solitude of the malls. In *Discrimination by Design,* architect Leslie Weisman writes that "the shopping mall is one of the few public spaces, in our age-segregated society, where older people and younger people can see each other, since they are the two groups who most regularly use the mall for social purposes" (45). The architectural introversion of the mall can be compared to the courtyard house depicted in *He, She and It.* Both the mall and the courtyard are interior worlds, which, as sheltering enclosures, resemble the womb: the mall is one of the rare spots in which Mary can rest. Yet the mall is a less positive image than the courtyard house. An icon of profit-minded commercialism, the mall, "the quintessential embodiment of patriarchal dichotomies," is a "racially and economically homogeneous, culturally arid [environment]" (4). For many Americans, the mall is practically the only public space still available in a car-oriented society, yet it is anything but a public space. Privately owned, it is a rigorously, virtually scientifically controlled milieu, whose primary purpose is to sell merchandise.

Only temporarily does Mary arrogate a space of her own, together with a bag lady, Beverly Bozeman, and two street characters, Houdini and Mouse. Moving into a rat-infested, abandoned building, implausibly, feels like regaining "a place of [their] own" (LOW 324). Ironically, only in this dangerous, shadowy territory, which will be exploited by drug dealers and other criminals, will Mary, originally a middle-class woman stemming from *Centralia* and *Normal,* Illinois (actual places), find real connection and real bonds. From this site a reversal occurs, in which Mary and her bag lady friend define themselves as selves in their own right and see people from the wealthy mainstream, those wealthy enough to afford cleaning ladies, as "the Others, the people with homes" (LOW 326). Their new home is appropriately named "Houdini's Ritz," Houdini being the man who found the squat, indicating both the unexpected comforts and the transience of marginality. In the core of placelessness, Mary finds a home: "Staying here was flirting with life outside the pale, life on the streets, yet she had not felt so at-home with anyone in years" (LOW 347). Horribly, Houdini's Ritz is burned down, but this leads to positive change for Mary. She is able to escape, since the doors are not locked: perhaps a suggestion that patriarchal structures are neither monolithic nor impenetrable. A recurring and ambiguous symbol in Piercy's work, fire is negatively destructive at the same time as it shrivels down deceit and lies, clearing the way toward a different construction of knowledge, even though it might be of an inadmissible kind. After the fire that consumes "Houdini's Ritz," Leila becomes a detective, trying to piece together Mary's real situation—strongly motivated, of course, by the fact that Mary, seriously ill after the fire, has collapsed in Leila's bed, thus invading Leila's own sanctuary. A newspaper article puts Leila onto the truth about Mary's "invisible home" (LOW 369), which will subsequently cave in, because for Mary, Leila's knowledge makes her feel as if "the whole card house of her life had collapsed" (LOW 371).

However, when dreaming of spaces of their own, neither Mary nor Beverly fantasize about houses anchored in one, safe spot. Mary's reveries revolve around the idea of having a secondhand car, a symbol Piercy invests with both a sense of connection and continuity (since the car is second- or thirdhand) and the suggestion of an equilibrium between the attractions of space and the amenities of place: a car is both a safer place for Mary to sleep in *and* a vehicle of mobility, opening up possibilities of exploring other spaces. "What she dreamed about was much more elemental: to have a place, even a movable place like an old car, that she could call home" (LOW 376). Similarly fusing spatial mobility and the comforts of place, Beverly's ideal site, palatial to Beverly, who has no home, is "one of them mobile homes. . . . Winnebagos, they call them" (LOW 345). For Mary, a car would be a shell, like that of a snail (LOW 189). In *Small Changes,* a turtle was a significant symbol for the painstakingly slow progress of individual and collective consciousnessraising, here the snail similarly represents slow mobility, progress and survival. Although all three women in *The Longings of Women* cherish the idea of the house and are likened to rooms or houses, this sense of place does not imply stasis but rather something like what James Clifford has called "dwelling-in-travel" (108). In a Heraclitian vein, Leila, for example, tells her husband, who likes the idea of travel that always allows him to return to his wife: "But I don't stay in the same place. I'm not exactly the same river you step in" (LOW 143). In *Anna Karenina,* which looms over *The Longings of Women,* husbands and lovers move about freely, asserting their "masculine independence" while the women are confined to their domestic spaces. In the Tolstoy novel when Anna leaves her husband for Vronsky, her space becomes even more constricted, while Count Vronsky's mobility remains unimpeded. While Anna initially moves without encumbrance between towns, houses, and salons, her disgrace increasingly encloses her in a salon, albeit an elegant one. In the final passage, significantly, Anna exits her claustrophobic chambers, driving recklessly about on the streets of Moscow, moving toward her suicide, the almost inevitable result of *her* longing for independence and freedom.

For Becky, who has grown up in the overcrowded house of a poor family, success and happiness seem encapsulated in the idea of a spacious, well-appointed home of her own. Briefly, she is able to enjoy the condo she shares with her husband, purchased with the help of his parents but the maintenance for which Becky has to shoulder after Terry has been laid off. This house develops into *the* central focus of her life, possessing and luxuriating in this condo becoming a life-and-death issue for her, overruling all other passions. Both rebelling against and buying into the American dream of material success, moreover, Becky is entirely taken in by, while reluctantly taken into, the spaces created by the bourgeois Burgesses, who are buttressed by codes of supremacy and living a kind of immutable order and flawlessness approaching sterility. Constantly snubbed by her mother-in-law, Becky, Pandora-like, puts away "All those insults and innuendoes . . . like pins in a metal box, for the time they would be needed" (LOW 178); focusing on a future time when she will secure her revenge. Place is seen by Becky, as by Leila and Mary, as supremely empowering, as a springboard from which to plunge, benevolently or maliciously. Even Debbie, Leila's impetuous and disorganized sister, essentially elects her home before her husband: "When it came to choosing between him and this place, I want this place" (LOW 356)—just as Becky at one point ponders the "truth" "that she wanted the condo far more than she wanted him" (LOW 357). Consequently, Becky's worst nightmares are dreams of being abandoned by Terry, the worst aspect of which is the loss of her house which he has taken with him while she walks around in miserable and futile search for it—dreams that foreshadow the end in which she in fact does lose her home. Sentenced for the murder of her husband, Becky finishes in a very small space; she will be "stuck in a box" (LOW 439). As she is incarcerated in the House of Correction, a deathly sense of enclosure descends on Becky: "Those metal grates closing made a definite and terrible sound, like fate" (LOW 427)—an enclosure that alters her sense of time: "Time passed like the growth of an oak. Time halted, spread out stagnant, glazed over, froze to the bottom. Time dripped on her closed eyes" (LOW 440).

Like caryatids and snails, all three women 'carry' the houses they inhabit, Becky and Leila taking care of the maintenance of their houses and Mary managing the houses of her clients. While Leila is forced to move after her divorce from Nick, she finds a different, more liberating home of her own, and Mary, too, gains a home in the end, as live-in help to Leila's pregnant sister, Debbie.

For the major part of the narrative, Mary is one of the homeless. In creating the character of Mary, Piercy seems to build on a very minor figure in her first novel, *Going Down Fast,* an old woman who has been evicted but who clings to her home, "barnacle-like," despite the cut-off electricity, gas, and heat, a woman who is like "a greatgrandmother, outliving her children, forgotten by her descendants. In the daytime she crouched at a window with cracks stuffed with rags, looking out at the busy street" (GDF 60). This figure resurfaces both in Mary Burke and in her even worse-off friend and 'other,' Beverly Bozeman, a bag lady who dies in the fire. Homelessness is a central issue in *The Longings of Women,* and in the end, influenced by what she has learned from Mary, Leila becomes a champion of the homeless, in particular of homeless women. That Mary, despite her education, willingness and ability to work, cannot afford a roof over her head and can expect no help or even sympathy from society, is a terrible indictment of the extreme individualism and class inequities of American society, even though the picture of the homeless, as seen through Leila's eyes and, in part, through the presentation of Mary, may be somewhat simplified. The homeless women are presented as 'ordinary,' middle-class women, in Mary's case, with a college degree, who, through no fault of their own but because of deserting husbands or through urban renewal or condoizations have lost their own homes and who lack the sizable sum demanded for an initial investment in a new house. There may also be other sociocultural parameters to the representation of homelessness. While blameless and luckless individuals certainly enter into the picture, Myron Magnet says in *The Dream and the Nightmare* that "40 percent of the homeless have done jail time" (101) and that the majority of the the rest of the homeless are mental patients who should not be out in the streets; "a recent, authoritative psychiatric study of the homeless in Baltimore found that almost half the women and 42 percent of the men suffered from a major mental disorder. . . . Two thirds of the New York homeless who live on the streets, rather than in the shelters, are schizophrenic, another study found" (82). In Magnet's view, the mentally ill have been and are still released thanks to effects of a 1960s counterculture ideology steeped in the ideas of Thomas Szasz, Ervin Goffman, and R.D. Laing, who erroneously perceived mental illness as either mythic or as the *result* of, not the reason for, being in mental hospital, ideas leading to the disastrous conclusion that the mentally ill ought not to be institutionalized (83-96).

To be sure, in *The Longings of Women* homelessness in not only a reality but a metaphor for women's condition. As long as women's homelessness is invisible, homeless women dwell in a borderland zone with society's outsiders, outside all protection of the law. Mary comes to the conclusion that "the homeless were either invisible in their expected hangouts, or stridently visible if they appeared beyond their grates and doorways" (LOW 344), an insight that can be related to Becky's discovery of how she is looked askance on after transgressing the codifications upheld by her husband and his social milieu. Blending metaphors of space and mobility with the invisibility trope, Piercy shows how women's transgressions rendered visible appear intolerable and threatening.

Part and parcel of the spatial imagery suggesting a transgression or erosion of boundaries is the exploration in *The Longings of Women* of female anger and violence. Anger against men erupts here and there throughout Piercy's work. Notable are the lines from her poem "What's that smell in the kitchen?" from the section entitled "Mrs. Frankenstein's Diary" in *Stone, Paper, Knife*. In *Woman on the Edge of Time*, in which novel, according to Rachel Blau du Plessis, "Piercy shows how politicized anger becomes the final outpost that hegemonic society attempts to colonize" (1985 185), Connie is imprisoned in a mental hospital because of her alleged violence, while the violence done to her is overlooked. In *Braided Lives*, Jill's childhood friend, Callie, receives a life sentence after killing her husband, a policeman, when he had pushed their daughter down the stairs. In *The Longings of Women*, similarly, a reference is made to a woman who killed her husband when he was beating their daughter. In Piercy's work, female violence is not condoned or exculpated but explored with the view of understanding it. Anger, and thoughts of or acts of violence against men who exploit, abandon, or betray, is one of the crucial links between the female characters in *The Longings of Women*. Even the apparently placid Mrs. Burgess, Terry's mother, is smoldering with a rage that cannot be spoken, projected at Becky, whom she finds a totally unsuitable match for her son. Perhaps Mrs. Burgess's rage stems in part from the restraints imposed on her by her husband's heart disease. He needs to be protected from strong emotions and upheavals, and it is Mrs. Burgess's duty to form a protective and concealing wall between her husband and the real world. In this sense, the walled-in persona of Mrs. Burgess, whose cover-ups echo those of Mary and Becky, can be linked to the mall metaphor.

The three main characters all deal with anger differently, ranging from an indulgence in vengeful fantasies to explosions of rage and even to murder. Several details in the novel, such as the manner in which the characters are linked, suggest that these reactions inhabit the same spectrum, simply placed at more or less extreme points. Leila becomes linked to Becky when she decides to write a book about Becky and her crime, the murder of a husband. Interestingly, Leila's decision to take on this book is fueled by her wish to be less of a victim herself and to direct her pain outward instead of being consumed by it. Furthermore, Leila and Becky are linked through the symbol of the vase: just as Leila actually throws a vase at Nick, so Becky relishes a *fantasy* of smashing a vase over Terry's head. While Mary has not committed any violent crimes, she has resorted to petty larceny and to an illicit trespassing into other people's homes. She, too, has fantasized about violent retaliation: "Thinking of doing violence to someone who was hurting you could be soothing, in a minor way. She remembered daydreaming about poisoning Jim [her ex-husband]" (LOW 43).

All three women have thus harbored an explosive rage toward and fantasies of killing their husbands, and one of them will actually realize her fancy. On one level a reference to Tolstoy's *Anna Karenina, The Longings of Women* challenges the masculinist ideology described in such a masterly way through metaphors of mobility and stasis in that novel. *The Longings of Women* explores themes of betrayal and vengeance, contrasting the effects of internalizing versus externalizing one's anger, in particular, an anger and resentment at a self-asserted "masculine independence" of unlimited mobility that presupposes feminine confinement. The reason Anna Karenina is so dangerous is her suppressed but flammable fury, first her animosity at the temporarily heroic but otherwise limited Karenin, then her increasing anger, when the all-consuming passion is spent, at Vronsky for not offering the transformation she had hoped but rather an equally stultifying existence. While Anna Karenina suppresses and internalizes her anger until its toxins make her suicidal, Becky instead externalizes her anger and murders her husband. In fact, Becky's anger is so externalized as to lead to a total disavowal of her own accountability.

Leila, early on, tells her lover, Zak: "I have trouble with anger. I just sit on it like a big hot egg" (LOW 241). It is not only the fact of Nick's infidelity that finally makes her explode, but the immaturity, self-indulgence, and unfairness he discloses in his attempts to project the guilt on Leila by blaming his affairs on his lonesomeness or on his insecurity while away on tours. He reproaches her for not being flexible, generous, and understanding enough as a wife—as if she has not exhibited all those qualities to a fault during the years of his philandering. When Nick solicits her approval for his not abandoning a pregnant girl-friend, "she realized that the thing in her, the force that was rising like hot thick liquid, like lava in her body, rising up to her brain, was rage" (LOW 241). This is when she grasps a vase and hurls it at her husband, who, shocked and drenched in flowers and water, thinks that she could have killed him—yet seems compelled to diminish her outburst by comparing it to a child's temper tantrum. Quite literally, through her breaking the vase, Leila's boiling rage collapses the boundaries that, in place throughout her marriage to Nick, have prohibited a ventilation of her anger at his perpetual philandering. Symbolically, Leila's anger is linked to the murderous wrath of Becky, since Leila now better understands women who are driven to violence by male abuse, a category of violence she perceives as a kind of self-defense.

For Becky, in like manner, it is infidelity, as linked to the threat of her losing her home, that feeds her glowing resentment. Her very survival seems at stake, when Terry no longer desires her and comes to adopt his mother's point of view, that Becky's and his class backgrounds are irreconcilable. Analogously, in *Anna Karenina,* society's hypocritical disapprobation and ostracization is transmitted to Vronsky through his mother. A very basic sense of powerlessness fuels Becky's fantasies of fatal accidents befalling both men who have betrayed her, first Ted Topper, then Terry Burgess.

The murder of Terry Burgess is recapitulated in graphic and gruesome detail, resembling scenes from Helen Zahavi's *The Weekend* (1991). Bella, Zahavi's heroine, chooses a hammer for her first deed of retaliation against the perverted aggressor who has invaded her peace and threatened to intrude into her home. Choosing neither flight through escape or suicide nor passive endurance and suffering, as so many of their precursors in literature have done, Bella and Becky both choose revenge, thus transgressing the boundaries of both written laws and unwritten stipulations as to how a woman may behave. As for Bella's demands, they are fairly simple:

> What Bella wants. What Bella wants is what she can't have. What she wants is open windows on summer nights. Lone walks along the shore. No fear of the motorway breakdown. No terror of the dark. No horror of the gang. No comments in the street. No furtive touchings on the Tube. No more stroking their egos for fear of the fist in the face, the broken nose, the blood and snot running into her mouth. Bella was born free and is everywhere in chains. (Zahavi 72-73)

Male savagery against women is omnipresent. In *The Longings of Women,* the assault on and stabbing of Beverly Bozeman, whose body, in incident also echoing a passage in *The Weekend*, is pushed into a dumpster is a reminder of women's physical vulnerability, occurring just a few blocks from Leila's house. The main novelty in *The Weekend,* indeed, is the explicit female violence against men. Had the protagonist been a man who responded thus to threats of brutality against his person, it would not have caused the stir that this novel did, since such novels abound. Neither does male violence against women, common as it is in literature and in life, provoke any censure approaching that which has befallen Zahavi's novel. Female anger in general and female violence in particular have indeed been taboo subjects in literature until quite recently. Marilyn French writes in the *Women's Review of Books* (July 1991):

> Until the last five years, films never showed females in groups attacking males. While the recent *Thelma and Louise* sympathetically shows two women pushed by male predation into a binge of violence, they are ultimately defeated, and the film has aroused considerable male outrage. An Australian film of a few years back, *Shame,* showed a righteous white woman taking vengeance on white male rapists. It was barely reviewed and within a few weeks disappeared from the single movie house in New York that showed it. The same treatment is accorded the brilliant films of Dutch film-maker Marlene Gorris, *A Question of Silence* (which depicts women killing a man

seemingly for no reason) and *The Broken Mirror* (which depicts male predation on women). Women writers are careful to avoid what is called "male-bashing"—which simply means blaming men as a group for their real acts. (4)

Not surprisingly, since men have been very quick to decry any type of reverse discrimination, John Leo in *U. S. News & World Report* (April 26, 1993), for example, cautions his readers to look out for what he calls "the race-and-gender people," whose "doctrine is that America will increasingly be divided by a truculent tribalism, with nonwhites and white women ganging up in a grand alliance to wrest power from white males." Leo vociferates: "Attention, men of the Caucasoid persuasion. Have you made a terrible mistake by being born white males?"

Perhaps John Leo's fears are warranted. In the mid-nineties, Piercy is right on target in her exploration of female anger and violence. According to FBI statistics, female violence is on the rise: "The number of women involved in violent crimes including murder, robbery and aggravated assault jumped 62 percent from 1981 to 1990" (Claude Lewis K-4). In 1991, America could even boast its "first known female serial killer."

In *The Longings of Women*, Becky lets Sam, her lover, wield a hammer, while she swings a golf club at her husband. Becky "stood up and hit him with all her strength" (LOW 378). Her participation in the brutal murder is for Leila hard to comprehend: "Becky was small. Her bones seemed as fine as those of a fish. This was the woman supposed to have beaten to death a husband described as six feet tall and an avid skier and golfer and squash player?" (LOW 35). In *The Weekend,* similarly, we learn that "Even Bella, even brittle little Bella, can lift a hammer. Even she can hold it in her hands, and swing it high, and bring it down" (Zahavi 58). In Zahavi's novel, in particular, female violence is depicted with a certain relish, which comes from the gratification of securing a space both individual and collective that has been threatened or violated. "She hammered her message home the only way she could. She bludgeoned him for all her silent sisters" (60). To men who molest, rape and kill women, Bella has a warning:

> If you see a woman walking, if she's stepping quietly home, if you see her flowing past you on the pavement. If you'd like to break her brittle bones, and you want to hear the hopeless pleading, and you want to feel the pink flesh bruising, and you want to taste the taut skin bleeding.
> If, in fact, you see her and you want her.
> Think on. Don't touch her. Just let her pass you by. Don't place your palm across her mouth and drag her to the ground.
> For unknowingly, unthinkingly, unwittingly you might have laid your heavy hand on Bella. And she's woken up this morning with the knowledge that she's finally had enough. (187)

In both novels, the violence of Bella and Becky arises from a wrath at the trespassing of their territories. They both respond by transgressing a boundary most women would never cross, yet one that many are able to sympathize with: among her fellow inmates, Becky is told that her crime is no big deal. "Not one of us didn't think of that some time. You did it" (LOW 431). A neighbor comments: "'She's a good woman. A good wife,' Helen said bluntly, of a woman she must suspect killed her husband" (LOW 551). Piercy manages to show how Becky is catapulted into murder both because of her own psychology and due to external factors ranging from social class to chance occurrences. Zahavi's heroine is both much more aware of what she is doing and more rational in that most of her victims are violent, criminal characters who do not deserve to continue their horrific abuse of women. Becky's actions, by contrast, are less defensible, since her life is not threatened, although, in her own interpretation it is. For her, having to return to a life of poverty and lack of opportunities represents a kind of death.

Becky's development is convincingly rendered in its almost imperceptible slide toward lawlessness. Just where does she cross the line? Intimations of a vengeful personality hidden behind a girlish mask are discernible in her reaction to Ted Topper's betrayal, when Becky visualizes, in minute detail, the violence she would do to him if she could. Inverting the hierarchy that ruled their relationship, she sees herself as a Roman aristocrat enjoying Ted Topper's being "hacked up" (LOW 93) and dying in the claustrophobically enclosed space of the arena.

Who, or what, is propelling Becky's crime? One important aspect fueling her vision of revenge is her own sense of powerlessness and ostracization. Her increasing despair at being able to defend 'her own space' in the form of the condo as well as of creating her own space professionally (so as to achieve the visibility and money to buy a place really her own) escalates into murderous rage. Had she not felt the threat, expressed in her nightmares, of being turned out on the street or shoved back where she came from—an unthinkable prospect—the murder would never have been planned or executed. Society, in the shape of Mrs. Burgess, is co-responsible for the outcome: a society that, while proffering the American dream as a possibility within any capable individual's reach, peremptorily bars access to some of its members, not through physical obstruction but through the psychological harassment of class insult. For Becky, the affront also acquires a tinge of gender insult when Terry tells her that she and her whole family smell of fish (LOW 322). Consistently, Becky is associated with the ocean and with fish; Leila, for example, musing that "her bones seemed as fine as those of a fish" (LOW 35), and, when watching Becky on television, observing that "more and more details effloresced like plankton in the light of the TV moon" (LOW 35). Relying upon Sandor Ferenczi, Camille Paglia has asserted in an interview that "there's an ancient analogy between the smell of marine life and the female genitals," and that "the substance in decaying fish is the actual chemical in female genital secretions" (see Kalbach 133). The juxtaposition of symbols in *The Longings of Women* reinforce an association of Becky with the mythical Pandora. Like Pandora, Becky is connected with boxes which are increasingly receptacles of misery and evil waiting to be uncovered. Also, Becky is linked to the 'fishy' aspects of the sea. These two strains of symbolism come together in a drawing by Paul Klee from 1920, *Die Büchse der Pandora als Stilleben*, in which Pandora's box (originally a jar) "is rendered as a kantharos-shaped vase containing some flowers but emitting evil vapors from an opening clearly suggestive of the female genitals" (Panofsky 113). In my view, Klee's drawing could also be interpreted as a distorted face of a woman which is simultaneously an image of the female reproductive organs. Klee's drawing thus powerfully echoes a whole complex of related themes in Piercy's novel.

The Burgesses, who see Becky as a vixen, are bent on blocking out everything she represents. Spatially rendered, their very bearing is "pinched and tight" (LOW 166). They barricade themselves behind a wall of codes concerning speech, dress, and demeanor, a chilly response that only adds to Becky's sense of a grievance she needs to correct, and if impossible to amend, to take revenge upon. As Leila phrases it: "[Becky's] anger finally loosed itself. Women were often terrified to let their anger out, for fear it would destroy everything. Usually it did no more than break a dish. Becky had been different. For being a woman who had used up her husband with no more regard or remorse than men frequently showed towards women, she had removed herself from the circle of women into infamy" (LOW 454).

Leila suggests that "Perhaps it takes only a certain lack of imagination, of empathy, to kill a person" (LOW 251). Through her crime, Becky has "removed herself from the circle of women" (LOW 454), she has flung herself outside a pattern of reciprocity and affiliation and ended up in a cramped and constricted space that is the very opposite of her dreams. Unlike Mary and Leila, Becky has cut herself off from a female principle, alienating herself from her female co-workers and from Leila, whom she in the end, in utter disapproval, refuses to talk to. Indeed, Becky appears to be increasingly marked by a phallic identification, as when she wants to *be* Terry: "she wanted to melt into his side, the rib given back" (LOW 163). If Mary and Leila, then, are transgressing patriarchal spaces and in varying degrees toiling to establish their own, Becky sinks into the chilly womb of detention that is the prison cell.

At the end, we may visualize the fates of the three women as placed inside an upside-down triangle without any clear-cut, insurmountable borders, but with Mary and Leila inhabiting the larger spaces at the top, and Becky squeezed into the small point at the bottom. Leila and Mary have managed to create their own bases or centers radiating outward toward, and supported by, a web of friendships and work. For them, as the novel closes, a new life is commencing.

Conclusion

> Together we are the rose, full, red as the inside
> of the womb and head of the penis,
> blossoming as we encircle, we make that symmetrical
>   fragrant emblem,
> then separate into discrete workday selves.
>   Marge Piercy, "Doing it differently," *Circles on the Water*

In an almost Tolstoyan passage in *Gone to Soldiers*, the elusiveness inherent in the process of creating art is rendered in Jeff Coates's musing (recalling the artist Mikhailov in *Anna Karenina*): "In order to paint well he had to abandon control. Everything constantly changed before him and everything moved and he stood in a swirl of chaos and humbly addressed it . . . All he could ever paint was a tiny flash of what truly showed itself to him, a seizure on one moment" (GTS 58). Whatever the authorial intentions, however, as finished products in circulation, an author's books may be used and interpreted in a multitude of ways, as expressed in the poem "Your cats are your children" (from *My Mother's Body*), in which Piercy's view of her cats merges with a vision of her books:

> Then they march off into the world
> to be misunderstood, mistreated, stolen,
> to be loved for the wrong reasons,
> to be fondled, beaten, lost.

Marge Piercy's novelistic panorama spans several centuries and decades, from the seventeenth century and into the future, encompassing the terrors and indignities of World War II, the Freudian and functionalist credos of the 1950s and 1960s, the 1970s counterculture reaction followed by the ambivalent 1980s and by the even more uncertain future of the twenty-first century. Central questions throughout Piercy's temporal and spatial panorama concern power as struggled over in various sites: in the marital dyad, in the construction of male and female sexuality, in what are euphemistically called urban renewal programs, and in questions of women's reproductive freedom with the issue of legal abortion high on the agenda.

Freud saw a fundamental conflict between eros and thanatos, that is, a principle of generation and reproduction versus the cutting off of a death principle, depending, of course, upon how we see death, as an irreversible vanishing or as reversibility, transformation, and rebirth in a different shape. While patriarchal Christianity has focused on the Cross, which is what kills, the matriarchal Eleusinian mysteries focused on the pomegranate seed (Ochs 21-22). Despite both obvious and subtle changes in narrative outlook and form from Marge Piercy's first published novel to her most recent, the commitment has been to the pomegranate seed: to the maternal metaphor, or the impulse of stitching together and repairing, to *tikkun*, "the process of cosmic restoration and reintegration" (Scholem 1974 140). "In all of Piercy's social fiction," writes Carol Farley Kessler, "a nurturing community, either implicitly or explicitly, is necessary for the emergence of what she considers to be the best in human potential—behavior both responsive to group needs and assertive of individual rights" (196).

Diane Freedman has pointed out that "the vocabulary of both quilting and gardening clearly crops up throughout Piercy's corpus and her commentary on it" (153). Piercy's title for her collection of critical essays and interviews, *Parti-Colored Blocks for a Quilt*, evokes an image of her writings as a whole, as does her poem "Looking at quilts" (in *Circles on the Water*): a quilt is, indeed, an appropriate metaphor for her texts. Formally, her fiction is marked by both contradiction and cohesion. Thematically, however, I find it remarkably cohesive. All of Piercy's prose works propose solutions to issues of urgency, as do her "utopian" scenarios, even though many questions and tensions are left unresolved. Yet, despite these tensions, contradictions, and questions left hanging, one may perceive certain characteristic responses, certain constants, throughout her work. Marge Piercy's commitment to a redressing of social grievances and to a vindication of the rights of all oppressed is a scarlet thread woven through her texts. The decoding of cultural constructions of power and powerlessness, in all forms and as they intersect with issues of ethnicity and class, pervade her oeuvre. As a part of the theme of a maternal principle in Piercy's work are frequently occurring maternal metaphors. References to pregnancies, literal or metaphorical, in imagery as well as in the titles of some of her poems, such as "The maternal instinct at work" and "Magic Mama" (from *My Mother's Body*), are significant. In the beautiful poem "Going Into the Storm," the lyrical personae "stagger out of the belly of the snow/ plucked of words naked and steaming" (from *My Mother's Body*; also in *The Earth Shines Secretly*). In "Hot, Hotter" (in *Mars and Her Children*; also in *The Earth Shines Secretly*),

> The world is a womb, hot and wet
> and laboring to be delivered of August,
> panting, gasping in the fever of afternoon,
> sizzling night sweats and poached mornings.

In "Your cats are your children" (in *My Mother's Body*), Piercy looks at writing itself as a maternity:

> My children are my books
> that I gestate for years,
> a slow-witted elephant
> eternally pregnant, books
> that I sit on for eras like the great
> auk on a vast marble egg.

In *Woman on the Edge of Time*, according to Libby Falk Jones, the birth and rebirth imagery can be "self-distortion," as with "Connie carried in the belly of the bus to the madhouse," but it can also be self-generation and "a re-creation of self . . . as in Connie's dream of comothering in the future world" (124). Part of the maternal metaphor are also references to and the imagery pertaining to the earth and the ocean, so ubiquitously present in Piercy's work. In many cosmogonic myths, the earth is born out of the sea, as, for example, the raising of Mount Ararat. As explained by Sandor Ferenczi in *Thalassa: A Theory of Genitality*, the maternal body is often symbolized by the sea in dreams and in neurosis, the sea symbolism being of a more archaic, primitive character, while the earth symbolism stems from a later evolutionary period (47). Ferenczi writes that "certainly the psychoanalytic day's work supplies gross examples of regression to the mother symbolism of earth or of water" (48)—not surprisingly, since, according to Ferenczi, from birth onwards, we carry the wish to regress to the womb, or to "the reestablishment of the intrauterine situation," as he puts it (20).

The maternal metaphor, then, is part and parcel of the most urgent themes in Piercy's fiction, a closer look at which reveals that a major tension in her work is between 'feminine' and 'masculine' principles, not as innate, essential qualities but as clusters of characteristics such as they have been constructed throughout history, sites from which a dichotomy between a principle of separation and a principle of connection stem. Piercy does not imply that these are genetically or hormonally caused characteristics; if anything, her explication is a cultural-constructionist one, as shown in a quote from "Me and

My Novel" where she states that "as long as women are given as part of our common daily work the emotional labor, the work of understanding, making the social glue stick, nurturing, socializing, comforting, negotiating, balancing, then we will have to understand men better than they have to understand us" (19). Of the 1950s she writes: "Mutually exclusive sex roles divided humanity into winners and losers, makers and made, doers and done, fuckers and fuckees, yin and yang, and who the hell wants to be passive, moist, cold, receptive, unmoving, inert: sort of a superbasement of humanity" (PCBQ 124). It is thus not the socially prescribed role of woman that Marge Piercy's work extols, but a maternal principle, which, whether biological or cultural or both, comprises the positive values that are traditionally associated with women, such as caring, emotionality and compassion, while a masculine or patriarchal principle involves rationality, a lack of empathy, aggressiveness, and so on. A "masculine" principle is generally linked to the concept of separation, as shown, for example, in the character of Billy, in *Dance the Eagle to Sleep*, who is cut off from intimate bonds with others and envious of someone who is connected with others in a profound sense. In their care-giving capacities or roles most women characters necessarily develop connecting abilities, part of which is identification and empathy, involving a social responsibility and hands-on solidarity: values advocated in Piercy's work over abstract and idealist proclamations. Piercy counterposes these principles in (couple) relationships and shows the detrimental effects of a governing "masculine" principle. Moreover, she applies the same theory to larger scale relationships, that is, to American society and culture. What is necessary at the moment, for the benefit or even survival of humanity, is that a maternal principle be allowed to govern and for male aggressiveness to be kept in check. "We must be taught, we must teach each other, to see and feel the connections," Piercy writes. "Without that sense of being part of a web—a social network of labor and society, a total community of rock and lizard and bird and coyote and person, a maze of past from which we issue and the future which issues from us—we necessarily do more injury than good to ourselves and to others" ("What Rides The Wind" 62). In the second stanza of "The seven of pentacles" (*Circles on the Water*), Piercy writes:

> Connections are made slowly, sometimes they grow underground.
> You cannot tell always by looking what is happening.
> More than half a tree is spread out in the soil under your feet.
> Penetrate quietly as the earthworm that blows no trumpet.
> Fight persistently as the creeper that brings down the tree.
> Spread like the squash plant that overruns the garden.
> Gnaw in the dark and use the sun to make sugar.

Integral to Piercy's thematics are her attempts to balance the Apollonian and the Dionysian, a balance perhaps symbolized by the cat imagery so prevalent in Piercy's work. Camille Paglia has seen the cat, which was loved and venerated by the ancient Egyptians, as symbolizing such a synthesis between the Apollonian and the Dionysian in Egyptian culture, a synthesis that made Egyptian culture more stable than classical Greek culture, which privileged the Apollonian. That Piercy appears to perceive such a synthesis in cats is suggested in her review in the *New York Times Book Review* of D.J.R. Bruckner's *Van der Steen's Cats*, where she refers to "the emotional life of cats, their richness of gesture, their curiosity, their self-satisfaction, their ability to leap from calm to lunacy in an instant, their intensity of regard and reaction" (36). In Piercy, there is an accenting of the Dionysian in form, content, outlook on life, in the embracing of what Paglia has called "the Dionysian empathic" (1991 602)—as expressed in the first stanza of "The queen of pentacles" (*Circles on the Water*):

> Empathy flows through my fingers: I need to touch.
> I am at home in that landscape of unkempt garden,
> mulch and manure, thorny blackberry and sunflower and
>   grape coiling.
> tomato plants mad with fecundity bending their stakes,
> asparagus waving fronds in the wind.

Literally and symbolically, for example, Piercy's own garden in Wellfleet is rampantly Dionysian in its lush mixing of plants, flowers, herbs, and vegetables in unorthodox ways and in inviting birds and bugs to be part of that alluring landscape ("Rooms Without Walls" 36); "It is not the kind of garden strangers want to walk into. It suggests that they might not escape intact" ("A Writer's Garden" 72). The threatening and chaotic aspects of the Dionysian principle are also present in Piercy's texts. In *Dance the Eagle to Sleep*, for example, one critic found "Dionysiac revels which involve eating 'bread' (a new psychedelicacy) and dancing out their moods without clothes" (Seelye 25). In Piercy's short story, "Love Me Tonight, God," moreover, a Dionysian revelry or sparagmos, "a fire that shrieks" (200), is superimposed on a contemporary tale of two teenage boys who become worshiped rock musicians descended on by wild female fans, something that leads to the death of one of the boys. Political struggle can also be marked by an Apollonian-Dionysian tug-of-war, as expressed in the last two stanzas of "Report of the Fourteenth Subcommittee on Convening a Discussion Group" (in *Mars and Her Children*), in which it is "true virtue" "to wade on through the muck/ wrestling to some momentary small agreement/ like a pinhead pearl prized from a dragon-oyster," while inside "lurks a tyrant" who, violently and undemocratically, determines that there be "No more committees but only picnics and orgies and dances."

In her striving to re-pair opposites into a balanced dynamic, Piercy as author could be seen as a *shadkan*, the traditional Jewish matchmaker, a role talmudic rabbis would recognize as demanding unique acuity. According to Maurice Lamm, the Jewish community needed the *shadkan* most during the dispersion of the Jews: the matchmaker helped preserve Jewish society (7). When the communities became more stable, the need for the *shadkan* diminished, although among orthodox Jews in New York they are still available today. The large panorama of characters in Piercy's fiction, first, parallels the equally large group of families a matchmaker had to know, and second, just as a *shakdkan*, Piercy intertwines separate strands into the *shidukh*, or match—braided patterns of optimal puissance. Furthermore, just as the *shadkan* paralleled God as the original matchmaker, and even "[traced] his lineage . . . to God himself" (Lamm 19), the role of author has often been compared to that of creator. Piercy as author and as *shadkan* can be seen as moving her intertwined themes and characters toward a sense of mutuality and complementarity, something that has a bearing also on her vision of feminism. Piercy writes: "What I call feminism involves, in its essence, replacing a habitual and permeating way of dividing the world into dualities and with a different way of looking at things, which is unity underlying diversity" ("What Rides the Wind" 61).

Piercy's feminism and "her different way of looking at things" has obviously influenced her creation of both male and female characters. As concerns the female characters, Pia Thielmann has argued that it is only in *Woman on the Edge of Time* that Piercy has created ideal role models that can inspire women. I would instead like to argue that rather than searching for individual, "acceptable" role models for women or men, one could see Piercy's oeuvre in its entirety as a coherent vision of a maternal principle as a potential savior of humankind and our world. I would question Thielmann's thesis that Piercy's novels develop toward an ideal or a climax in *Woman on the Edge of Time* and that her subsequent novels, up to and including *Fly Away Home* are regressions toward a liberal ideology. Undeniably, Piercy desires to see female characters on the pages of literature that are less stereotyped and more fleshed-out than those of many male writers. In D. M. Thomas's *Ararat*, for example, Piercy found "no female human beings . . . only orifices with a few visual characteristics such as red gold hair, a too skinny body, a too fat body—too skinny or too fat for Rozanov or Surkov to wish to bed them" ("Thomas Caught in a Tangled Web of Stories" 35). In an interview, Piercy has lamented the dearth of strong female characters in American literature (Betsky 1980 37). Yet, creating role models for women is not Piercy's primary mission. "Writing politically," according to Piercy, "doesn't mean creating impossible, good, heroic, pure, strong, healthy, no-fault, no-ulcers women who run around in seven-league boots, righting wrongs before breakfast. Writers aren't in the business of fulfilling anyone's fantasies, even those of the oppressed" ("Active in Time and History" 118).

Nevertheless erring on the side of didacticism, some of Piercy's early nonfiction displays a hectoring tone at which one bristles, as when she herself is out "running around in seven-league boots righting wrongs before breakfast," as in the fifth stanza of "The homely war" (*Circles on the Water*):

> I lack a light touch.
> I step on my own words,
> a garden rake in the weeds.
> I sweat and heave when I should slip away.
> I am earnest into sermons when I should shrug.
> I ram on.

In her fiction and poetry, thematically an extension of her nonfiction, the mordant timbre is muted, although the jaunty gestures of Piercy's prescriptive passages can occasionally jar the lyricism. That is the case with some parts of *Woman on the Edge of Time*, about which Margarete Keulen has observed, "Since the self-confident Luciente is convinced of the superiority of her society and Connie is relegated to the role of pupil-to-be-convinced, Piercy is not able to avoid a certain sermonizing, to which the utopian genre is indeed prone" (45). Margaret Atwood has also pointed to the perils lurking in any utopia: "inhabitants of utopias somehow cannot help coming across as slightly sanctimonious and preachy; they've been like that since Thomas More" (275). Atwood also points out that the utopian "is a genre more at home in 19th-century England than the America of the 1970s, where moral earnestness seems to have gone out of fashion" (276).

However, even though what Atwood has called "Piercy's earthy aesthetic" (277) may seem unfashionable, it is still compelling, challenging, and necessary. Political passivity, Piercy emphasizes again and again, is dangerous, one example being the dystopian scenario in *Woman on the Edge of Time*, and another her depiction of World War II in *Gone to Soldiers*. What Anne Cranny-Francis proposes of contemporary feminist utopias as a whole would be as valid an assessment also of Piercy's work as a whole:

> Feminist utopia writers, by constructing a feminist reading position in their texts, show readers the nature of their society from a different (feminist) perspective. Beliefs, values, institutions traditionally represented as natural or obvious or inevitable are revealed as ideological constructs and the nature of that constructing ideology (patriarchal or heterosexist) is analyzed. They also show that social change is not only possible, but constantly in process, and that a feminist perception or understanding constitutes a continual intervention

in the dominant patriarchal ideology and its practice; that a feminist consciousness is necessarily activist. (140-41)

In Piercy's fiction an impulse toward continuity and connection is uppermost. Empathy marks Piercy's writing from the writing process to the frameworks of reception as she visualizes them. Her characters represent not a recreation of herself, but an entry into lives she has not lived. This perspective colors also Piercy's view of the role of literature and the effect that novel-reading has on readers. If we are able to identify with characters who are vastly different from ourselves, Piercy argues with ardor, we might also in real life be more open and understanding towards those who belong to a different race or religion:

> The conviction that those who talk differently, or look different, feel less than we do is exceedingly popular. "They don't know the value of human life in the Orient," we say, dropping bombs on them, or in Central America, or Africa, or wherever we're doing business. But one of the effects of the novel can be to induce us to identify with a character who resembles us in some way, or whom we wish we resembled, even if in ordinary life we wouldn't recognize that resemblance because the externals are so dissimilar. The novelist may even seduce the reader into identifying with characters whom he or she would refuse to know in ordinary life. . . . I consider fiction one way of persuading people to cross those borders of alienation and mistrust into the existence of someone in whose mind and body a reader may find enlightening to spend some time. ("Active in Time and History" 114)

As Thomas Moylan has stated, "The belief in a beautiful and just world and the anger at the denial of it by the dominant power structure have persisted in all Piercy's writings" (1982 136), a belief that has been strengthened by Piercy's own active engagement in political and ecological movements. Piercy perceives in Audre Lorde's poetry a quality "of embattled connection and opposition, often intermingled" ("From Where I Work" 11): this is a quality I find also in Piercy's own work, in which the fundamental battle in Piercy's work is not usually between individual men and women, even though such battles do occur, but between an impulse of separation and hierarchy and a maternal, healing impulse. The opposition of matriarchal and patriarchal principles is clearly present in some of Piercy's novels, for example, *Woman on the Edge of Time* and *He, She and It*, an opposition that in our culture is "far more pervasive, deep-rooted, and influential than generally acknowledged" (Ochs x).

But the duality is never absolute. As Carol Ochs suggests, "the opposition of matriarchy and patriarchy can be overcome not by opting for one rather than the other, not even by combining the two" (xi). Piercy writes that in recognizing the unity of the ground of being, the sense of being part, you also recognize how diverse and varied and peculiar are the flowers upon that ground. You don't expect all division to fall neatly into two. Many colors blend into one another, many ways of making a living on this planet, many ecological niches, many ways of making love, many kinds of love to be made, many choices of emphasis. Praise the dung beetle as well as the honeybee. ("What Rides in the Wind" 61-62)

In her propositional as in her poetic discourses, Marge Piercy is striking many notes that blend into a resonant chord of empathy and connectedness, orchestrated into her song to *tikkum olam*—the repair of the self and the world. In the last stanza of "The seven of pentacles" (*Circles on the Water*), she exhorts us to

reach out, keep reaching out, keep bringing in.
This is how we are going to live for a long time: not always,
for every gardener knows that after the digging, after
        the planting,
after the long season of tending and growth, the harvest comes.

Bibliography

Writings by Marge Piercy

NOVELS, CHRONOLOGICALLY LISTED

Going Down Fast. 1969. Rpt. New York: Fawcett Crest, 1984.
Dance the Eagle to Sleep. 1970. Rpt. New York: Fawcett Crest, 1982.
Small Changes. 1973. Rpt. New York: Fawcett Crest, 1974.
Woman on the Edge of Time. 1976. Rpt. New York: Fawcett Crest, 1985.
The High Cost of Living. New York: Fawcett Crest, 1978.
Vida. 1979. Rpt. New York: Fawcett Crest, 1985.
Braided Lives. 1982. Rpt. New York: Fawcett Crest, 1983.
Fly Away Home. 1984. Rpt. New York: Fawcett Crest, 1985.
Gone to Soldiers. 1987. Rpt. New York: Fawcett Crest, 1988.
Summer People. 1989. Rpt. New York: Fawcett Crest, 1990.
He, She and It. 1991. Rpt. New York: Fawcett Crest, 1993.
The Longings of Women. New York: Fawcett Columbine, 1994.

POETRY, CHRONOLOGICALLY LISTED

A recent bibliography compiled by Marge Piercy lists several hundred poems published individually since 1956. Since most of these poems are included in the collections of poetry listed below, I will not list them separately. A list of individual poems is included in the bibliography compiled by Sue Walker et al. (155-68); see below under "Bibliographies."

Breaking Camp. Middletown, CT.: Wesleyan UP, 1968.
Hard Loving. Middletown, CT.: Wesleyan UP, 1969.

4-Telling Poems (with Emmett Jarrett, Dick Lourie, Robert Hershon). Trumansburg, NJ: The Crossing Press, 1971.
To Be of Use. Illustrated by Lucia Vernarelli. Garden City, NY: Doubleday, 1973.
Living in the Open. New York: Knopf, 1976.
The Twelve-Spoked Wheel Flashing. New York: Knopf, 1978.
The Moon Is Always Female. New York: Knopf, 1980.
Circles on the Water. New York: Knopf, 1982.
Stone, Paper, Knife. New York: Knopf, 1983.
My Mother's Body. New York: Knopf, 1985.
Available Light. New York: Knopf, 1988.
Mars and Her Children. New York: Knopf, 1992.

SHORT STORIES

"A Dynastic Encounter." *Aphra* 3 (Spring 1970), 3-10. Rpt. in *The Looking Glass* (1977).
An excerpt from "Maud Awake." *December Magazine* 4 (Winter 1963), 184-90. Also in *The Bold New Women*. Ed. Barbara Alson. Greenwich, CT: Fawcett, 1965. Rpt. in *Modern Girl* 1 (Aug 1971), 22-27.
"And I Went Into the Garden of Love." *Off Our Backs* (Summer 1971), 2-4.
"Do You Love Me?" *Second Wave* 1, no. 4 (1972), 26-27, 40.
"God's Blood." *Anon*, no. 8 (1974), 50-59.
"Going Over Jordan." *Transatlantic Review* 22 (Fall 1966), 148-57.
"I Will Not Describe What I Did." *Mother Jones* 7, no. 11 (Feb/Mar 1982), 45-56.
"Like a Great Door Closing Suddenly." *Detroit Discovery* (Mar/Apr 1974), 45-50.
"Little Sister, Cat and Mouse." *Second Wave* 3, no. 1 (Fall 1973), 9-12+.
"Love Me Tonight, God." *Paris Review* 43 (Summer 1968), 185-200.
"Of Chilblains and Rotten Rutabagas." *Lilith*, no. 12-13 (Winter-Spring 1985), 9-12.
"Somebody Who Understands You." *Moving Out* 2, no. 2 (1972), 56-59.
"Spring in the Arboretum." *Michigan Quarterly Review* 21, no. 1 (Winter 1982), 96-98.
"The Cowbirds in the Eagle's Nest." *Maenad* 1, no. 1 (Fall 1980), 17-32.
"The Retreat." *Provincetown Poets* 2, no. 2-3 (1976), 9-11.

REVIEWS BY PIERCY

"A Fuller Life: How Hard It Was 100 Years Ago." Rev. of *The Woman and the Myth: Margaret Fuller's Life and Writings*, by Bell Gale Chauvigny. *Seven Days*, June 6, 1977, 34-35.
"A Historian Obsessed By Ghosts of Past." Rev. of *The Chaneysville Incident*, by David Bradley. *Chicago Tribune* Book World, Apr 26, 1981, 4.
"A Touching Detective Story: Who Really Killed Rosie at 27?" *Chicago Tribune* Book World, June 11, 1979, 6.
"A Well Made Quilt." Rev. of *Star Quilt*, by Roberta Hill Whiteman. *American Book Review* 8, no. 2 (1986), 17.

"Asking For Help Is Apt to Kill You." Rev. of *Women and Madness,* by Phyllis Chesler. *Village Voice,* Nov. 30, 1972, 25-26.

"Daily Life, Daily Struggle." Rev. of *Eye of a Hurricane,* by Ruthann Robson. *Women's Review of Books* 7, no. 8 (May 1990), 22.

"Doris Lessing and the Days of Darkness." Rev. of *Shikasta,* by Doris Lessing. *Washington Post* Book World, Nov. 4, 1979, 5.

"Firewheels of Whiskers." Rev. of *Van der Steen's Cats,* by D.J.R. Bruckner. *New York Times Book Review,* Feb. 3, 1985, 36.

"Godwin Details Strains, Stresses of Family Life." Rev. of *A Mother and Two Daughters,* by Gail Godwin. *Chicago Tribune* Book World, Jan. 10, 1982, 3.

"Gritty Places and Strong Women." Rev. of *The Diviners,* by Margaret Laurence. *New York Times Book Review,* June 23, 1974, 6.

"Hellman: Twilight Memories of a Dramatist." Rev. of *Maybe,* by Lillian Hellman. *Chicago Tribune* Book World, May 11, 1980, 1.

"Margaret Atwood: Beyond Victimhood." *American Poetry Review* 2 (Nov-Dec 1973), 41-44.

"No Final Answers." Rev. of *Who Killed Karen Silkwood?,* by Howard Kohn. *Sojourner* (Dec 1981), 18.

"Other Planets, Other Cats." Rev. of *Motherlines,* by Suzy McKee Charnas; *Watchtower,* by Elizabeth Lynn; and *Godsfire,* by Cynthia Felice. *Sojourner,* Apr 1979, 16-17.

Rev. of *Daughters of the Moon,* by Joan Haggerty, and *Memoirs of an Ex-Prom Queen,* by Alix Kates Schulman. *Second Wave* 2, no. 1, 1972, 46.

Rev. of *Keeper of Accounts,* by Irena Klepfisz. *American Book Review* 5, no. 6, Sept-Oct 1983.

Rev. of *Meridian,* by Alice Walker. *New York Times Book Review,* May 23, 1976, 5, 12.

Rev. of *Migrants, Sharecroppers, Mountaineers* and *The South Goes North,* by Robert Coles. *New York Times Book Review,* Febr. 13, 1972, 1, 20.

Rev. of *Monster,* by Robin Morgan. *New* 21 (Spring-Summer 1973), 64-67.

Rev. of *Zami: A New Spelling of My Name,* by Audre Lorde. *13th Moon* 7, no. 1-2, 1983, 187-90.

"Sacrificed to the Mills of Fate." Rev. of *Emmeline,* by Judith Rossner. *Washington Post* Book World, Sept 14, 1980, 3, 15.

"Shining Daughters." Rev. of *The Two of Them,* and *Kittatinny,* by Joanna Russ. *Sojourner,* Oct 1978, 14.

"Ship Out on a Corrupt Cruiser in the Middle of World War II." Rev. of *Time and Tide,* by Thomas Fleming. *Chicago Tribune* Book World, Aug. 9, 1987, 6.

"Short Fiction: Witty Parables, Eroticism, and Magic." Rev. of *The Queen of Egypt* and *The Bible of the Beasts of The Little Field,* by Susan Fromberg-Schaeffer. *Chicago Tribune* Book World, Jan 27, 1980, 3.

"Small Cameos, A Grand Portrait, and Twilight Sketches." Rev. of *Stories,* by Doris Lessing. *Chicago Tribune* Book World, May 14, 1978, 1.

"The Feminist Gospel According to Adrienne Rich." Rev. of *On Lies, Secrets, and Silence: Selected Prose 1966-1978,* by Adrienne Rich. *Chicago Tribune* Book World, Apr 15, 1979, 1-2.

"The Little Nuances of History." Rev. of *You Can't Keep A Good Woman Down,* by
Alice Walker. *Washington Post* Book World, May 31, 1981, 11.
"The Repair of the World." Rev. of *On Being a Jewish Feminist: A Reader.* Ed. and
introd. Susannah Heschel. *Women's Review of Books* 1, no. 5 (Feb 1984), 5-6.
"Thomas Caught in a Tangled Web of Stories." *Chicago Tribune* Book World, Nov.
25, 1984, 35.
"Together in Space: Old Style, New Locale." Rev. of *Mysteries of Motion,* by Hortense
Calisher. *Washington Post,* 31 Dec 1983, C2.
"Tom Robbins With a Bad Case of the Cutes." Rev. of *Still Life with Woodpecker,* by
Tom Robbins. *Chicago Tribune* Book World, Sept. 14, 1981, 3.

CRITICISM AND ESSAYS BY MARGE PIERCY

"A Symposium on Contemporary American Fiction." *Michigan Quarterly Review* 27,
no. 1 (Winter 1988), 105-7.
"A Writer's Garden." *Organic Gardening* 36, no. 6 (June 1989), 72.
"Active in Time and History." In *Paths of Resistance: The Art and Craft of the Novel.*
Ed. William Zinsser. Boston: Houghton Mifflin, 1989, 90-123.
"Autobiography." Vol. 1 of *Contemporary Authors Autobiography Series.* Ed. Dedria
Bryfonski. Detroit, MI: Gale, 1984, 267-81.
"Autobiography." *Cream City Review* 4, no. 1 (Spring 1990), 3-5.
"E.M. Broner." *Contemporary Novelists.* 4th edition. London: St. James Press, 1986,
144-46.
"Feminist Perspectives." *Sojourner* 4, no. 4 (Jan 1979), 7.
Foreword. *Back Rooms: Voices from the Illegal Abortion Era.* Ed. Ellen Messer and
Kathryn E. May. New York: St. Martin's Press, 1988, i-x.
Foreword. *Lost in Space,* by Marleen S. Barr. Chapel Hill, NC: U of North Carolina
P, 1993.
"From Where I Work." *American Poetry Review* 5, no. 2 (March/April 1976), 11.
"From Where I Work." *American Poetry Review* 6, no. 3 (May/June 1977), 27.
"How I Came to Walt Whitman and Found Myself." *Massachusetts Review* 33, no. 1
(Spring 1992), 98-100.
"Inviting the Muse." *Negative Capability* 2, no. 1 (Winter 1981), 5-15.
"Joanna Russ." *Contemporary Novelists.* 4th edition. London: St. James Press, 1986,
791-92.
"Lost and Found." Foreword to *The Zanzibar Cat,* by Joanna Russ. Arkam, 1983, vii-
xii.
"Me and My Novel." *The Boston Review* 12, no. 3 (June 1987), 19.
"Memory Annex." In *Ariadne's Thread: A Collection of Contemporary Women's
Journals.* Ed. Lyn Lifshin. New York: Harper and Row, 1982, 58-61.
"My, Haven't You Lost Weight!" *Woman's Day* 51, no. 15, Oct 25, 1988, 226.
"Of Arms and the Woman." *Harper's Magazine,* 274, no. 1645, June 1987, 30-32.
"On Jewish Identity." *Smate* 2, no. 8, 1984, 25-27.
"Poets on Poetry." *Literary Cavalcade* (Oct 1984), 24-25.
"Reminiscence of Esther Epstein." *Mai Pen Rai* 25, no. 2 (Apr 1991).

"Rooms Without Walls." *Ms.* (Apr 1988), 36-37.

"Simone de Beauvoir." In *Daughters of de Beauvoir.* Ed. Penny Forster and Imogen Sutton. London: Women's Press, 1989, 112-23.

"Starting Support Groups for Writers." In *Literacy in Process.* Ed. Brenda Miller Power and Ruth Hubbard. Portsmouth, NH: Heinemann, 1991, 14-18.

"The Dark Thread in the Weave." In *Testimony: Contemporary Writers Make the Holocaust Personal.* Ed. David Rosenberg. New York: Random House, 1989, 171-91.

"The Foreign Policy Association: Fifty Years of Successful Imperialism." *CAW* no. 1 (Feb 1968), 6-10.

"The Grand Coolie Dam." *Leviathan* (Nov 1969), 16-18.

"The Turn-On of Intimacy." *Ms.* (Feb. 1984) 46-48.

"The White Christmas Blues." With Uta West. *Provincetown Advocate,* Jan. 9, 1975.

"Through the Cracks." *Partisan Review* 41, no. 2 (1974), 202-16.

"Tom Eliot Meets the Hulk at Little Big Horn: The Political Economy of Poetry." With Dick Lourie. *Triquarterly: Literature in Revolution,* no. 23-24 (Spring 1972), 57-91.

"What Are We Leaving the Children?" *Woman's Day* 52, no. 15, Oct. 24, 1989, 57-58.

"What I Do When I Write." *Women's Review of Books* 6, no. 10-11 (July 1989), 25-26.

"What Rides the Wind." *Tikkun: A Bimonthly Jewish Critique of Politics, Culture & Society* 4, no. 2 (Mar/Apr 1989), 58-62.

"Women's Liberation: Nobody's Baby Now." *Defiance,* no. 1, 1970, 134-62.

"Writer's Choice." *Partisan Review* 42, no. 1 (1975), 156-57.

OTHER WORKS BY PIERCY

Early Ripening: American Women's Poetry Now. Ed. and introd. Marge Piercy. London: Pandora, 1987.

Parti-Colored Blocks for a Quilt. Ann Arbor: U of Michigan P, 1982.

The Earth Shines Secretly: A Book of Days. With paintings and drawings by Nell Blaine. Cambridge, MA: Zoland Press, 1990.

The Last White Class. Play co-authored with Ira Wood. Trumansburg, New Jersey: The Crossing Press, 1980.

BROADSIDES AND CHAPBOOKS

(List Compiled by Marge Piercy)

"A work of artifice." Detroit: Red Hanrahan Press, 1972.

"Closing."

"For shelter and beyond." Woman's Day broadside, 26 August, 1976.

"For the young who want to." The Zoland Books Poetry Postcard Collection, 1989.

"In the dark all cats fly." Iron Mountain Press broadside, 1988.

"Short season." Folger Shakespeare Library broadside.

"Softly during the night." *Zone* 3 (Winter), 1988.

"The faithless." Ill. David Diaz. E. P. Wilson Letterpress, 1988.

"The world comes back, like an old cat."

"To be of use." Broadside for Commonwork awards, City of Boston Emergency Shelter Commission, 1989.

"When the drought broke." Unicorn Press.

"To be of use."

"When a friend dies."

TAPES AND RECORDINGS

(List Compiled by Marge Piercy)

At the core. Cassette of reading. Watershed tapes, Washington, DC, 1976.

Interview. American Audio Prose Library. Cassette. 1986.

Interview and Poetry Reading. New Letters on the Air. University of Missouri-Kansas City. 1989. 30 minutes.

Interview with Ira Wood and Marge Piercy. *Pulp* 8, no. 1, 1982.

Laying down the tower. Also included in Black Box no. 1, cassette mag, 1972.

Laying down the tower. Sequence of 11 poems recorded in 1972, Radio Free People, 133 Mercer Street, New York, NY. 10012. Time: 30 minutes. (Both items on tape and cassette).

Marge Piercy: Poems. 12 poems, some recorded in 1968, some in 1969, by Radio Free People, 133 Mercer Street, New York, N.Y. 10012. Time: 30 minutes.

Readings and Thoughts. Marge Piercy, Women's Studies Series, Everett/Edwards, Inc., Deland, FL.

Readings of excerpts from *Braided Lives* and *Woman on the Edge of Time*, and poetry. Cassette, American Audio Prose Library, Columbia, MO, 1986. 65 minutes.

Reclaiming Ourselves. Radio Free People, 133 Mercer Street, New York, N.Y. 10012. Marge Piercy reading her poems, some alone, sometimes with guitar accompaniment, and Painted Women's Ritual Theater with Jeriann Hilderly performing some of her songs.

Record: Atomic Love. Katzberg and Snyder. "What's. That Smell in the Kitchen?" from *Circles on the Water*, read by Kate Katzberg. Manufactured at A&R Records, Dallas, TX. Recorded at Celebration Sounds, Pawtucket, RI, 1983.

Sorrells, Rosalind. *Be careful, there's a baby in the house*. Green Linnet Records, Inc., "Right to Life." Compact disc. 1991.

Writings About Marge Piercy's Work

BIBLIOGRAPHIES

Hansen, Elaine Tuttle, and William J. Scheick. "A Bibliography of Writings by Marge Piercy." In *Contemporary American Women Writers: Narrative Strategies*. Ed. Catherine Rainwater and William J. Scheick. Lexington: UP of Kentucky, 1985, 224-27.
Piercy, Marge. "Bibliography: Marge Piercy." (Unpublished bibliography).
Walker, Sue, et al. "Bibliography." Walker, *Ways of Knowing*, 153-80.

INTERVIEWS WITH MARGE PIERCY

(See also "Tapes and Recordings")

Dong, Stella. "Marge Piercy." Interview. *Publishers Weekly*, Jan 18, 1980, 18-19.
Hamner, Eugenie Lambert, and Sue Walker. "Interview with Marge Piercy." Walker, *Ways of Knowing*, 148-52.

SELECTED REVIEWS OF PIERCY'S WORK

Allison, Dorothy. "Marge Piercy Makes War." Rev. of *Gone to Soldiers*, by Marge Piercy. *Village Voice*, May 19, 1987, 45, 52.
Betsky, Celia. Rev. of *Miss Herbert (The Suburban Wife)*, by Christina Stead, and *Woman on the Edge of Time*, by Marge Piercy. *New Republic*, Oct 9, 1976, 38-40.
Biggs, Mary. Rev. of *Gone to Soldiers*, by Marge Piercy. *Women's Review of Books* 4, no. 10-11, July-August 1987, 23.
Blackburn, Sara. 1973. "What Happens to Women Who Struggle, What Happens to Those Who Don't." Rev. of *Small Changes*, by Marge Piercy. *New York Times Book Review*, Aug 12, 1987, 2-3.
Bosse, Malcolm. "A Cyborg in Love." Rev. of *He, She and It*, by Marge Piercy. *New York Times Book Review*, Dec 22, 1991, 22.
Broyard, Anatole. "Critic's Fiction." Rev. of *The High Cost of Living*, by Marge Piercy. *New York Times Book Review*, Jan 22, 1978, 14.
Caplan, Brina. "Not So Happy Days." Rev. of *Braided Lives*, by Marge Piercy. *Nation*, Mar 6, 1982, 280-82.
Chatain, Robert. "Marge Piercy's Friendly Cyborg." Rev. of *He, She and It*, by Marge Piercy. *Chicago Tribune* Book World, Dec 1, 1991, 6.
Clute, John. "Seeing the light." Rev. of *Fly Away Home*, by Marge Piercy. *Times Literary Supplement*, June 15, 1984, 658.
Craig, Patricia. "Self-fulfilling Destinies." Rev. of *American Appetites*, by Joyce Carol Oates, and *Summer People*, by Marge Piercy. *Times Literary Supplement*, Sept 15, 1989, 997.

Duffy, Martha. "Stiff Upper Lib." Rev. of *Small Changes*, by Marge Piercy. *Time*, Aug 20, 1973, 81-82.

Flower, Dean. Rev. of *The High Cost of Living*, by Marge Piercy. *Hudson Review* 31, 1978, 349-50.

Fruchter, Norm. Rev. of *Dance the Eagle to Sleep*, by Marge Piercy. *Village Voice*, Feb 11, 1971, 6, 34, 36, 40.

Gerrard, Nicci. "Sixties People." Rev. of *Summer People*, by Marge Piercy. *New Statesman & Society*, Aug. 11, 1989, 26-27.

Gornick, Vivian. "Bombed Under." Rev. of *Vida*, by Marge Piercy. *Village Voice*, Feb 18, 1980, 43-44.

Hawes, Norma B. Rev. of *Vida*, by Marge Piercy. *National Review*, May 30, 1980, 675-76.

Isaacs, Susan. "Willie & Susan & Dinah & Tyrone." Rev. of *Summer People*, by Marge Piercy. *Washington Post* Book World, July 23, 1989, 4.

Israel, Betty. Rev. of *Braided Lives*, by Marge Piercy. *Ms.* (June 1982) 18.

Kuehl, Linda. Rev. of *Dance the Eagle to Sleep*, by Marge Piercy. *Commonweal*, Apr. 2, 1971, 92-94.

Langer, Elinor. "After the Movement." Rev. of *Vida*, by Marge Piercy. *New York Times Book Review*, Feb 24, 1980, 1, 36.

Leonard, John. "Two Good Books, Two Different Realities." Rev. of *The House of Akiva*, by William Butler, and *Going Down Fast*, by Marge Piercy. *New York Times*, Oct 21, 1969, 45.

——————. "1973: An Apology and 38 Consolations." *New York Times Book Review*, Dec 2, 1973, 2 (mentions *Small Changes*).

——————. "Written on Bandages." Rev. of *Dance the Eagle to Sleep*, by Marge Piercy. *New York Times*, Oct. 23, 1970, 39.

Levin, Martin. Rev. of *Going Down Fast*, by Marge Piercy. *New York Times Book Review*, Nov 9, 1969, 70.

Lindsey, Karen. Rev. of *The High Cost of Living*, by Marge Piercy. *Ms.* (July 1978) 31.

Loewenstein, Andrea Freud. "Iron-Fisted Fiction." Rev. of *Gone to Soldiers,* by Marge Piercy. *Nation* 4, no. 11 (July), 24-27.

Mernit, Susan. "Suburban Housewife Makes Good." Rev. of *Fly Away Home*, by Marge Piercy. *Women's Review of Books* 1, no. 11, Aug 8, 1984, 18.

Miner, Valerie. "Marge Piercy and the Candor of our Fictions." Rev. of *Fly Away Home*, by Marge Piercy. *Christian Science Monitor*, May 4, 1984, B3.

O'Reilly, Jane. "Utopias and Firebugs." Rev. of *Fly Away Home*, by Marge Piercy. *New York Times Book Review*, Feb 5, 1984, 7.

Pollitt, Katha. "A Complete Catalogue of Suffering." Rev. of *Braided Lives*, by Marge Piercy. *New York Times Book Review*, Feb 7, 1982, 7, 30, 32.

Rosen, Lynn. "Piercy Takes On War: Piercy Wins." Rev. of *Gone to Soldiers*, by Marge Piercy. *New Directions for Women*, Sept/Oct 1987, 14.

Schiff, Stephen. "Red-Hot Pastorale." Rev. of Marge Piercy's *Summer People*. *New York Times Book Review*, June 11, 1989, 26.

Schulder, Diane. "Two Women." Rev. of *Small Changes*, by Marge Piercy. *New Republic*, Oct. 27, 1973, 30-31.

Scruton, Roger. "Bodily Tracts." Rev. of *Braided Lives*, by Marge Piercy. *Times Literary Supplement*, July 23, 1982, 807.

Seelye, John. "The Greening Grows Dark: *Dance the Eagle Down* [*sic*] by Marge Piercy." Rev. of *Dance the Eagle to Sleep*, by Marge Piercy. *New Republic*, December 12, 1970, 24-25.

Sweet, Ellen. Rev. of *Fly Away Home*, by Marge Piercy. *Ms.* March 1984, 32.

Uglow, Jennifer. "Weighing Up the Seventies." Rev. of *Vida*, by Marge Piercy. *Times Literary Supplement*, March 7, 1980, 56.

Updike, John. "If At First You Do Succeed, Try, Try Again." Rev. of *Dance the Eagle to Sleep*, by Marge Piercy. *New Yorker*, Apr. 10, 1971, 143-44, 147-48, 150, 153.

Waltzer, Judith B. Rev. of *Vida*, by Marge Piercy. *New Republic* 182, no. 69 (Feb 1980), 38-40.

Wynn, Judith. "Piercy's Big War: 'Soldiers' Is Not the 'Good' Fight Nostalgia Recalls." Rev. of *Gone to Soldiers*, by Marge Piercy. *Chicago Tribune* Book World, May 10, 1987, 3.

Yardley, Jonathan. "Marge Piercy's Big War Novel." Rev. of *Gone to Soldiers*, by Marge Piercy. *Washington Post* Book World, May 3, 1987, 3.

SELECTED CRITICISM

Adams, Karen C. "The Utopian Vision of Marge Piercy's *Woman on the Edge of Time*." Walker, *Ways of Knowing*, 39-50.

Albrecht, Lisa Diane. "The Woman Writer Empowered: A Study of the Meanings of Experience of Ten Published Feminist Women Writers." Diss. State U of New York at Buffalo, 1984.

Annas, Pamela J. "New Worlds, New Words: Androgyny in Feminist Science Fiction." *Science Fiction Studies* 5 (1978), 143-57.

Atwood, Margaret. "Marge Piercy: *Woman on the Edge of Time, Living in the Open*" (1976). In *Second Words: Selected Critical Prose*. Toronto: Anansi, 1982, 272-78.

Augustine, Jane. "Piercy, Marge." *Contemporary Poets*. Ed. James Vinson and D.L. Kirkpatrick. 4th ed. New York: St. Martin's Press, 1985, 1180-83.

Barnouw, Dagmar. *Die Versuchte Realität Oder von der Möglichkeit, Glücklichere Welten zu Denken:Utopische Diskurs von Thomas Morus zur Feministischen Science Fiction*. Studien zur Phantastischen Literatur, Band 1. Meitingen, Germany: Corian-Verlag Heinrich Wimmer, 1985.

Barr, Marlene S. *Alien to Femininity: Speculative Fiction and Feminist Theory*. Westport, CT: Greenwood Press, 1987.

——————. *Feminist Fabulation: Space/Postmodern Fiction*. Iowa City: U of Iowa P, 1992.

——————. "Permissive, Unspectacular, A Little Baffling: Sex and the Single Feminist Utopian Quasi-Tribesperson." In *Erotic Universe: Sexuality and Fantastic Literature*. Ed. Donald Palumbo. Westport, CT: Greenwood Press, 1986, 185-96.

Bartkowski, Frances. "Marge Piercy's *Woman on the Edge of Time*." In *Feminist Utopias*. Lincoln and London: U of Nebraska P, 1989, 41-80.

——————. "Toward a Feminist Eros: Readings in Feminist Utopian Fiction."
    Diss. U of Iowa, 1982.

Bazin, Nancy Topping. "Marge Piercy's *Small Changes*." Walker, *Ways of Knowing*,
    127-38.

Beis, Patricia S. "Cold Fire: Some Contemporary American Women Poets." *DAI* 43
    (1974): 5157A. St. Louis U.

Bell, Pearl K. "Marge Piercy and Ann Beattie." *Commentary* 70 (1980), 59-61.

Bender, Eleanor. "Marge Piercy's *Laying Down the Tower*." In Walker, *Ways of
    Knowing,* 101-10.

——————. "Visions of a Better World: The Poetry of Marge Piercy." Walker,
    Ways of Knowing, 1-14.

Bender, Robert. "A Sense of Place in the Work of Marge Piercy." Walker, *Ways of
    Knowing*, 120-31.

Berkson, Dorothy. "So We All Became Mothers." In *Feminism, Utopia, and
    Narrative*. Ed. Libby Falk Jones and Sarah Webster Goodwin. Knoxville: U of
    Tennessee P, 1990, 100-15.

Betsky, Celia. "Talk With Marge Piercy." *New York Times Book Review*, Feb 24,
    1980, 36-37.

Burton, Deidre. "Linguistic Innovation in Feminist Utopian Fiction." *Ilha do Desterro:
    A Journal of Language and Literature* 14, no. 2 (1985), 82-106.

Caruso, Barbara Ann. "Circle without Boundaries: Feminist Criticism and the
    Contemporary Woman Poet." *DAI* 38 (1978): 5455A. Bowling Green State.

Contoski, Victor. "Marge Piercy: A Vision of the Peaceable Kingdom." *Modern
    Poetry Studies* 8 (1977), 205-16.

Cranny-Francis, Anne. *Feminist Fictions: Feminist Uses of Generic Fiction*.
    Cambridge, Oxford: Polity Press, 1990.

Delaney, Sheila. *Writing Woman*. New York: Schocken Books, 1983.

Dobbs, Jeannine. "Not Another Poetess: A Study of Female Experience in Modern
    American Poetry." *DAI* 34 (1973): 255A. U of New Hampshire.

Du Plessis, Rachel Blau. 1979. "The Feminist Apologues of Lessing, Piercy, and
    Russ." *Frontiers* 4, no. 1 (1980), 1-8.

——————. *Writing Beyond the Ending: Narrative Strategies of Twentieth-Century
    Women Writers*. Bloomington: Indiana UP, 1985.

Ecker, Gisela. "The Politics of Fantasy in Recent American Women's Novels."
    Englisch-Amerikanische Studien 6 (1984), 503-10.

Empey, John Theodore. "The Androgynous Vision in the Novels of Marge Piercy."
    M.A. thesis. U of Texas, Arlington, 1979.

Felski, Rita. "The Novel of Self-Discovery: A Necessary Fiction?" *Southern Review:
    Literary and Interdisciplinary Essays* 19, no. 2 (July 1981), 131-48.

Ferns, Chris. "Dreams of Freedom: Ideology and Narrative Structure in the Utopian
    Fictions of Marge Piercy and Ursula Le Guin." *English Studies in Canada* 14, no.
    4 (December 1988), 453-66.

Fitting, Peter. "Positioning and Closure: On the 'Reading-Effect' of Contemporary
    Utopian Fiction." In *Utopian Studies* 1. Ed. Gorman Beauchamp, Kenneth
    Roemer, and Nicholas D. Smith. New York: UP of America, 1987, 23-36.

Foster, David L. "Woman on the Edge of Narrative: Language in Marge Piercy's Utopia." In *Patterns of the Fantastic*. Ed. Donald M. Hassler. Mercer Island, WA: Starmont House, 1983, 47-56.

Fredette, Jean M. "Close-Up: Marge Piercy Poet." In *1986 Poet's Market: Where & How to Publish Your Poetry*. Ed. Judson Jerome and Jean M. Fredette. Cincinnati: Writer's Digest Books, 1986, 269.

Freedman, Diane P. "An Alchemy of Genres: Cross-dressing Writing by American Women Poet-Critics." Diss. U of Washington, 1989.

Frye, Ellen. "Piercy Poetry...and Prose." *Off Our Backs* (March 1978), 21.

Fucci, Marie Lucille. "Women's Novels of the Seventies in the United States and France." Diss. U of Michigan, 1976.

Gardiner, Judith Kegan. "Evil, Apocalypse, and Feminist Fiction." *Frontiers* 7, no. 2 (1983), 74-80.

———————. "On Female Identity and Writing by Women." In *Writing and Sexual Difference*. Ed. Elizabeth Abel. Chicago: U of Chicago P, 1982, 177-91.

Gates, Elizabeth Charlene. "The Tarot Trumps: Their Origin, Archetypal Imagery, and Use in Some Works of English Literature." Diss. U of Oregon, 1982.

Gould, Jean. *Modern American Women Poets*. New York: Dodd, Mead, 1984.

Grödal, Hanne Tang. "Words, Words, Words." *Dolphin* 18, Aarhus, Denmark, Dept. of English, 18 (1990), 21-26.

Gygax, Franziska. "Demur—You're Straightways Dangerous: *Woman on the Edge of Time*." Walker, *Ways of Knowing*, 51-59.

Halischak, Kathleen. "Small Changes in Feminist Fiction." In "Recent Voices in American Feminist Literature." Diss. U of Notre Dame, South Bend, IN, 1982, 40-81.

Hamner, Eugenie Lambert. "Becoming One's Own in Piercy's *Fly Away Home*." Walker, *Ways of Knowing*, 91-100.

Hansen, Elaine Tuttle. "Marge Piercy: The Double Narrative Structure of Small Changes." In *Contemporary American Women Writers: Narrative Strategies*. Ed. Catherine Rainwater and William J. Scheick. Kentucky: UP of Kentucky, 1985, 209-23.

Hardwick, Elizabeth. "Militant Nudes." In *Bartleby in Manhattan, and Other Essays*. New York: Random, 1983, 29-40.

Harris, Marie. "Let Me See That Book." *Parnassus: Poetry in Review* 3, no. 1 (1974), 149-58.

Hartman, Patricia L. "The Politics of Language in Feminist Utopias." Diss. Ohio U, 1986.

Hassan, Ihab. "Cities of the Mind, Urban Worlds: The Dematerialization of Metropolis in Contemporary American Fiction." In *Literature and the Urban Experience: Essays on the City and Literature*. Ed. Michael C. Jaye and Ann Chalmers Watts. New Brunswick, NJ.: Rutgers UP, 1981, 93-112.

Hicks, Jack, ed. *Cutting Edges: Young American Fiction for the '70s*. New York: Holt, Rinehart and Winston, 1973.

———————. *In the Singer's Temple*. Chapel Hill: U of North Carolina P, 1981.

Hicks, Walter J. "An Essay on Recent American Fiction." *DAI* 35 (1974): 3744A. U of North Carolina.

Huckle, Patricia. "Women in Utopias." In *The Utopian Vision: Seven Essays on the Quincentennial of Sir Thomas More*. Ed. E. D. S. Sullivan. San Diego: San Diego State UP, 1983, 115-36.

Iannone, Carol. "A Turning of the Critical Tide?" *Commentary* 88, no. 5 (Nov 1989), 57-59.

Jerome, Judson. "'Grabbing the Gusto': Marge Piercy's Poetry." *Writer's Digest* 61 (1981), 56-59.

Jones, Libby Falk. "Gilman, Bradley, Piercy, and the Evolving Rhetoric of Feminist Utopias." In *Feminism, Utopia, and Narrative*. Ed. Libby Falk Jones and Sarah Webster Goodwin. Knoxville: U of Tennessee P, 1990, 116-29.

Kakutani, Michiko. "Making a Literary Lunge into the Future." *New York Times*, 21 Feb. 1992, C1, C 31.

Keinhorst, Annette. *Utopien von Frauen in der zeitgenössischen Literatur der USA*. Frankfurt-am-Main: Peter Lang, 1985.

Kessler, Carol Farley. "Fables Toward Our Future: Two Studies in Women's Utopian Fiction." *Journal of General Education* 37, no. 3 (1985), 189-202.

——————. "Woman on the Edge of Time: A Novel *To Be Of Use*." *Extrapolation* 28, no. 4 (Winter 1987), 310-18.

Keulen, Margarete. *Radical Imagination: Feminist Conceptions of the Future in Ursula Le Guin, Marge Piercy and Sally Miller Gearhart*. Frankfurt-am-Main: Peter Lang, 1991.

Khanna, Lee Cullen. "Women's Utopias: New Worlds, New Texts." In *Feminism, Utopia, and Narrative*. Ed. Libby Falk Jones and Sarah Webster Goodwin. Knoxville: U of Tennessee P, 1990, 130-40.

Khouri, Nadia. "The Dialectics of Power: Utopia in the Science Fiction of Le Guin, Jeury, and Piercy." *Science Fiction Studies* 7 (1980), 49-60.

Kramarae, Cheris, and Jana Kramer. "Feminist's Novel Approaches to Conflict." *Women and Language News* 11, no. 1 (Winter 1987), 36-39.

Kress, Susan. "In and Out of Time: The Form of Marge Piercy's Novels." In *Future Females: A Critical Anthology*. Ed. Marleen Barr. Bowling Green, Ohio: Bowling Green State U Popular P, 1981, 109-22.

Ladenson, Joyce R. "Marge Piercy's Revolutionary Feminism." *Newsletter: Society for the Study of Midwestern Literature* 10, no. 2 (1980), 24-31.

——————. "Political Themes and Personal Preoccupations in Marge Piercy's Novels." Walker, *Ways of Knowing*, 111-20.

——————. 1980. "Surviving in a Man's World." *USA Today*, Jan 2, 60-62.

Lebow, Jeanne. "Bearing Hope Back into the World: Marge Piercy's *Stone, Paper, Knife*." Walker, *Ways of Knowing*, 60-72.

"Marge Piercy." In *Rising Tides*. Ed. Laura Chester and Sharon Barba. NY: Pocket Books/Simon and Schuster, 1973, 274.

"Marge Piercy." In *No More Masks: An Anthology of Poems by Women*. Ed. Florence Howe and Ellen Bass. Introd. by Ellen Bass. Garden City, NY: Anchor Books, 1973, 386.

Marks, Patricia R. "Re-Writing the Romance Narrative: Gender and Class in the Novels of Marge Piercy." Diss. U of Oregon, 1990.

Marshall, Linda Krum. "A Study, for Oral Interpretation, of Selected Poetry by Contemporary American Women." Diss. Syracuse U, 1978.

Masinton, Martha, and Charles G. Masinton. "Second-class Citizenship: The Status of Women in Contemporary American Fiction." In Springer, Marlene, ed. *What Manner of Woman: Essays on English and American Life and Literature.* New York: New York UP, 1977.

Mellor, Anne K. "On Feminist Utopias." *Women's Studies* 9 (1982), 241-62.

Mernit, Susan. "Poets Who Write Fiction: What's Your Primary Form?" *Coda: Poets and Writers' Newsletter* 13, no. 5 (1976), 14-19.

Michael, Magali Cornier. "Feminism and the Postmodernist Impulse: Doris Lessing, Marge Piercy, Margaret Atwood, and Angela Carter." *DAI* 51, 5 (1990): 1609A.

Michelsen, Anne. "Piecemeal Liberation: Marge Piercy, Sara Davidson, Marilyn French, Grace Paley." In *Reaching Out: Sensitivity and Order in Recent American Fiction by Women.* Metuchen, NJ and London: Scarecrow Press, 1979.

Miner, Madonne. "Not Just Playing Around: The Word as Weapon in Piercy's *Small Changes.*" Walker, *Ways of Knowing,* 15-26.

Mitchell, Felicia. "Marge Piercy's *The Moon is Always Female*: Feminist Text, Great Books Context." *Virginia English Bulletin* 40, no. 2 (1990), 34-45.

Moylan, Thomas. "Figures of Hope: The Critical Utopia of the 1970s. The Revival, Destruction, and Transformation of Utopian Writing in the United States: A Study of the Ideology, Structure, and Historical Context of Representative Texts." Diss. U of Wisconsin-Milwaukee, 1981.

——————. "History and Utopia in Marge Piercy's *Woman on the Edge of Time.*" In *Science Fiction Dialogues.* Ed. Gary Wolfte. Chicago: Academy Chicago, 1982, 133-52.

——————. "Marge Piercy: *Woman on the Edge of Time.*" In *Demand the Impossible: Science Fiction and the Utopian Imagination.* New York: Methuen, 1986, 121-55.

Nelson, Ronald. "The Renewal of the Self By Returning to the Elements." Walker, *Ways of Knowing,* 73-90.

Nowik, Nan. "Mixing Art and Politics: The Writings of Adrienne Rich, Marge Piercy, and Alice Walker." *The Centennial Review* 30, no. 2 (Spring 1986), 208-18.

Nunnally, Tina, and Fran Hopenwassser Peterson. "Mothers and Daughters in Recent North American Literature." *Edda,* 1980, 23-31.

Olderman, Raymond M. "American Fiction, 1974-1976: The People Who Fell to Earth." *Contemporary Literature* 19 (1978), 497-530.

Pearson, Carol S. "Towards a New Language, Consciousness & Political Theory: The Utopian Novels of Dorothy Bryant, Mary Staton and Marge Piery." *Heresies* 4, no. 1 (1981), 84-87.

Peck, Elizabeth. "More Than Ideal: Size and Weight Obsession in Literary Works by Marge Piercy, Margaret Atwood, and Andre Dubus." *Platte Valley Review* 18, no. 1 (Winter 1990), 69-75.

Pykett, Lyn. "Marge Piercy." *Contemporary Novelists.* 4th edition. London: St. James Press, 1986, 729-31.

Rankin, Ginny. "Women and Science Fiction Possible Futures." *Second Wave* (Summer/Fall 1978), 7-10.

Rigney, Barbara Hill. *Lilith's Daughters: Women and Religion in Contemporary Fiction*. Madison: U of Wisconsin P, 1982.

Robson, Ruth. "Women's Writing / Male Subjects." *Kalliope* 9, no. 3 (1987), 72-78.

Roller, Judi M. *The Politics of the Feminist Novel*. Westport, CT: Greenwood Press, 1986.

Rosenbaum, Jean. "You Are Your Own Magician: A Vision of Integrity in the Poetry of Marge Piercy." *Modern Poetry Studies* 8, no. 3 (Winter 1977), 193-205.

Rosinsky, Natalie. "Feminist Theory in Women's Speculative Fiction, 1966-81." Diss. U of Wisconsin-Madison, 1982.

Ruppert, Peter. *Reader in a Strange Land: The Activity of Reading Literary Utopias*. Athens: U of Georgia P, 1986.

Sargent, Lyman Tower. "A New Anarchism: Social and Political Ideas in Some Recent Feminist Eutopias." In *Women and Utopia: Critical Interpretations*. Ed. Marleen Barr and Nicholas D. Smith. Lanham, New York, and London: UP of America, 1983, 3-33.

Sauter-Bailliet, Theresia. "Marge Piercy: Woman on the Edge of Time (1976)." In *Die Utopie in der angloamerikanischen Literatur: Interpretationen*. Ed. Hartmut Heuermann and Bernd-Peter Lange. Düsseldorf: Bagel, 1984, 349-70.

Schweickart, Patrocinio. "A Theory for Feminist Criticism." Diss. The Ohio State U, 1980.

Seidel, Kathryn. "Envisioning the Androgynous Future." *Sun & Moon: A Quarterly of Literature and Art* 3 (1976), 98-101.

——————. "Marge Piercy." In *Contemporary Novelists*. Ed. D.L. Kirkpatrick. London: St. James Press, 1986, 673-75.

Shinn, Thelma J. *Radiant Daughters: Fictional American Women*. Westport, CT: Greenwood Press, 1986.

——————. *Worlds Within Women: Myth and Mythmaking in Fantastic Literature by Women*. Westport, CT: Greenwood Press, 1986.

Sizemore, Christine W. "Masculine and Feminine Cities: Marge Piercy's *Going Down Fast* and *Fly Away Home*." *Frontiers* 13, no. 1 (1992), 90-110.

Snitow, Ann Barr. "The Front Line: Notes on Sex in Novels by Women, 1969-1979." *SIGNS: Journal of Women in Culture and Society* 5, no. 4 (1980), 702-18.

Specter, Judith. "The Functions of Sexuality in the Science Fiction of Russ, Piercy and Le Guin." In *Erotic Universe: Sexuality and Fantastic Literature*. Ed. Donald Palumbo. Westport, CT: Greenwood Press, 1986, 197-207.

Stephanchev, Stephen. "The Present State of Poetry/ VIII." *New York Quarterly* 34 (1987), 105-21.

Thielmann, Pia. *Marge Piercy's Women: Visions Captured and Subdued*. Frankfurt (Main): R. G. Fischer, 1986.

Tiger, Virginia. "Alice and Charlie and Vida and Sophy—A Terrorist's Work Is Never Done." *New York Times Book Review*, Nov. 10, 1985, 11.

Uphaus, Susanne Henning. "Marge Piercy." In *American Women Writers*. Ed. Lina Mainero. Vol. 3. New York: Frederick Ungar, 1981, 389-91.

Walker, Nancy A. *Feminist Alternatives: Irony and Fantasy in the Contemporary Novel by Women*. Jackson and London: UP of Mississippi, 1990.

Walker, Sue. "Marge Piercy: An Overview (31 March 1936-)." Walker, *Ways of Knowing*, 132-47.

Walker, Sue, and Eugenie Hamner, eds. *Ways of Knowing: Essays on Marge Piercy.* Mobile, AL: Negative Capability Press, 1991.

Wallin, Hilja-Katarina. "Dygden som underhållning: Marge Piercy's författarskap." *Kvinnobulletinen* 6 (1983), 32-34.

Waugh, Patricia. *Feminine Fictions: Revisiting the Postmodern.* New York: Routledge, 1989.

West, Celeste. "Foreword: Closing the Media Gap." In *Words in Our Pockets: The Feminist Writers Guild Handbook on How to Gain Power, Get Published & Get Paid.* Paradise, CA: Dustbooks, 1985, 1-11.

Wynne, Edith J. "Imagery of Association in the Poetry of Marge Piercy." *Publications of the Missouri Philological Association* 10 (1985), 57-63.

Zee, Nancy Scholar. "Marge Piercy: A Collage." *Oyez Review* 9, no. 1 (1975), 87-94.

Øverland, Janneken. "Bøkene Mine Handler Om Å Overleve: Et Møte med Marge Piercy." *Vinduet* 34, no. 3 (1980), 64-66.

Additional Works Consulted

"After 23 Years, Double Life Is Over." *Kansas City Star*, Sept 16, 1993, A-1, A-13.

Brown, Rosellen. "Transports of Delight." Rev. of *Women Pilots of World War II*, by Jean Hascall Cole, and *Confessions of a Fast Woman*, by Lesley Hazleton. *Women's Review of Books* 9, no. 12 (September 1992), 6-7.

Brownmiller, Susan. *Femininity.* New York: Linden Press/Simon & Schuster, 1984.

"'Cabin Fever' Nears End for Crew of Biosphere 2." *Kansas City Star* 19 Sept. 1993, A-13.

Casey, John. "The Promise of American Life." Rev. of *Natural History* by Maureen Howard. *New York Times Book Review*, Oct 18, 1992, 1, 46.

Cheatham, Annie and Mary Clare Powell. *This Way Daybreak Comes: Women's Values and the Future.* Afterword by Gloria Anzaldúa. Philadelphia, PA: New Society Publishers, 1986.

Chesler, Phyllis. *Women and Madness.* 1972. Rpt. New York: Avon, 1983.

Chesnoff, Richard Z. "The Hatred That Endures." *U.S. News and World Report*, Apr 26, 1993, 64.

Cleaver, Eldridge. *Soul on Ice.* Introd. Maxwell Geismar. New York: Dell, 1968.

Clifford, James. "Traveling Cultures." In *Cultural Studies.* Ed. L. Grossberg, C. Nelson, P. Treichler. New York: Routledge, Chapman and Hall, 1992, 96-112.

De Lauretis, Teresa. *Technologies of Gender: Essays on Theory, Film, and Fiction.* Bloomington: Indiana UP, 1987.

Donovan, Josephine. "Toward a Women's Poetics." In *Feminist Issues in Literary Scholarship.* Ed. Shari Benstock. Bloomington: Indiana UP, 1987, 98-109.

Du Plessis, Rachel Blau. "For the Etruscans." In *The New Feminist Criticism: Essays on Women, Literature, and Theory.* Ed. Elaine Showalter. New York: Pantheon Books, 1985, 271-91.

Ebersole, Lucinda, and Richard Peabody, eds. *Mondo Barbie*. New York: St. Martin's Press, 1993.

Ehrenreich, Barbara. "What Do Women Have to Celebrate?" *Time*, Nov. 16, 1992, 55-56.

Eklundh, Jenny. "Biblens Bedrövliga Kvinnosyn." *Sveamagasinet*, Oct 1992, 18-19.

Faludi, Susan. *Backlash: The Undeclared War Against American Women*. 1991. Rpt. New York: Anchor Books, 1992.

Felski, Rita. *Beyond Feminist Aesthetics: Feminist Literature and Social Change*. Cambridge, MA: Hutchinson Radius, 1989.

Ferenczi, Sandor. 1933. *Thalassa: A Theory of Genitality*. Rpt. New York: W. W. Norton, 1968.

Freibert, Lucy M. "World Views in Utopian Novels by Women." *Journal of Popular Culture* 17 (1983), 49-60.

French, Marilyn. "A Choice We Never Chose." *Women's Review of Books* 8, no. 10-11 (July 1991), 3-4.

Gartshore, Pamela. "Marge Piercy and the American Feminist Movement in the Last Ten Years from Her Novel *Small Changes*." M.A. thesis. Université de Paris, 1976.

Gershuny, Lee H. "The Linguistic Transformation of Womanhood." In *Women in Search of Utopia: Maverics and Mythmakers*. Ed. and introd. Ruby Rohrlich and Elaine Hoffman Baruch. New York: Schocken Books, 1984, 189-99.

Gilbert, Sandra M. and Susan Gubar. *The Madwoman in the Attic: The Woman Writer and the Nineteenth-Century Literary Imagination*. New Haven, CT: Yale UP, 1979.

Goldman, Anita. *Våra Bibliska Mödrar*. Stockholm: Natur och Kultur, 1988.

Haraway, Donna. *Simians, Cyborgs, and Women: The Reinvention of Nature*. London: Free Association Books, 1991.

Hellman, Lillian. *The Little Foxes*. In *Four Plays*. New York: The Modern Library, 1942.

Huet, Marie-Hélène. *Monstrous Imagination*. Cambridge, MA: Harvard UP, 1993.

Irigaray, Luce. "An Interview by Lucienne Serrano and Elaine Hoffman Baruch." In *Women Writers Talking*. Ed. Janet Todd. New York and London: Holmes & Meier, 1983, 231-45.

Jardine, Alice. "Introduction to Julia Kristeva's 'Women's Time.'" *SIGNS: Journal of Women in Culture and Society* 7, no. 1 (1981), 5-12.

Johnson, Diane. "An Interview by Janet Todd. In *Women Writers Talking*." Ed. Janet Todd. New York and London: Holmes & Meier, 1983, 121-34.

Jung, Carl G. *Psychological Reflections: An Anthology of the Writings of C. G. Jung*. Ed. Jolande Jacobi. New York: Pantheon Books, Bollingen Series 41, 1953.

Kalbach, Warren. "20 Questions: Camille Paglia." [Interview]. *Playboy*, Oct 1991, 132-33, 170-72.

Kinder, Maria. Rev. of *Scenes from a Marriage*, by Ingmar Bergman. *Film Quarterly* 28, no. 2 (1974-75), 48-53.

Kramarae, Cheris. "Proprietors of Language." In *Women and Language in Literature and Society*. Ed. Sally McConnell-Ginet, Ruth Borker and Nelly Furman. New York: Praeger, 1980.

Kristeva, Julia. "Women's Time." Trans. Alice Jardine and Harry Blake. *SIGNS: Journal of Women in Culture and Society* 7, no. 1 (1981), 13-35.

Lamm, Maurice. *The Jewish Way in Love and Marriage*. New York: Harper & Row, 1980.

Lauter, Estelle. *Women as Mythmakers: Poetry and Visual Art by Twentieth-Century Women*. Bloomington, Indiana UP, 1984.

Leo, John. "The Demonizing of White Men." *U.S. News & World Report*, Apr. 26, 1993, 24.

Lewis, Claude. "Women Are Turning to Violence." *Kansas City Star*, July 25, 1993, K-4.

Lewis, Jill. "Mothers, Daughters, and Feminism." In *Common Differences: Conflicts in Black and White Feminist Perspectives*. Garden City, NY: Anchor-Doubleday, 1981, 127-48.

Magnet, Myron. *The Dream and the Nightmare: The Sixties' Legacy to the Underclass*. New York: W. Morrow, 1993.

Marill, Michele Cohen. "Will Motherhood Cost You Your Job?" *Redbook*, May 1993, 84, 86-88.

Miller, Jean Baker. *Toward a New Psychology of Women*. 2nd Ed. Boston: Beacon Press, 1986.

Miner, Valerie, and Helen E. Longino, eds. *Competition: A Feminist Taboo?* With a foreword by Nell Irvin Painter. New York: The Feminist Press at the City University of New York, 1987.

Modleski, Tania. *Feminism Without Women: Culture and Criticism in a "Postfeminist" Age*. New York: Routledge, 1991.

——————. *Loving with a Vengeance: Mass-Produced Fantasies for Women*. New York: Methuen, 1982.

Ochs, Carol. *Behind the Sex of God: Toward a New Consciousness—Transcending Matriarchy and Patriarchy*. Boston: Beacon Press, 1977.

Paglia, Camille. *Sex, Art, and American Culture: Essays*. New York: Vintage, 1992.

——————. *Sexual Personae: Art and Decadence from Nefertiti to Emily Dickinson*. New York: Vintage Books, 1991.

Panofsky, Dora and Erwin Panofsky. *Pandora's Box: The Changing Aspects of a Mythical Symbol*. Bollingen Series 52. New York: Pantheon Books, 1956.

Polen, Nehemia. "Miriam's Dance: Radical Egalitarianism in Hasidic Thought." *Modern Judaism* 12, no. 1 (February 1992), 1-21.

Polyzoides, Stefanos, Roger Sherwood, and James Tice. *Courtyard Housing in Los Angeles: A Typological Analysis*. New York: Princeton UP, 1982.

Pratt, Annis. With Barbara White, Andrea Loewenstein, and Mary Wyer. *Archetypal Patterns in Women's Fiction*. Bloomington: Indiana UP, 1981.

Rich, Adrienne. "Compulsory Heterosexuality and Lesbian Existence." *SIGNS: Journal of Women in Culture and Society* 5, no. 4, 1980, 631-60. Also in Adrienne Rich. *Blood, Bread, and Poetry: Selected Prose 1979-1985*. New York: W. W. Norton, 1986, 23-75.

Ruddick, Sara. *Maternal Thinking: Toward a Politics of Peace*. Boston: Beacon Press, 1989.

Russ, Joanna. "Recent Feminist Utopias." In *Future Females: A Critical Anthology.*
    Ed. Marleen S. Barr. Bowling Green, OH: Bowling Green State U Popular P,
    1981, 71-85.
Scholem, Gershom. *Kabbalah.* New York: Quadrangle, 1974.
————————. *On the Kabbalah and Its Symbolism.* Trans. Ralph Manheim. London:
    Routledge and Kegan Paul, 1965.
Schrof, Joannie. "The Gender Machine: Congress is Looking for Ways to Remove Old
    Barriers to Girls' Success." *U.S. News & World Report,* Aug 2, 1993, 42-44.
Shima, Alan. *Skirting the Subject: Pursuing Language in the Works of Adrienne Rich,
    Susan Griffin, and Beverly Dahlen.* Uppsala, Sweden: Acta Anglistica Upsaliensis
    82, 1993.
Shkop, Esther M. "The Implications of Feminine Imagery in the Bible." *Tradition: A
    Journal of Orthodox Jewish Thought* 27, no. 1 (Fall 1992), 42-47.
Singer, Isaac Bashevis. Foreword. In *Golem! Danger, Deliverance and Art.* Ed. Emily
    D. Bilsky. With essays by Moshe Idel and Elfi Ledig. New York: Jewish
    Museum, 1988, 6-9.
Stimpson, Catherine. "Feminism and Feminist Criticism (1983)." In *Where the
    Meanings Are.* New York: Methuen, 1988, 116-29.
Tracy, Laura. *The Secret Between Us: Competition Among Women.* Boston: Little,
    Brown, 1991.
Tuan, Yi-Fu. *Space and Place: The Perspective of Experience.* Minneapolis: U of
    Minnesota P, 1977.
Weisman, Leslie Kanes. *Discrimination by Design: A Feminist Critique of the Man-
    made Environment.* Urbana and Chicago: U of Illinois P, 1992.
Wiesel, Elie. *The Golem: The Story of a Legend.* Ill. Mark Podwal. Trans. Anne
    Borchardt. New York: Summit Books, 1983.
Wikborg, Eleanor. "The Ambivalent Narrator: Conflicts in the Narrator's Attitude to
    the Ideal Lover and the Ideal City in Doris Lessing's *Children of Violence.*" In
    Papers on Language and Literature. Presented to Alvar Ellegård and Erik
    Frykman. Ed. Sven Bäckman and Göran Kjellmer. Göteborg, Sweden: Acta
    Universitatis Gothoburgensis, 1985, 385-99.
Woolf, Virginia. *A Room of One's Own.* 1929. Rpt. London: Grafton Books, 1985.
Zahavi, Helen. *The Weekend.* New York: Donald I. Fine, 1993.

Index

About the Author

KERSTIN W. SHANDS teaches English and American literature at Stockholm University. She holds a doctorate in English from Uppsala University, Sweden, and is the author of several books on North American women writers and feminist theory, including *Voices and Visions in Feminist Theory* (1992), *Awakening Women: North American Women Writers of the 20th Century* (1992), and *Escaping the Castle of Patriarchy: Patterns of Development in the Novels of Gail Godwin* (1990). Her current project aims to explore the significance of spatial metaphors in feminist texts.

ISBN 0-313-29257-4

90000>

EAN

9 780313 292576

HARDCOVER BAR CODE